Capital Transport

LONDON
GREEN • LINE
TRANSPORT

A history by
LAURIE AKEHURST

AUTHOR'S ✦ NOTE

First published 2005

ISBN 185414 290 9

Published by
Capital Transport
P.O. Box 250, Harrow

Printed by
CS Graphics, Singapore

The Green Line coach first appeared in 1930 to provide an express service from various towns in the Home Counties to central London. It was the brainchild of the London General Omnibus Company in response to the many independent coach operators who had introduced services throughout the area of the LGOC and its associated companies, taking their longer distance bus passengers. There was a ready demand for express motor coach travel and Green Line quickly became held in high public esteem. Politically inflicted licensing to control the numbers of coaches, the formation of the London Passenger Transport Board and the acquisition of the independents' services and vehicles led to the system being completely revised. By the late 1930s Green Line had been re-equipped with modern coaches and was firmly established as part of the modern London scene, contemporary with the trolleybuses and the Charles Holden designed Underground stations. The story continued with the fortunes of war, the post-war revival, the continuing demand for Green Line travel and the establishment of additional routes to serve the rapidly developing new towns. Post-war prosperity with the associated increase in private motoring brought about a decline in the use of public transport in general and Green Line was not exempt. Despite the introduction of new and refurbished coaches and some innovative service changes, demand for Green Line travel fell substantially during the 1960s and a spiral of service reductions became normal.

This book covers the story of Green Line and its origins going back well before 1930 until the Country Bus and Coach operations of London Transport were transferred at the start of 1970 to London Country Bus Services, a subsidiary of the National Bus Company. The story of Green Line during the London Country years, 1970 to 1986, has been told in *London Country* (second edition) published by Capital Transport in 2001. The name Green Line survives to this day but is used primarily as a marketing name by a consortium of operators.

Green Line has always been special to me and I well remember my first childhood journey, on an RF, and the friendly crew, the deep seats, the saloon heater, doors to keep out the cold and the faster journey compared with the bus. Upon arriving at our destination we alighted at a coach only compulsory stop quite away from where the buses stopped. My father worked for London Transport for 26 years and became a conductor on the coaches during the 1960s, opting for early retirement in 1972 as a result of the all-conquering one-man operation. I have been researching Green Line since the early 1960s and I contributed to two books published in 1980 at the time of Green Line's golden jubilee. My researches have continued during the intervening twenty-five years and a considerable amount of additional information has come to light which has been included in this new book.

I must thank several people who have helped with this book: Ken Glazier went through the text and clarified a number of points; Philip Hopcroft who not only read through the draft but checked the cross-references; David Ruddom and Graham Page for their assistance over the years. I am also indebted to John Herting, Fred Ivey, Bruce Jenkins, Barry LeJeune and David Manning of the Essex Transport Group who kindly loaned me some of their colour slides.

Regrettably, with the passing of the years, a number of people who rendered assistance are now no longer with us. These include my friends Mervyn Gibson, who was often able to answer my searching questions, and Albert McCall, one time Green Line inspector, who gathered a considerable amount of information from the many staff he had known who worked on the coaches. I am grateful to two ladies, Peggy Healey and Jean Tuck, who allowed me unrestricted access to the London Transport photographic collection over many years when it was under the auspices of the Publicity Office.

I spent my entire working career with London Transport and its successors during which time I met many staff who had an association with Green Line. I particularly acknowledge the following, most of whom are sadly no longer with us: chief inspector Alec Smith (Hitchin and Stevenage), drivers Percy Bishop (Epping and Harlow), Cecil Brown (Amersham and Garston), Bill Winzaar (Leavesden Road), conductors Ted Bowden (Epping and Harlow), Heather Hawkins (Garston), Mr Peacock (Swanley), Ray Taylor (Dorking) and Winnie Youngs (Staines). These people were pleased to talk about their experiences on Green Line, loan photographs and official material and attempt to answer some of the difficult questions I posed.

In conclusion I dedicate this book to Irene Glen.

Laurie Akehurst, Watford 2005

CONTENTS

Cover painting: Barry Pearce
Title page photos: Old Motor (upper), Fred Ivey (lower)

ORIGINS
BEFORE 1929

The advent of the motor bus in London in the early 1900s meant that routes could be extended as operators were no longer reliant on animal power. Early motor buses were, however, notoriously unreliable but this did not stop an enterprising operator, the London Motor Bus Co. Ltd which used the fleet name Vanguard, starting a service from Northumberland Avenue to Brighton via Croydon on 30th August 1905. The company may have had plans for other such ventures but the service was brought to an end by disaster striking on 12th July 1906 when a Vanguard double deck bus on a private hire to Brighton suffered a severe mechanical failure while descending Handcross Hill. The bus was left with only the steering operable and crashed out of control with ten fatalities amongst top-deck passengers plus many injuries.

With its origins dating from 1855 the London General Omnibus Co. Ltd was the pre-eminent omnibus operator but by 1907, it found itself in fierce competition with two other formidable motor bus operators, the London Road Car Company and Vanguard. In 1908 General struck agreements to merge with the two rival concerns thus becoming unassailably the largest and most powerful operator in London with the resources to design and manufacture its own buses. In October 1910 it produced the B type which was vastly superior to all previous designs.

The availability of reliable buses meant that it was viable to establish longer routes and to this end in June 1912 General proposed some 27 so-called 'Country' services all radiating from Charing Cross.

Chesham via Harrow and Rickmansworth
Chesham via Uxbridge and Gerrards Cross
Beaconsfield via Uxbridge and Gerrards Cross
Watford via Edgware and Stanmore
St Albans via Edgware and Elstree
St Albans via Golders Green, Barnet and London Colney
Hatfield via Highgate, Barnet and Potters Bar
Maidenhead via Brentford, Hounslow and Slough
Windsor via Brentford, Hounslow and Slough
Ascot via Kew, Richmond, Teddington, Kingston and Staines
Hertford via Tottenham, Enfield, and Waltham Cross
Epping via Leytonstone, Woodford and Epping Forest
Loughton via Leytonstone and Woodford
Guildford via Putney, Richmond, Kingston and Esher
Abridge via Leytonstone, Woodford and Chigwell
Chelmsford via Romford and Brentwood
Dorking via Clapham Junction, Tooting and Epsom
Dorking via Stockwell, Tooting, Sutton and Banstead Heath
Reigate via Stockwell, Tooting, Sutton and Kingswood
Southend via Barking, Rainham, Aveley and Benfleet
Gravesend via Blackheath, Welling and Dartford
Brighton via Croydon, Crawley and Handcross
East Grinstead via Croydon, Upper Warlingham, and Caterham
Edenbridge via Croydon and Warlingham
Maidstone via Lewisham, Sidcup and Farningham
Sevenoaks via Peckham, Lewisham, Bromley and Farnborough
Westerham via Peckham, Lewisham, Bromley and Cudham Wood

Details of days of operation or frequency are not stated but some of the proposed routes do bear a remarkable similarity to Green Line routes later to be established. Quite where some 27 routes would stand at Charing Cross was not explained. These proposals were not implemented but some of the country terminals were to see General buses in the not too distant future.

In 1912 the London General Omnibus Company was taken over by the Underground Electric Railway of London of which Albert Stanley, later to become Lord Ashfield, was the managing director. The company was now in a very powerful position as part of the so-called London Traffic Combine.

It became the policy of General that, as

far as possible, the buses that took people to work on Monday to Saturday should not remain idle on Sunday when they could be deployed to take leisure traffic to London's countryside. The first example was service 61 from Brixton to Whyteleafe which commenced on 16th June 1912 followed on 3rd August by Saturday and Sunday service 84 from Golders Green to St Albans. Two daily services commenced on 1st August, 81 from Hounslow to Windsor Castle and 82 from Harlington Corner to Staines. The years 1913 and 1914 saw further expansion and prior to the First World War it became possible to reach Burnham Beeches, Dorking, Epping, Godstone, Hatfield, Leatherhead, Maidenhead, Redhill, Reigate, Virginia Water, Watford and Wormley by General omnibus. Some services quickly became established as daily operations. The First World War checked such operations as vehicles were requisitioned for war service and staff joined the armed forces but by the early 1920s General buses were running to Ascot, Brentwood, Dartford, Farningham, Guildford, Harpenden, Ongar, Upminster, Ware, West Wycombe and Woking.

This expansion into London's countryside posed the question of the General's territory and it decided on a policy of making boundary agreements with neighbouring large operators rather than indulging in damaging competition.

In 1920 General moved into Watford to fill a void that was created by the demise of the London & North Western Railway bus services which had been withdrawn during the First World War. A garage was built in Leavesden Road and operations commenced on 25th August with two, later three 'country' routes plus an allocation on established routes 140 and 142. This combination led to industrial unrest as the crews on the country routes were paid a lower rate than the men working on the

140 and 142. General's solution to the difficulty was to enter into an agreement with the National Omnibus and Transport Co. Ltd. to operate the country routes on its behalf and to reallocate the 140 and 142 to other garages. This company was the descendent of Thomas Clarkson's National steam bus empire which had been reconstituted on 13th February 1920 with operational areas based on Chelmsford, Bedford, Stroud and Yeovil. The agreement provided for General to supply the vehicles and equipment and to build the garages. National established a new area defined as Watford and North London and was responsible for operating and developing the route network. The main advantage was that an economy in operation was forthcoming as the National rates of pay were lower than those paid by General.

A similar agreement was signed on 7th July 1921 with East Surrey to operate services for and on behalf of General in the area north of the Valley Road (the present A25) and south of the Metropolitan Police area. A further agreement was made with the Thames Valley company to operate routes beyond Uxbridge from 14th June 1922 but the operation was never fully developed and the routes concerned were worked by General from 1st January 1929 when Thames Valley terminated the agreement. It was these operating agreements in conjunction with boundary agreements that largely determined what would become the London Passenger Transport Board area in 1933.

In the mid-1920s the availability of reliable vehicles, the pneumatic tyre, the improved standards of road surfaces and the building of arterial roads out of London resulted in a network of long-distance coach services being progressively established. In addition vehicle design underwent considerable enhancement between 1925 and 1930. Until this time the main line railways has enjoyed a virtual monopoly of long and intermediate-distance traffic but the coaches offered a cheaper and often a more convenient, albeit slower, service. Lord Ashfield was on record as having assured Sir Herbert Walker, General Manager of the Southern Railway, that General had no intention of entering the coastal coach business. Events were to move on and in 1926 some coach operators were offering fares for journeys solely within General's area. Such practice might well have started in an informal way – if the driver of a London bound long-distance coach was setting down passengers at, say, Barnet Church he may well have offered to convey any waiting bus or tram passengers to central London for a fare of one shilling.

A market for this intermediate-type traffic obviously existed and in 1927 four examples of what might be termed London suburban coach services commenced operation. The very first operator was Empress

Motors, later New Empress Saloons, which started on 27th May running from Wood Green to Southend. Glenton Coaches began the operation of six daily journeys from Victoria to Sevenoaks via Bromley in August. The through fare was 2/6 single, 4/- return but a range of intermediate bookings was also offered. The timetable leaflet made clear that it was a coach, not an omnibus service, and bookings had to be made in advance. It stated that the fares were cheaper than by rail and that the coach was more agreeable than rail travel. Redcar Services commenced a service on 16th September of four daily journeys plus a 'theatre car' on Wednesday and Saturday from Tunbridge Wells to Buckingham Palace Road near Victoria Station. The handbill makes clear that seats had to be pre-booked and that seats could not be guaranteed for the return journey unless the passengers specified the journey upon which they wished to return with the booking agent on arrival at their destination. Eight booking agents were listed along the line of route. The fourth service was that of R. W. Priest who, under the fleet name Imperial Motor Services, commenced running from Kings Cross to Luton sometime in November.

These four operators were to prove to be fairly typical of the many others to follow. New Empress was eventually acquired by the City Omnibus Company Ltd of Peckham which, after its London bus interests had been acquired, was reconstituted as the City Coach Company. Redcar suspended their service from the start of 1928 but recommenced in the spring and was acquired by Maidstone and District in 1935 but not before indulging in competition with the Autocar Company which was acquired by East Surrey. Glenton withdrew their service after a matter of months, probably due to lack of patronage. Priest extended his service to Bedford for a period and also established other routes but after some months of competition, sold the Luton service as a going concern to A. J. Smith of Holloway. Smith subsequently went bankrupt and the service passed to Venture Transport of Hendon.

The following years saw a profusion of such services with many operators trying their luck at this type of operation. Many were running entirely within what General considered to be its area but others continued to towns within a 60-mile radius of London, including Aldershot, Bedford, Chelmsford, Oxford, Reading and Southend. The histories of some services are extremely complicated with proprietors often selling the operation to another concern, while some companies reformed or merged sometimes altering the fleet name. Others sold out to rivals in the face of competition while some simply withdrew unprofitable services after a matter of months. Some proprietors may have been established bus, long-distance or tour coach operators diversifying their businesses while others invested their savings into this new venture. It is difficult to classify operations precisely as London suburban operations because some routes ran beyond General's area, but some 14 other operators started up in 1928, to be joined by 27 more in 1929 and a further 18 the following year. It must be appreciated that for reasons explained above not all operations were concurrent and some operators ran more than one route.

One of those to try its luck in 1928 was East Surrey which on 7th August commenced two routes to Northumberland Avenue, route A from Redhill via Reigate and Sutton and route B from Reigate via Redhill and Croydon. Initially five journeys were run on each route with no Sunday service. A Sunday service of three journeys via Croydon was added on 11th November at which time the fares of 2s 6d single, 3s 6d return were both reduced by 6d. Both routes ran for the last time on 3rd March 1929.

Initially the long distance-coach operating practice of advance booking was a prerequisite and to this end a network of booking agents would be established along the line of route. Some services were advertised as non-stop from the terminal town to London but it soon became apparent that successful operations had to offer a greater degree of flexibility by inserting intermediate stops. The coaches were initially worked by drivers only with some operators requiring all passengers to be in possession of a pre-booked ticket, but the more enterprising stated that the driver would issue tickets on the coach if accommodation was available. Where services ran at convenient times for London business travel (the word commuter had not crossed the Atlantic in the 1920s) weekly, monthly and quarterly tickets were offered at discounted rates. As the coaches were in competition with the main line railways some services terminated at the appropriate London station but in a desire to develop the leisure market, most were eventually extended to Oxford Circus or the Victoria Embankment at Charing Cross, often causing considerable congestion.

With London suburban coach operations rapidly expanding some services lasted only a matter of months while others prospered with frequencies being increased and routes extended. How were services made attractive? Some operators offered use of travelling rugs and fitted their coaches with saloon heaters, luggage racks, deep seats and curtains. Late night coaches from London were provided for theatre traffic with one operator, Skylark, advertising spare coaches guaranteeing to get passengers home! When this operator had commenced operations from Guildford to Oxford Circus on 14th December 1928 it even offered the first 40 tickets on a complimentary basis! The requirement to

pre-book tickets was not ideally suited to this type of service and an enterprising operator, E. Gray and Sons (Transport) Ltd., which operated two routes from Strand to Oxford, one via Uxbridge and High Wycombe and a more circuitous route via Rickmansworth, Amersham, Beacons-

Most operators produced handbills to publicise their services and established a network of booking agents along the line of route. This example from 1928 for the East Surrey services also contains a map which features onward connections.

TRAVEL TO LONDON BY ROAD.

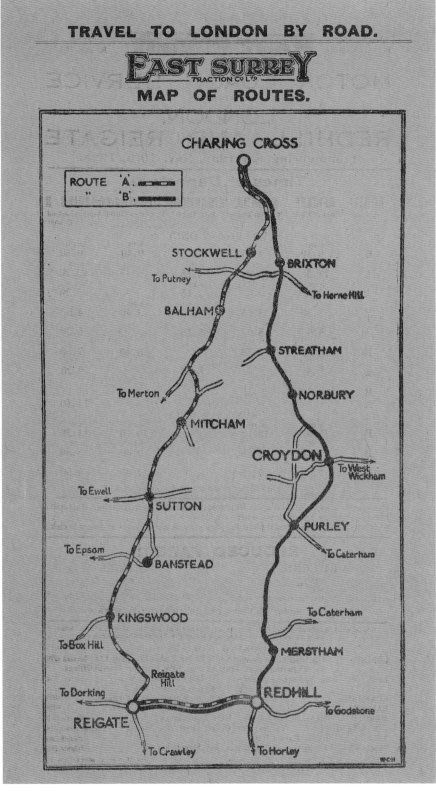

EAST SURREY TRACTION Cº Lᵀᴰ
MAP OF ROUTES.

ROUTE 'A'. ━━━━━
    " 'B'. ━━━━━

CHARING CROSS

STOCKWELL — BRIXTON
To Putney
To Herne Hill
BALHAM
STREATHAM
To Merton — NORBURY
MITCHAM
CROYDON — To West Wickham
To Ewell
SUTTON
PURLEY
To Epsom
BANSTEAD — To Caterham
To Caterham
KINGSWOOD
To Box Hill — MERSTHAM
Reigate Hill
To Dorking — REDHILL
REIGATE — To Godstone
To Crawley — To Horley

---

solicit traffic by announcing fares when the coach stopped at intermediate points. For example, on the busy routes out to the east of London if a Hillman's coach stopped at, say, Ilford Broadway the conductor would announce to the queue the fares to Romford or Brentwood in order to entice would be General bus passengers onto his coach. In addition to competing with the railways the coaches were now competing with the parallel General, East Surrey and National bus services.

How was such operation possible within the scope of the licensing arrangements? Within the Metropolitan Police area The London Traffic Act of 1924 had been created to curb and control the many independent, so-called pirate, bus operations in central London. The number of buses plying for hire along certain thoroughfares (so-called 'restricted streets'), the terminals and in some cases stopping places were strictly controlled by the police. The Act also established a larger London Traffic Area extending approximately 20 to 25 miles from Charing Cross but the restrictions only applied within the Metropolitan Police area. Coaches running into the area could be licensed as stage carriages in the same way as buses, provided that they conformed to the Metropolitan Police standards as regards dimensions and weights. They would receive a licence plate subject to satisfactory annual inspection by the Public Carriage Office, while drivers and conductors were also licensed being issued with numbered enamel badges. A copy of the fares list had to be submitted to the Commissioner of Police. Outside London matters were much different with local councils having powers through watch committees to license vehicles plying for hire within their boundaries. In practice some councils did not require vehicles to be licensed. Similarly some licensed drivers and conductors but others did not. This situation presented a loop hole in the 1924 legislation as a limited stop coach service running into the Metropolitan Police area was not considered subject to the severe restrictions imposed on omnibuses.

Frank Pick, managing director of General, complained that bus operators hampered by 'restricted street' regulations were facing unfair competition from coach services which were not subject to such restrictions. The position was confused and Pick maintained that the coaches were operating illegally but was obliged to accept that the police could not allocate resources to clarifying matters so the whole thing had to go by default. General unquestionably felt that it had the divine right to operate and was extremely concerned at the abstraction of traffic within its area, caused by the newly formed coach services. Thus it decided that the solution was to enter the market itself on the basis that "if you couldn't beat them, join them".

---

field and Henley dispensed with pre-booking and put a conductor on the coach. This proved to be the key to success as with a conductor to collect the fares and assist with luggage the service could be speeded up. Prior to this the driver might well have pulled up at a convenient spot en route to

check the tickets and collect the fares from any casual passengers.

Many other operators eventually followed suit finding that the provision of a conductor permitted additional local fares to be inserted into the faretable in the outer districts. The conductor could also

FORMATION
1929–1930

General commenced its 'London suburban coach' operations on 2nd October 1929. Taking advantage of the winter lull in private hire work they deployed AEC Reliance 'all-weather' coaches from their private hire fleet to establish a service from Watford Market Street to Golders Green via Bushey Heath and Watford By-Pass. Two bookings were available – Watford to Golders Green 1/- single, 1/6 return and Watford to London via the Underground at 1/6 single, 2/- return. The through tickets permitted passengers to continue their journey to specified Underground stations in central London. The garage in Leavesden Road was reopened to work the service which ran every 15 minutes, daily. National had outgrown the accommodation and moved to new premises in Watford Lower High Street in about July 1925 since when the Leavesden Road premises had been let. The tickets were sold by the drivers on the coaches and, in addition, they could also be obtained at Leavesden Road garage, the National garage, the National enquiry office in Market Street or at 55 Broadway, SW1. The tickets could not be purchased at Underground booking offices for outward journeys.

The creation of this first route was in response to Mr Thomas Edward Greenwood, an existing bus and coach proprietor, who acquired an interest in Bucks Garage (Watford) which was situated in Watford Parade. Greenwood had commenced a half-hourly service under the fleet name Empress Coaches from Watford to Oxford Circus via Stanmore, Edgware and Kilburn on 26th September 1929.

GENERAL MOTOR COACHES
EVERY 15 MINUTES DAILY

WATFORD (MARKET STREET)
Via Golders Green Station

To LONDON

Through Tickets are issued to the following UNDERGROUND Stations in the City and West End.

Aldwych	Edgware Road	Oxford Circus
Angel	Euston	Paddington
Baker Street	Goodge Street	Piccadilly
Bank	Hampstead	Post Office
Belsize Park	Holborn	Regent Street
Blackfriars	Hyde Park Corner	Russell Square
Bond Street	King's Cross	Strand
British Museum	Leicester Square	St. James' Park
Camden Town	Mansion House	Temple
Chalk Farm	Marble Arch	Tottenham Court
Chancery Lane	Marylebone	Road
Charing Cross	Mornington	Trafalgar Square
Covent Garden	Crescent	Victoria
Dover Street	Moorgate	Warren Street
Down Street	Old Street	Westminster

THROUGHOUT FARE 1/6 Single 2/- Return.

Golders Green Station only 1/- " 1/6 "

Available on day of issue only.

The coach service from Watford to Golders Green Underground station started on 2nd October 1929 using AEC Reliance 32-seater all-weather coaches in green and cream livery from the LGOC private hire fleet. The bodies were designed so that the canvas section of the roof could be folded back when the weather allowed. When new the coaches were not allocated fleet numbers – YW8015 poses for the camera in May 1929. *London's Transport Museum*

This was the very first leaflet issued for the new motor coach service from Watford to Golders Green.

TIMES OF DEPARTURE.

FROM WATFORD (Market Street)

First Coach.		Last Coach.	
Weekdays.	Sundays.	Weekdays.	Sundays.
a.m.	a.m.	p.m.	p.m.
7.0	9.0	11.30	10.30

FROM GOLDERS GREEN Station

First Coach.		Last Coach.	
Weekdays.	Sundays.	Weekdays.	Sundays.
a.m.	a.m.	p.m.	p.m.
7.35	9.35	12.5	11.5

Service every 15 minutes.

BOOKINGS FROM

NATIONAL OMNIBUS & TRANSPORT CO. LTD.
GARAGE, HIGH STREET, WATFORD, } Telephone No.:
MARKET STREET, WATFORD } WATFORD 1642

or

LONDON GENERAL OMNIBUS CO. LTD. GARAGE,
LEAVESDEN ROAD, WATFORD, or
55, BROADWAY, WESTMINSTER, LONDON, S.W.1.
Telephone, VICTORIA, No. 6800.

GENERAL

500. 2/10/29.

WATERLOW & SONS LIMITED, LONDON, DUNSTABLE & WATFORD.

The back of the first leaflet for the service between Watford and Golders Green.

Below left This leaflet was produced in April 1930 to advertise the Watford to Charing Cross service. The overprint refers to the weekly tickets offered in competition with Bucks Express and the conditions still refer to booking seats with the driver. Conductors were provided on the route from 18th May 1930.

Below right The original leaflet for the Windsor via Slough service in April 1930 shows the operation marketed under the General name. The 3d fares offered at the country end of the route proved to be very short-lived.

In November Greenwood set up a new company, Bucks Expresses (Watford) Ltd, with the coaches carrying the fleet name 'Bucks Express'. Intermediate fares were offered as well as weekly, monthly and quarterly season tickets and additional coaches were soon added at peak times. The service was in competition with General service 142 running from Watford Junction to Kilburn Park.

Both operations fell foul of Watford Council which had not issued the necessary licences and at the Council's request both services were withdrawn after 12th November pending the next meeting of the Watch Committee. Eventually the Council issued the necessary licences and the Bucks Express service recommenced on 15th December but General waited until the start of the pay week on 18th December when it re-introduced the Golders Green service on a 30-minute headway Monday to Saturday, 60 minutes Sunday. Intermediate fares were now provided and tickets could be obtained at specified Underground stations for outward travel, a practice which was to become standard as other coach routes were introduced. The reduction of the headway on the Golders Green route permitted some coaches to be used on a new route, in direct competition with

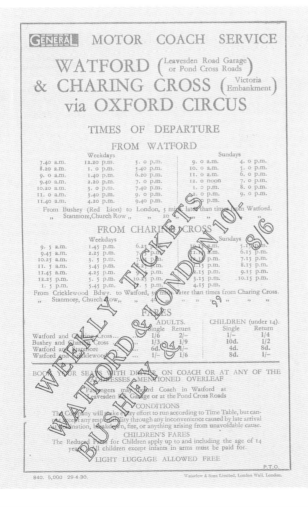

GENERAL EXPRESS COACH SERVICE

WINDSOR CASTLE
SLOUGH, COLNBROOK
& CHARING CROSS

TIMES OF DEPARTURE

FROM WINDSOR, ("LORD RAGLAN")

WEEKDAYS.				SUNDAYS.			
6.45 a.m.	10.45 a.m.	2.45 p.m.	6.45 p.m.	8.45 a.m.	12.45 p.m.	4.45 p.m.	8.45 p.m.
7.15 a.m.	11.15 a.m.	3.15 p.m.	7.15 p.m.	9.15 a.m.	1.15 p.m.	5.15 p.m.	9.15 p.m.
7.45 a.m.	11.45 a.m.	3.45 p.m.	7.45 p.m.	9.45 a.m.	1.45 p.m.	5.45 p.m.	9.45 p.m.
8.15 a.m.	12.15 p.m.	4.15 p.m.	8.15 p.m.	10.15 a.m.	2.15 p.m.	6.15 p.m.	10.15 p.m.
8.45 a.m.	12.45 p.m.	4.45 p.m.	8.45 p.m.	10.45 a.m.	2.45 p.m.	6.45 p.m.	
9.15 a.m.	1.15 p.m.	5.15 p.m.	9.15 p.m.	11.15 a.m.	3.15 p.m.	7.15 p.m.	
9.45 a.m.	1.45 p.m.	5.45 p.m.	9.45 p.m.	11.45 a.m.	3.45 p.m.	7.45 p.m.	
10.15 a.m.	2.15 p.m.	6.15 p.m.	10.15 p.m.	12.15 p.m.	4.15 p.m.	8.15 p.m.	

WINDSOR CASTLE 5 minutes (approx.) after leaving WINDSOR ("LORD RAGLAN")
ETON .. 9 " " " " "
SLOUGH .. 12 " " " " "
COLNBROOK .. 24 " " " " "
'PEGGY BEDFORD' 30 " " " " "

FROM CHARING CROSS (Victoria Embankment)

WEEKDAYS.				SUNDAYS.			
8.15 a.m.	12.15 p.m.	4.15 p.m.	8.15 p.m.	10.15 a.m.	2.15 p.m.	6.15 p.m.	10.15 p.m.
8.45 a.m.	12.45 p.m.	4.45 p.m.	8.45 p.m.	10.45 a.m.	2.45 p.m.	6.45 p.m.	10.45 p.m.
9.15 a.m.	1.15 p.m.	5.15 p.m.	9.15 p.m.	11.15 a.m.	3.15 p.m.	7.15 p.m.	11.15 p.m.
9.45 a.m.	1.45 p.m.	5.45 p.m.	9.45 p.m.	11.45 a.m.	3.45 p.m.	7.45 p.m.	11.45 p.m.
10.15 a.m.	2.15 p.m.	6.15 p.m.	10.15 p.m.	12.15 p.m.	4.15 p.m.	8.15 p.m.	
10.45 a.m.	2.45 p.m.	6.45 p.m.	10.45 p.m.	12.45 p.m.	4.45 p.m.	8.45 p.m.	
11.15 a.m.	3.15 p.m.	7.15 p.m.	11.15 p.m.	1.15 p.m.	5.15 p.m.	9.15 p.m.	
11.45 a.m.	3.45 p.m.	7.45 p.m.	11.45 p.m.	1.45 p.m.	5.45 p.m.	9.45 p.m.	

HYDE PARK CORNER .. .. .. 6 minutes (approx.) after leaving CHARING CROSS
229, HAMMERSMITH ROAD (opposite Kings Theatre) .. 17 " " " " "
CHISWICK (Needhams, next Chiswick Empire) .. 23 " " " " "

FARES

	WINDSOR		SLOUGH		COLNBROOK		"PEGGY BEDFORD"	
	Single	Return	Single	Return	Single	Return	Single	Return
SLOUGH	3d.	—						
COLNBROOK	6d.	—	3d.	—				
"PEGGY BEDFORD" ...	9d.	—	6d.	—	3d.	—		
CRANFORD	1/-	—	9d.	—	6d.	—		
OSTERLEY, Thornbury Rd.	1/3	—	1/-	—	9d.	—		
GUNNERSBURY STN. ...	1/6	—	1/3	—	1/-	—		
HAMMERSMITH	1/9	3/-	1/6	2/6	1/3	2/-		
CHARING CROSS ...	2/-	3/6	1/9	3/-	1/6	2/6	1/3	2/-

BOOK YOUR SEATS ON THE COACH—OR AT ANY
OF THE ADDRESSES MENTIONED OVERLEAF

Passengers may board coach in WINDSOR at the CASTLE or at the "LORD RAGLAN" opposite Cambermere Barracks.

CHILDREN'S FARES.
Children under 14 years of age HALF PRICE. Halfpennies are reckoned as Pennies.
All Children, unless in arms, must be paid for.

CONDITIONS.
The Company will make every effort to run according to Time-table but cannot accept any responsibility for any inconvenience caused by late arrival at destination, breakdown, fire or anything arising from unavoidable cause.

LIGHT LUGGAGE ALLOWED FREE

P.T.O.

T 155 in the General red and black livery, one of a batch of 150 rear-entrance Regal coaches, poses for the camera when new in May 1930. The practice of providing route details on the louvres was soon discontinued in favour of side boards. *London's Transport Museum*

The splendid and welcoming interior of T 155. The deep seats, luggage racks, light fittings, mirror, clock and saloon heater all add to the passengers' feeling of well-being. A journey by Green Line insulated passengers from the cares and troubles of the outside world. *London's Transport Museum*

Bucks Express, from Watford to Charing Cross running every 40 minutes Monday to Saturday, 60 minutes on Sunday. Watford Council, like many other local authorities, tended to favour local businesses rather than the powerful Combine and placed restrictions on the coaches stopping within the borough. Passengers could only board the General coaches at Leavesden Road garage or at Pond Cross Roads while Bucks Garage was more favourably placed towards the centre of Watford.

Bucks Express proved to be formidable competition and General very soon established a network of booking agents on the line of route and in central London and in March 1930, weekly tickets were introduced on both General routes. The possibility of General enhancing the Watford operations or introducing further routes was restricted as additional coaches were not available – a matter that had to be addressed.

The T class single-deck 30-seat buses based on the AEC Regal 662 chassis were introduced by General in 1929 and one of the batch, T 38, was developed as a suburban coach. The vehicle had six bays and the internal floor was much higher than on the buses to enable all 28 seats to face forward. Due to the maximum permitted length of 26 feet it was not possible to fit a sliding door to the rear entrance thus necessitating the provision of a swing door. A batch of 150 Regal coaches based on T 38 but with a number of detail differences was ordered. They had seven bay bodywork, a more rounded back and roof and a recessed swing door which reduced the seating capacity to 27. The bodies were by Hall Lewis (later to become Park Royal Vehicles) and Short Brothers and they were numbered T 51–149, 155, 157–206.

Windsor had long been a popular destination – General first reached the town in 1912. In December 1929, Highways Ltd. started an hourly daily service from the town to Oxford Circus via Slough at through fares of 2/6 single, 3/6 return, the Slough fares being 6d cheaper. The coaches ran non-stop between Slough and Hammersmith. They were soon joined by the Premier Omnibus Co. Ltd, a London independent operator which diversified into the suburban coach business under the name Premier Line. Premier commenced an approximately 40-minute service from Windsor to Aldwych via Slough on 27th January 1930 charging the same fares as Highways. The Premier coaches were worked initially only by a driver. Premier had plans to run similar services to various towns and optimistically lettered this route A. Additional stops were added on 19th February and the service was increased to 20 minutes every day on 7th April.

General commenced a 30-minute service on 20th April 1930 from Windsor to Charing Cross via Slough and Colnbrook using the new T type coaches which were finished in red and black livery. Aware of Premier competition they departed from Charing Cross via Temple Station and Aldwych in order to call at the Premier terminus at Bush House. As no convenient operating base was available premises were rented in Alpha Street, Slough. The coaches carried conductors, which was now to become normal for General services and a full range of intermediate fares was offered with a 3d minimum west of the Peggy Bedford at the junction of Bath Road and Colnbrook By-Pass. The through single fare was set at 2/- rather than the competitors' 2/6. General had one advantage over the independents in that tickets available to central London allowed passengers the option of changing to the Underground at Hammersmith in order to complete their journey to specified stations.

The gauntlet had been thrown down and competition was on. Premier increased their service to 15 minutes and introduced a range of intermediate bookings and reduced the through single fare to 2/- on 12th May. Five days later General withdrew the 3d bookings thus leaving a 6d minimum west of the Peggy Bedford and on 30th May increased their service to 15 minutes. Premier had offered season tickets from an early date and from 15th June General offered similar facilities and on the following day passengers could book outward single and return journeys from central London Underground stations and change to the coach at Hammersmith. From 1st July General had the last word and stepped their service up to 10 minutes. Highways ceased operating in July but were to make a comeback in November.

As more of the T type coaches became available they were put on the Watford services in May, with the Charing Cross service being increased to half hourly daily from 18th May when conductors were provided on the coaches. From 1st July both routes offered season tickets.

In the meantime four new routes using the new T type coaches were established on 6th June. General, which had acquired control of East Surrey in 1929, supplied coaches in red and black livery with the East Surrey fleet name to operate from Dorking to Oxford Circus via Epsom, Reigate to Oxford Circus via Sutton, and Redhill to Oxford Circus via Croydon, all initially on a 60-minute headway, worked from Reigate garage. The fourth service, from Tunbridge Wells to Oxford Circus, was operated by the Autocar company of Tunbridge Wells which East Surrey had acquired in 1928. The frequency was every 60 minutes and the coaches were supplied in the red and black livery with the Autocar fleet name. As more new coaches became available the Tunbridge Wells, Reigate and Dorking routes were increased to 30 minutes on 24th June with the latter being transferred to Leatherhead garage. There was competition from the Skylark Motor Coach Co. Ltd. which had started a 60-minute service on 4th December 1929 from Dorking via Reigate and Tooting to Oxford Circus and on to High Wycombe. It was Skylark who pioneered the practice of cross-London running. Seemingly the East Surrey services proved too much for Skylark who withdrew operation of their route south of London on and from 19th December. Valliant Super Motor Coaches commenced an hourly daily service from Reigate to Oxford Circus via Redhill and Croydon on 25th March 1930 but it was short-lived, possibly being withdrawn in July. The Autocar service was in competition with the hourly Redcar service the origins of which went back to 1927. Competition had its effect as Redcar publicity dated 5th August specifically stated "no tickets sold on the coaches" while the

next issue made clear that tickets were sold on the coaches!

New routes were now coming at a pace and on 10th July 1930 a 30-minute service from Windsor to Charing Cross via Staines and Hounslow commenced running under the General fleet name. The coaches left Charing Cross via Bush House and passengers were offered the option of changing to and from the Underground at Shepherds Bush station. No existing garage facilities were available so a new garage was opened in London Road, Staines. Season tickets were offered during August but they were

The Dorking to Oxford Circus route, marketed under the East Surrey name, started on 6th June 1930 as an hourly service but was increased to run every 30 minutes from 24th June as more new coaches became available.

not inter-available on the alternative route via Slough. Grimwood Parlour Coaches had started running from Staines to London via Ashford and Hounslow early in 1929 with the service being extended to Egham on 15th June 1929. It is not known when the service ceased.

The Tunbridge Wells to Oxford Circus route was worked by the Autocar company with T type coaches in red and black livery with the Autocar fleet name. T 65, fitted with side route boards, is seen in Regent Street at Oxford Circus before returning to Tunbridge Wells.
C. Klapper

The beginnings of a suburban coach network had been established but lacked a corporate identity. Coaches in red livery – did the public appreciate that it was a new type of service or did they think that the vehicles were merely a new type of single deck bus? The network needed to be marketed as a separate entity and it was Lord Ashfield who suggested the name 'Green Line'.

On 9th July 1930 Green Line Coaches Ltd with a capital of £20,000 was formed to operate the services as a wholly-owned subsidiary of the LGOC. Lord Ashfield, Frank Pick and Daniel Duff were the directors with J. C. Mitchell as the secretary. As a precaution to prevent competitors taking similar names, Red Line, Blue Line and Yellow Line companies were also registered.

Green Line has arrived! The Watford services were allocated new coaches in green livery carrying the Green Line fleet name from 17th July 1930. Brand new T 122 poses for the camera equipped with side route boards for the Watford to Charing Cross service. The coach was actually allocated to the Guildford route.
London's Transport Museum

Green Line Coaches Ltd was incorporated as a company on 9th July 1930 and on 17th July the first route marketed under the Green Line name commenced between Guildford and Oxford Circus. The non-standard fares on the fare table reflect the competition with the Skylark company.

GREEN LINE

COACH SERVICE
GUILDFORD
RIPLEY, COBHAM, ESHER &
CHARING CROSS
(Embankment)
Via Hammersmith & Oxford Circus
Every 30 minutes

Departure Points.	WEEKDAYS.			SUNDAYS.		
	First Coach.	Then at Minutes past each hour.	Last Coach.	First Coach.	Then at Minutes past each hour.	Last Coach.
TO CHARING CROSS from	a.m.		p.m.	a.m.		p.m.
Guildford	6 22	52 & 22	10 22	7 52	22 & 52	9 22
Ripley	6 42	12 & 42	10 42	8 12	42 & 12	9 42
Cobham	6 52	22 & 52	10 52	8 22	52 & 22	9 52
Esher	7 0	30 & 0	11 0	8 30	0 & 30	10 0
TO GUILDFORD from			a.m.			
Charing Cross (Embankment) ...	8 17	47 & 17	12 17	9 47	17 & 47	11 17
Aldwych (Bush House) ...	8 21	51 & 21	12 21	9 51	21 & 51	11 21
Trafalgar Square	8 24	54 & 24	12 24	9 54	24 & 54	11 24
Oxford Circus	8 30	0 & 30	12 30	10 0	30 & 0	11 30
Hammersmith (Greyhound Motors)	8 45	15 & 45	12 45	10 15	45 & 15	11 45

FARES

FARE STAGES.		Guildford.	Ripley. (Post Office.)	Cobham. ("White Lion")	Esher. ("The Bear.")	Malden. (Cross Roads.)
Ripley (Post Office) ... ...Single		6d.				
Cobham ("White Lion") ... ... ,,		10d.	5d.			
Esher ("The Bear") ... ... ,,		1/-	9d.	—		
Malden (Cross Roads)... ... ... ,,		1/4	1/-	8d.	5d.	
HAMMERSMITH	Single	2/3	2/-	1/9	1/6	—
	Return	3/9	3/3	2/9	2/6	
*CHARING CROSS	Single	2/6	2/3	2/-	1/9	1/4
	Return	4/-	3/9	3/3	2/9	2/-

* These tickets entitle passengers to travel to and from Underground stations in the central area, as shown on the ticket, changing at Hammersmith.

Passengers may hail and board the Coach at any point en route.

CHILDREN'S FARES. Children under 14 years of age half-price, fractions of a penny being counted as a 1d. All children, except infants in arms, must be paid for.

CONDITIONS. The Company will make every effort to run according to Time-table, but cannot accept any responsibility for any inconvenience caused by late arrival at destination, breakdown, fire or anything arising from unavoidable cause.

LIGHT LUGGAGE ALLOWED FREE. ONLY LAP DOGS CARRIED.

TAKE YOUR TICKETS ON THE COACH, OR AT ANY OF THE ADDRESSES MENTIONED OVERLEAF.

GREEN LINE COACHES Ltd.
July, 1930.

P.T.O.

1379—10,000. 16-7-30.

WATERLOW & SONS LIMITED, LONDON WALL, LONDON.

The new company lost no time in making its mark and on 17th July a 30-minute service commenced from Guildford to Charing Cross via Ripley, Kingston By-Pass and Barnes. The coaches, which were kept in the premises of Rice & Harpers Ltd. in London Road, Guildford, were in the new green and black livery with 'Green Line' fleet name and the publicity was headed Green Line and, of course, printed in green ink. Passengers were allowed the option of changing to and from the Underground at Hammersmith, the through fare being 2/6 single, 4/- return. Until this time fares had been in multiples of 6d but the faretable for this service included single fares of 5d, 8d and 1/4 due to the Skylark competition. On the same day the Watford services were recorded as using the 'Green Line' fleet name on their newly-delivered coaches.

The Skylark Motor Coach Co. Ltd had pioneered the Guildford service running virtually hourly to Oxford Circus from 14th December 1928. Initially the operation was advertised as non-stop but intermediate traffic was clearly necessary to support the service and some two months later stops at Ripley and Cobham were added and from 4th December 1929 the route was extended through to Hertford. The Aldershot & District Traction Company was running a similar 60-minute service by 11th May 1929, with the two concerns offering identical fares and season ticket rates and effectively providing a 30-minute service although tickets were not inter-available. The Skylark service was temporarily strengthened to 30 minutes at busy times and all day Sunday by September 1929. This competition proved too much for the

Aldershot company which reduced their Monday to Friday operation to two-hourly from 21st October and, from 2nd December offered a mere five or six journeys according to the day of operation.

Green Line and Skylark embarked on a fares war from 1st September 1930 with the former reducing the through fare to 2/- single, 3/3 return. The Skylark publicity announced 'Amazing reduction of fares' but Green Line still managed to undercut them by 3d on the return fare. During December, however, Green Line increased the return fare to 3/6.

The Romford road offered potentially good pickings with a lot of traffic between Bow, Stratford, Ilford, Romford and Brentwood. Hillman's Saloon Coaches commenced operations on 7th December 1928 between Stratford and Brentwood with ten daily journeys. The service was extended to Chelmsford in 1929 and in 1930 Edward Hillman opened a coach station at 133 Bow Road, near the District Railway station. Frequency was progressively increased and the route was extended to Colchester and Clacton. During the off-peak period five coaches per hour were run as far as Brentwood with projections beyond and in the rush-hours a five-minute service was advertised to Romford and Brentwood. Hillman had used conductors from the start offering local fares on the coaches. The publicity offered return tickets available for any period plus season tickets and requested passengers to ensure that they boarded the royal blue and white coach!

A number of long-distance operators offered intermediate fares along this route and in January 1930 a true suburban operation was begun by Sunset Pullman Coaches running from Brentwood to Charing Cross. The service was gradually built up from nine journeys to more frequent than half-hourly. Competition was intense and cheap day tickets were offered on Monday to Saturday outside the rush-hours. It was hardly surprising that Green Line wanted a slice of the action and on 23rd July 1930 commenced a 20-minute service from Brentwood to Charing Cross. Temporary accommodation for the coaches was found in Metcalf's Works on Eastern

Avenue to the west of the junction with North Street, Romford. Mindful of short-distance traffic additional fare stages were provided from 31st August and at the same time weekly and monthly tickets were issued. The service was increased to 15 minutes during the rush-hours and on Sunday from 24th September.

23rd July 1930 also saw the introduction of a 60-minute service from Sunningdale to Charing Cross via Staines and Hounslow. This operation, marketed as 'General', was worked from the garage at Staines and after one week was increased to a 30-minute frequency as new coaches became available. Passengers were allowed

to complete their journeys to central London by changing to the Underground at Hammersmith if they so wished. A number of established operators were running into London via this route, notably Aldershot & District and Farnham Blue Coaches from Farnham, and Safeway Super Coaches and Thames Valley from Reading. On 31st July Thackray's Way commenced a Reading to London service via Ascot which proved to be the final straw for Safeway which withdrew sometime in August. From 1st September the Sunningdale service was cut to 60 minutes and the surplus coaches used to provide a service on the same headway from Ascot to Oxford Circus.

This smartly turned out Denis Arrow with a Thurgood body was in the fleet of Red Rover Saloon Coaches which started a service from Aylesbury to Seymour Street near Marble Arch in 1928. GT1657 initially became D 5 in the LPTB fleet but was subsequently renumbered DL 39. *J.F. Higham*

The Thames Valley was always a popular destination and having established itself with Windsor traffic, General coaches started a half hourly service between Maidenhead and Charing Cross on 2nd August 1930 with the coaches housed in an open-sided barn adjacent to Maidenhead Station. Passengers could opt to transfer to and from the Underground at Shepherds Bush. The primitive garage facilities at Maidenhead proved unsatisfactory and from 22nd October the coaches were transferred to Alpha Street in Slough. Again competition was fierce with Thackray's Way which had started running from Reading to London on 25th September 1929, using conductors on the coaches from the start, which forced the older established Safeway Super Coaches to switch their Reading operation to the Ascot route. Pring's Express Motor Coach Service started between Maidenhead and Charing Cross offering five journeys (four Sundays). In an attempt to gain any traffic Pring was even offering Slough to Colnbrook at 6d single but the might of General proved too much and the service did not last long.

The Combine now turned its attention to the north of London, firstly to the area beyond Watford. Red Rover Saloon Coach Service had commenced in the late summer of 1928 running from Aylesbury to Marble Arch and had built up the service level to ten journeys (eight on Sunday). Watford Council would not permit through services to stop in Watford High Street so, for this reason, Red Rover chose to run via Watford By-Pass. The train service to local stations north of Watford was extremely infrequent so Green Line started running a 30-minute service worked by Watford, Leavesden Road from Tring to Charing Cross on 8th September 1930. The coaches ran via Berkhamsted and King's Langley through Watford and then followed the route of the Watford service. Due to Watford Council's restrictions the coaches were not allowed to pick up or set down between Grovemill Lane and Bushey, Aldenham Road.

The Great North Road corridor had attracted various operators, the major players being Baldock Motor Transport Ltd and the old established bus operator, Birch Brothers Ltd. The former had commenced operations in October 1928 from Baldock via Hitchin, Stevenage, Welwyn, Barnet By-Pass and Barnet to the grandiosely titled Central London (Road Transport) Station in Cartwright Gardens near Russell Square. In the early days the service was projected to Biggleswade but the extension was short-lived. The Baldock company was taken over by Queen Line Coaches in 1930 and the service was eventually marketed as 'Queen Line'. Birch diversified into the suburban coaching business in November 1928 running from Aldwych to Bedford via Kings Cross, Barnet, Hatfield, Welwyn, Codicote and Hitchin. In September 1929 a companion service was run from Aldwych to Bedford via St Albans and Luton with projections as far as Kettering. By July 1931 the latter route had been withdrawn in favour of the original route which had been extended to Bedford with projections beyond to Rushden and Kettering. Flower & Etches, a local bus operator, put on a service of three journeys from Welwyn Garden City to Portman Square about August 1929 but the service was never expanded and they ceased operation in early 1931.

Green Line entered the scene on 17th September 1930 by providing an hourly service, increased to half-hourly just one week later, from Welwyn Garden City to Charing Cross via Hatfield, Potters Bar and Barnet with passengers being allowed to transfer to the Underground at Golders Green. Publicity makes clear that the service was run for Green Line by 'National' acting as operating agents. A suitable operating base proved difficult to find with the coaches initially being housed at Jenner Parsons Ltd. but from 15th November they were switched to Welwyn Stores.

On 20th September 1930 Green Line commenced operations from Harpenden to Charing Cross via St Albans, Radlett, Elstree and Golders Green with a half-hourly service. No convenient operating base was available so arrangements were made with Comfy Cars, a local bus company, to use its premises in Luton Road, Harpenden. Passengers were offered the option of transferring to the Underground at Golders Green. Green Line probably had its sights set on Luton but difficulties with licensing accounted for the coaches running only to Harpenden. Strawhatter Motor Coaches, which had started running on 1st October 1928, and Venture Transport (Hendon) Ltd which acquired the Imperial Motor Services route dating from November 1927, were both running from Luton to Kings Cross via Barnet. Over 90 percent of traffic on these services was reputedly end to end so there was little Harpenden business for Green Line to capture. At St Albans the situation was rather different with St Albans Coaches service, dating from September 1929, running from that city to Oxford Circus via Radlett, Elstree and Edgware Road providing seven journeys (five on Sunday). Once Green Line appeared on the road this operator's traffic was lost virtually overnight and the service was quickly withdrawn. District

Baldock Motor Transport's service commenced in 1928 running to the coach station in Cartwright Gardens near Russell Square. The company was taken over by Queen Line Coaches and by April 1931 the route had been extended to the so-called London Terminal station at 80 Clapham Road. The handbill advertises books of tickets at discounted rates for regular travellers and also offers cheap midday period returns.

By the autumn of 1930 posters advertising the new Green Line services were produced in this eye-catching and attractive style designed by Edward McKnight Kauffer. The Welwyn Garden City route started on 17th September 1930.
London's Transport Museum

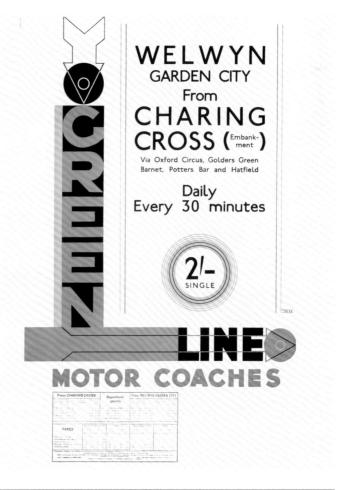

Omnibus Services started a service from St Albans to Oxford Circus via Barnet and Golders Green in about January 1930. This operator got into financial difficulties and the service was acquired by St Albans and District and withdrawn in May 1932. In St Albans the Green Line route crossed that of Beaumont Safeway Saloon Coaches, dating from December 1929, running some five journeys from Leighton Buzzard to Kings Cross via Dunstable, St Albans and Barnet.

The autumn of 1930 saw a number of new Green Line services worked from East Surrey garages. Firstly on 29th September came a 30-minute service from Godstone Green to Oxford Circus via Whyteleafe and Croydon with the coaches based at Godstone garage. On the same date the Redhill route was doubled in frequency to 30 minutes. On 1st October came Great Bookham and Oxford Circus via Morden with the 30-minute service being worked from Leatherhead garage. One week later

came Westerham to Oxford Circus via Bromley every 60 minutes with the coaches based at Dunton Green garage; on 18th October, it was extended to Sevenoaks. On 22nd October Oxted was linked to Oxford Circus via Chelsham and Croydon. A 30-minute service was operated from London to Chelsham garage with a two hourly projection through the sparsely populated countryside to Oxted. Alternate coaches on the Redhill route were extended to Crawley on 12th November with part of

Once the coaches had left the built-up area of London, which did not extend so far out in 1930 as it does today, there was often very little other traffic on the road. T 95 shares the Kentish countryside with a solo motorcyclist near Leaves Green while working from Sevenoaks to London via Westerham. *London's Transport Museum*

the allocation being transferred to the small East Surrey garage at Crawley. On the same date a new route was provided from East Grinstead to Oxford Circus via Caterham-on-the-Hill and Croydon, every 60 minutes with the coaches based at East Grinstead garage. Competition here was offered by Blue Belle Motors who had started running an hourly service on 1st October 1930 from Charing Cross via Croydon Aerodrome and Whyteleafe to Godstone. From Godstone certain coaches were extended to East Grinstead while others ran on to Westerham via Oxted. The coaches did not pick up after entering the Metropolitan Police area at Caterham unless seats had been pre-booked or the passengers were season ticket holders.

Organisational changes were made to the services with the Ascot, Sunningdale and Windsor via Staines routes becoming 'Green Line' on 1st October 1930 while on the same day the Guildford route was transferred to East Surrey but retained the Green Line fleet name. Similarly the Maidenhead and Windsor via Slough routes became Green Line from 18th October with the coaches gradually being repainted into the green livery.

October 1st also saw National commence a new 30-minute service on behalf of Green Line from Bishop's Stortford to Charing Cross via Epping, Loughton and Finsbury Park. The coaches were allocated to the National garage in Bishop's Stortford which had been built by General in 1928. Passengers were permitted to continue their journeys on the Underground from Finsbury Park. The established operator was Acme Pullman Services which had commenced on 5th October 1929 from Bishop's Stortford to Charing Cross via Epping, Epping Forest, Woodford and Stratford. Acme had conductors on the coaches from the start and offered bus fares north of the Metropolitan Police area boundary at the Wake Arms. By the time Green Line appeared, a 15-minute rush-hour frequency, half hourly at other times, was run as far as Bishop's Stortford with approximately hourly projections to Stansted and three daily journeys continuing to Newmarket. Acme was very popular with passengers, offering season tickets and special cheap return fares.

Further expansion in the Thames Valley took place on 11th October 1930 when Green Line started a half hourly service from Chertsey to Charing Cross via Weybridge, Thames Ditton, Kingston and Richmond. Passengers could change to the Underground at Hammersmith if they wished. There was no convenient operating base in the area so accommodation was rented in Weymann's Bodies' premises at Addlestone. Spartan Coaches of Acton had started a service of eleven journeys (five on Sunday) from Walton-on-Thames to Oxford Circus via Hersham, Esher and Kingston on 23rd June 1930 and extended it to Weybridge on 4th August. It is not known when this service was withdrawn.

The Lea Valley was an attractive area for a number of operators and Green Line proved to be rather late in entering the field. Others had been much quicker to realise the potential and no less than four operators were running in Autumn 1930. Skylark first ran from Hertford to Oxford Circus on 14th September 1929 (linked to Guildford on 4th December) and by this time an hourly service was running from Hertford Heath through to Guildford via Hertford, Ware, Cambridge Arterial Road, Finsbury Park and Oxford Circus. Regent Motor Services commenced operation on 9th October 1929 and at this time was running hourly from Hertford to Oxford Circus via Ware, Waltham Cross, Cambridge Arterial Road and Kings Cross. London & Counties Carriage Co. Ltd started an hourly service from Hertford to Charing Cross in Summer 1930 via Ware, St Margarets and Cheshunt running in London via Liverpool Street, Moorgate and Bank. On 20th October 1930 P & S Motor Services joined the throng running hourly from Hertford to Liverpool Street via Ware, St Margarets, Cheshunt and Tottenham. The proprietors were Prosser and Sanders but the first handbill was titled Punctuality and Service Motor Services. Competition was fierce and fare reductions had been applied when Green Line commenced on 22nd November running hourly from Hertford to Charing Cross via Ware, Waltham Cross and Enfield. Passengers were permitted the option of transferring to the Underground at Camden Town. The service was worked by National, acting as operating agents, from their garage in Ware.

As the system developed various adjustments were made to the services. From 1st November 1930 the practice of some routes leaving Charing Cross via Victoria Embankment and Bush House to Trafalgar Square was discontinued; the coaches now proceeded via Temple Station double running along Victoria Embankment to Northumberland Avenue. On 29th November the Ascot and Sunningdale routes were diverted away from the main road to run via Ashford and Feltham and the Ascot coaches were diverted away from Oxford Circus to terminate at Charing

Blue Belle Motors of Brixton started running from East Grinstead to Charing Cross on 1st October 1930 and in December the route was extended to terminate at Paddington. This AEC Regal with a London Lorries body carries a very informative route board. The coaches ran via Purley Way in order to serve Croydon Aerodrome. *N. Hampshire*

The publicity for the Bishop's Stortford route makes it clear that National were acting as operating agents for Green Line. The reverse of the timetable leaflet contains a list of booking agents, a list of other routes and wayside notes.

Coach **GREEN LINE** Service

OPERATED BY THE NATIONAL OMNIBUS & TRANSPORT CO., LTD.,
Local Office, South Street, Bishop's Stortford.   *Phone: Bishop's Stortford 172.*

BISHOP'S STORTFORD & LONDON (CHARING CROSS / EMBANKMENT)

via Harlow, Epping, Loughton, Woodford, Walthamstow, Finsbury Park, Camden Town

Every 30 Minutes

TICKETS MAY BE OBTAINED ON THE COACHES OR AT:—

CHARING CROSS	The Underground Station Booking Hall, Charing Cross.
SOUTHAMPTON ROW ...	The District Messengers' Office, 109, Southampton Row.
BISHOP'S STORTFORD ...	The National Travel Bureau.
	Matthews, Newsagents, Hockerill Street.
	Copley's, Printers, North Street.
SAWBRIDGEWORTH	Slater's Stores.
POTTER STREET ...	Thompson's Tea Rooms.
HARLOW	Cornwall Austin, The Library.
EPPING	Larlham's, Golden Iris.
LOUGHTON	Mr. Butcher, next to Loughton Cinema.
WOODFORD	Alderton's Coaching Agency.
	R. Brown, 112B, High Road.
WALTHAMSTOW	W. J. Knight, Forest Road, Motor Coach Agent.
SEVEN SISTERS ROAD ...	Mr. W. Stanley, Booking Agent.
CAMDEN TOWN	J. MacKinnon-Hart, 5, Camden Road, Camden Town Booking Agency.

AND AT ALL DISTRICT MESSENGER OFFICES.

GREEN LINE coach services also operate to and from London and

Chelsham	Chertsey	Harpenden	Tunbridge Wells
Crawley	Edenbridge	Hertford	Windsor (via Slough)
Dorking	Godstone Green	Sunningdale	Tring
East Grinstead	Great Bookham	Maidenhead	Watford
Ascot	Redhill	Reigate	Windsor (via Staines)
Brentwood	Guildford	Sevenoaks	Welwyn Garden City

WAYSIDE NOTES.

The route from Charing Cross to Woodford is via Kingsway, Euston, Camden Town, Holloway, Finsbury Park, South Tottenham, and the Forest Road through Walthamstow. From Woodford to Thorndon the course lies through Epping Forest. The "Wake Arms" is convenient for Theydon Bois; from Epping omnibuses run to North Weald and Ongar. Potter Street is convenient for Latton, Spellbrook for Little Hallingbury. BISHOP'S STORTFORD. Features of interest for the visitor are the fine Parish Church (early 15th Century), which has a memorial of Cecil Rhodes, who was baptised here; the adjacent Roman Catholic Church of St. Joseph and the English Martyr; the mount and remains of the keep of the old castle of the Bishops of London; and the 16th Century "Boar's Head" (in High Street) and "Black Lion" (in Bridge Street), and other picturesque old inns and houses. Hockerill is reached by way of Bridge Street. The School is in the Hadham Road; the Training College near Hockerill Church. Market day (cattle, poultry, and general) is Thursday.

Cross. From 6th December the Oxted route was extended to Edenbridge with an hourly service being provided south of Chelsham. This was soon to prove excessive and from 11th February the following year the projection was reduced to two-hourly.

This was a tremendous rate of expansion for Green Line involving the recruitment and training of staff, the acquisition of the vehicles and suitable garage facilities, route planning, licensing, timetable and duty schedule compilation, the preparation of faretables and tickets and the publicising of the services. No doubt problems and difficulties were encountered but the speed at which new services appeared would indicate that the organisation was adept at overcoming obstacles.

LEGISLATION
1930–1932

By the end of 1930 there had been a phenomenal increase in motor coach operation – in 1928 the Metropolitan Police had licensed 347 coaches, in 1929 some 811 and in 1930 the figure had risen to 1,762. A census was taken in central London on two Saturdays in September 1930 and some 3,500 coaches were noted in each direction. These figures included all types of motor coach operation, not just the suburban services. Such expansion was not without problems and increasing traffic congestion in central London was blamed, in part, on the coaches. The two main terminal points of Oxford Circus and the Embankment at Charing Cross were particular black spots. Some operators even pointed out in their publicity that the times quoted for Oxford Circus were approximate due to traffic congestion in the area. Extending from Charing Cross Underground facing east on the Embankment a line of parked coaches sometimes stretching over 100 yards could be seen. Green Line usually maintained the favoured position adjacent to the station while others had to be content with standing further east. Green Line crews were instructed that one of them had to remain by the vehicle at all times in order to assist in obtaining traffic.

Two actions were taken to help reduce traffic congestion caused by the coaches. The first and simplest was to link up services to run across London thus alleviating the need for stand time in central London, a practice which Skylark had pioneered in December 1929. Green Line followed suit on 10th December 1930 when the Reigate route was linked to Welwyn

Coaches standing at Charing Cross. T 186 working to Bishop's Stortford heads a line of coaches waiting for departure time on Victoria Embankment. *E.G.P. Masterman*

Garden City and Great Bookham was linked to Harpenden with both routes running via Oxford Circus. Green Line issued the first weekly traffic circulars to staff and officials from this date and the through running is dealt with at some length. When leaving the outer terminal crews were instructed to display 'London' on the destination blinds which were to be altered to show the appropriate country terminal on southbound journeys at Golders Green and on northbound journeys at Clapham Common. It was stressed that it was essen-

tial that the crews finished their duties at their home depot and they were instructed to study the timetables and duty schedule with care. In the pre-war period cross London running sometimes involved crews changing over at a suitable point to a coach proceeding in the opposite direction.

The second action, decidedly costly, was the building of purpose built coach stations where services could terminate off of the public highway. A number had been established for use by other operators such as Kings Cross, Cartwright Gardens (near

Left The authorities favoured purpose built coach stations where services could terminate without the need to stand on the public highway where they might have caused traffic congestion. The London Terminal Coach Station was located at 80 Clapham Road near the Oval. This busy scene clearly shows that the public readily took to this new form of travel and often saw it as offering a more convenient albeit slower means of travel than the main line railways. *AEC*

Right Cross-London running began on 10th December 1930 when Reigate was linked to Welwyn Garden City and Great Bookham was linked to Harpenden in an attempt to overcome the problems caused by coaches terminating in central London. Harpenden based T 180 is seen heading for Great Bookham after route letters had been allocated to the services in February 1931. *W. Noel Jackson collection – Alan B. Cross*

Russell Square), Lupus Street (near Vauxhall Bridge) and Clapham Road. Some locations were not conveniently situated for passengers wishing to continue their journeys by bus or Underground and some involved coaches traversing unsuitable thoroughfares in order to gain access. General acquired a former brewery site in Soho situated on the south side of Broad Street (Broadwick Street today) and constructed a terminal coach station. Finished in an art-deco style the building was quite an achievement, so much so that the contractors C. F. Kearley advertising in the trade press stated, "The new coach station erected here for the Green Line Coaches, and comprising waiting hall, platform, canteen, etc., etc., and new exit and distinctive front elevation was executed in record time by C. F. Kearley Ltd, enabling a service being run on Christmas Day". The building was named Poland Street Coach Station – it was actually opposite one end of that street but presumably was so named as Poland Street formed a junction with Oxford Street. As the advertisement stated it opened, incredibly, on Christmas Day 1930 when the Guildford and Windsor via Staines services were amended to terminate there. Other services were soon diverted to terminate at the new facility – Maidenhead on 4th January 1931, Ascot/Sunningdale and Chertsey one week later, to be joined on 14th January by Dorking, Edenbridge, Sevenoaks and Tunbridge Wells. On the same date the Hertford route was increased to every 30 minutes and diverted to the Coach Station with the East Grinstead route which also was diverted away from Caterham-on-the-Hill to run via Whyteleafe. It was originally proposed to link this route through to Uxbridge and publicity was produced but it never happened.

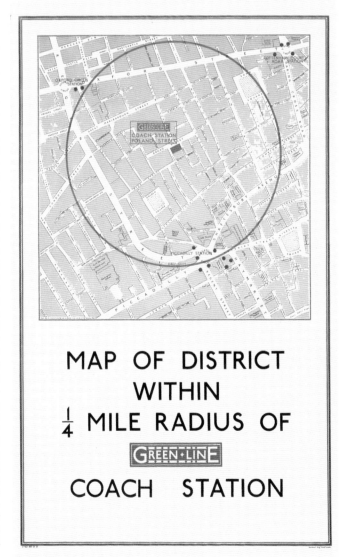

MAP OF DISTRICT WITHIN ¼ MILE RADIUS OF GREEN·LINE COACH STATION

This map, produced in a similar style to those exhibited at Underground stations, shows the exact location of Poland Street coach station in the very heart of Soho. *London's Transport Museum*

Facing page Green Line built their Poland Street coach station in this art-deco style. The frontage was in Broad Street (today named Broadwick Street) with the coaches entering from Lexington Street and departing via Ingestre Place. At night the building was impressively flood-lit. It opened on Christmas Day 1930. *London's Transport Museum*

Above The interior provided passengers with a heated waiting room and was also equipped with accommodation for staff and supervisors. As new services were introduced the coach station saw more activity. In this busy scene an unidentified T on the Byfleet route is accompanied by T 91 on the Dorking route and T 284, one of the second batch of Regals, heading for Tunbridge Wells. The Byfleet service started on 31st January 1931. *London's Transport Museum*

Where no convenient operating base existed Green Line rented accommodation to house the coaches. At Guildford space was rented in Rice and Harpers' yard in London Road where a withdrawn K-type bus sufficed as staff accommodation. *London's Transport Museum*

The 21 routes now established required 153 scheduled coaches on Monday to Saturday with two fewer on Sunday due to reduced running time being allowed on that day. The 151 Regals were supplemented by vehicles from the General and East Surrey private hire fleets.

It should be pointed out that most businesses worked a five-and-a-half day week thus the Saturday morning service was the same as Monday to Friday with a homeward peak between noon and 2pm. West End stores observed early closing on Saturday which tended to exacerbate the mid-day peak travel requirements from London. Many people chose to spend part of the weekend in London's countryside and seemingly everyone wished to return to the metropolis on Sunday evenings. As business travel became established some services had to be duplicated and on Sunday evenings, especially in summer, the timetable would apparently be discarded, all staff and coaches would be available and as soon as a coach filled up at the country terminal it would be despatched. Inspectors and other staff employed on such duties often had a difficult job. For example, when hop-pickers were returning from Tunbridge Wells, if a coach was not readily available they would adjourn to a near-by public house and when the coach arrived the despatcher would have the unenviable task of enticing them out of the pub! Further coaches would be deployed after the last scheduled departure time and everyone so desiring would be returned to London. These conditions were not, of course, unique to Green Line; the independent operators also had to cope with peaks of demand.

Green Line was becoming established and General, which started the venture in an attempt to eliminate the independents, who it saw as poaching their traffic, accepted that there was a significant market for this type of travel. Independent proprietors who might well have invested all their capital and borrowed further funds to set up their operations were competing with the seemingly limitless funds of the Combine.

Lord Ashfield and Frank Pick were astute businessmen and while the coaches were undoubtedly prestigious, the remainder of the operation was financed very frugally indeed. Crews were originally issued with caps and white tunics only but soon were turned-out in smart green uniforms. While bell punches were available for use by some conductors others were equipped with old pistol punches which had been used on the lorry buses running after the First World War. Garage accommodation was meagre with rented property or yards being used where no established base was available. The corrugated shed that was erected at Staines had previously seen service at Potters Bar while at Guildford a withdrawn K type bus served as staff accommodation. On 2nd March 1931 operations at Romford were switched from Metcalf's Works on Eastern Avenue to premises at 998 Hare Street at Gidea Park. It was no more than a muddy farm and a fitter, while peering under the bonnet of a coach, complained of being butted by a goat!

While Green Line was establishing its system the question of control of passenger road transport was being looked at by Herbert Morrison, the Minister of

At Staines some land was acquired in London Road and this corrugated structure erected. The shed had reputedly been dismantled from the Overground premises in Potters Bar and re-erected on this site. Coaches were provided for the Ascot, Sunningdale and Windsor via Staines routes. *London's Transport Museum*

Transport, appointed by the second Labour government which came to power in June 1929 with Ramsay MacDonald as Prime Minister. The proposals which were enacted as the Road Traffic Act, 1930 swept away existing licensing arrangements and divided the country into traffic areas, each one under a commissioner responsible to the minister. Vehicles were subject to inspection and approval and would then be licensed to ply for hire (Public Service Vehicle Licence) while Road Service Licences would be issued to control the bus and coach routes. The latter were divided into Stage Carriage Licences to cover ordinary bus services with at least one fare below one shilling and Express Service Licences to cover coach services with all fares of one shilling or more. The proposed route would be surveyed, operators were required to submit faretables and time-tables to the Commissioner and stopping places would also be considered. Operators were required to apply to the commissioners of each area through which the proposed route was to run but the procedure was simplified by the issuing of so-called backing licences in other areas. Traffic courts were to be established where all applications could be considered and objectors had the right to be heard. The Commissioner could approve or reject the application: in the latter case the operator could appeal to the Minister of Transport whose decision would be final. The intention was to restrict competition and thus reduce the number of vehicles on the road. Drivers and conductors would also to be licensed by the commissioners but licence badges issued in any one traffic area would be valid throughout the country.

The legislation received royal assent on 1st August 1930 but the complex and far reaching proposals could not be implemented overnight and the requirements of the act were to be phased in as directed by the Minister. The question of traffic congestion in central London caused by the coaches had not gone unnoticed and the Traffic Advisory Committee had studied the problem during 1930. This committee made proposals to the minister to ban absolutely coaches from large parts of the West End and City with further restrictions placed on the surrounding areas. The view was that the coaches should complement the railway services, not compete with them, and that all coaches should terminate at points on the periphery of the central area, off the public highway, in purpose-built premises. The minister announced on 19th December that he proposed to make restrictions but protests from the industry were considerable. The Minister then gave directions to the traffic commissioner for the metropolis that when he was considering road service licence applications he should have regard to restricting coach operation in the specified area and that control was required within six miles of Charing Cross. About the same time the Minister decreed that Road Service Licences would be required after 1st April 1931 and that any route started after 9th February could not continue after 31st March. If a route was in operation on or before 9th February the operator could use its existence as an established facility when arguing the case. It did not in itself guarantee that the licence would be issued.

A further batch of one hundred Regals was delivered between December 1930 and February 1931 to meet the needs of the expanding network. They differed from the original batch in having a front entrance and a revised style of destination box with the Green Line panel appearing below the destination. T 208 is seen outside its garage on the site of Weymann's body works in Station Road, Addlestone. Note the prominent timetable information display. *London's Transport Museum*

Further cross-London routes were introduced on 14th January 1931 including one from Bushey to Crawley. Conductor Winzaar of Leavesden Road garage, complete with Bell Punch ticket punch, stands proudly by brand new T 236 at Redhill shortly after the route's introduction. By this time crews were issued with smart green uniforms instead of just caps and white tunics. *Laurie Akehurst collection*

It was in the light of these circumstances that the race was on to establish services before 9th February. Green Line needed more coaches and a batch of one hundred Regals (T 207–306) had been ordered with the first examples entering service in December. They differed from the earlier batch in having a front enclosed sliding door, a rear emergency door, a modified blind box arrangement and seating 30 passengers. The independents were obtaining coaches as fast as they could and some even started new services after Green Line was established in the area. Most of these services either failed economically or were eventually forced to withdraw by the Minister of Transport.

Once the new coaches were available new routes could be quickly established and no time was lost. On 14th January 1931 more cross London running was introduced with the Crawley and Redhill route extended to Bushey Station with the coaches standing in Villiers Road. Leavesden Road provided some of the coaches but the refusal of Watford Council to license the route meant that the coaches had to terminate short of Watford. The Godstone Green service was diverted via Whyteleafe and linked to Tring on a 60-minute headway and a new hourly route was provided from Caterham Station to Hemel Hempstead via Old Coulsdon and Croydon then following the Tring route to Two Waters. Like the Tring route the coaches could not stop in Watford. Cross London running was not without its initial problems as a former conductor once explained that the National and Green Line crews from the north could do nothing right as far as the East Surrey inspectors were concerned. Word soon got round and the National inspectors started victimising the East Surrey crews but eventually all concerned managed to co-exist in a state of harmony. Also on 14th January the Brentwood route was increased in frequency to 15 minutes am and 12 minutes pm daily and another goal was reached when the Reigate to Welwyn Garden City route was extended to Hitchin. The unsatisfactory Welwyn Garden City garaging facilities were replaced by new facilities in the premises of A. E. Primes in Queen Street, Hitchin.

The next development was quite surprising to many observers at the time and involved the Amersham & District company of which General had bought control in August 1929 but allowed the local company to continue. Five of the rear entrance Regals were painted in the Amersham & District livery of green and cream to start an hourly service on 26th January 1931 from Amersham to Oxford Circus via Uxbridge. On 1st February the route was extended to Chesham. A number of independent operators had tried their luck in the Chilterns, the most notable being West London Coaches which commenced on 15th

LONDON—AYLESBURY
LONDON—CHESHAM
SERVICES

TRAVEL BY COACH—BUT

BE SURE IT'S
WEST LONDON

See inside for details

Five of the rear entrance Regals (T 69, 71, 89, 96 and 104) were painted in the green and cream livery of Amersham & District to work the service from Amersham to London which the Amersham company operated on behalf of Green Line from 26th January 1931. T 96 stands outside the Amersham & District garage in Amersham old town. Following a decision of the Southern Area Traffic Commissioner, the route which had been extended to Chesham was curtailed at Amersham and prevented from stopping in the Denham area from 22nd October 1931. The side route board reflects the revised arrangements with the destination Chesham having been amended to Amersham and Denham painted out.
J. F. Higham collection

West London Coaches started running from London to Aylesbury via Rickmansworth on 15th September 1928. A shuttle connected at Amersham for Chesham. This leaflet shows a splendid Duple bodied Damiler CF6 which eventually became DST 6 in the LPTB fleet.

September 1928 running five journeys from the Coach Station in Lupus Street to Aylesbury via Rickmansworth and Amersham. At Amersham New Town a shuttle met the coaches to convey passengers to Chesham. The fares varied over the years but shortly after the Amersham & District service and the Green Line operation to Rickmansworth commenced (see below) they were offering 1/- minimum fares over the entire route on their driver-operated coaches. At Gerrards Cross the

Amersham & District service joined the Skylark route from High Wycombe to Oxford Circus which was every 60 minutes but strengthened at busy times by a 30-minute service from Gerrards Cross. Another operator, Western Star Motorways Ltd of Hayes, was running some nine journeys a day from Chalfont St Giles to Oxford Circus but the service was reduced, eventually disappearing altogether. Western Star even tried a route of three daily journeys from Chesham to Oxford Circus via Rickmansworth, Harefield and Uxbridge.

Further changes were made on 28th January 1931 when a new route from Farningham to Poland Street Coach Station via Sidcup was introduced on an hourly headway worked from the East Surrey garage at Swanley. The Ascot, Sunningdale and Windsor via Staines routes were diverted away from Syon Lane to run via Brentford High Street. More significantly the Ascot and Sunningdale service was extended from London to Dartford. Swanley garage initially supplied the coaches at this end but from 1st April when the General garage at Crayford was handed over to East Surrey they were transferred there. On 31st January three half-hourly routes appeared all running to Poland Street Coach Station – one from Sunbury Common via Kingston and Richmond, one from West Byfleet via Cobham, Kingston By-Pass and Barnes and one from Rickmansworth via Pinner and Harrow. The Sunbury route was worked from temporary premises in Hanworth Road, Sunbury, the West Byfleet service shared garage facilities with the Chertsey route in Weymann's Works at Addlestone and the Rickmansworth service was worked from Watford Leavesden Road. Problems over licensing in Rickmansworth meant that passengers had to obtain tickets from agents before boarding the coach in that town. Finally on 7th February Green Line had proposed to introduce a service from Beaconsfield to Poland Street Coach Station but insufficient numbers of coaches precluded the service from running further than Uxbridge towards London. The 30-minute service was worked by coaches garaged in the Associated Equipment Company works at Southall.

The cut-off date of 9th February passed but it did not stop some operators including Green Line introducing new routes. On 18th February the Godstone Green to Tring service was extended to Aylesbury with temporary garage facilities found at Cubitt Works in Aylesbury and Leavesden Road retaining just one coach. On 21st February an hourly route from Upminster to Charing Cross via Barking appeared with Romford Metcalf's Works providing the coaches. One week later the delivery of additional coaches allowed a half-hourly frequency to be operated but a proposed route from Upminster via Ilford never

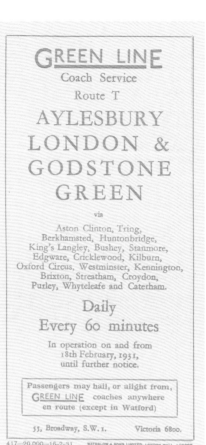

materialised. To comply with the requirements of the Road Traffic Act, the Aylesbury route was curtailed at Tring from 1st April and the Upminster route ran for the last time on 31st March. Some independents continued to operate routes introduced after 9th February but they went on to incur fines and the future of all such routes was ultimately doomed.

During February some organisational matters were tidied-up with the garages at Addlestone, Staines and Slough being transferred from General to East Surrey control. The coaches, of course, continued to run in Green Line livery. These organisational changes resulted in problems with the traffic commissioners over the legal lettering and later in the year an undertaking was given to the South East Area Traffic Commissioners that only vehicles bearing the name of Trevor Lloyd Davies (the company secretary of East Surrey) would be used on the Green Line services operated by Autocar and East Surrey. Other Green Line services would use vehicles showing the name John Christopher Mitchell as the secretary of Green Line Coaches Ltd.

By this time Green Line was running 27 routes with the country terminal being the only means of identification and this matter was addressed with the routes being allocated letters, officially from 21st February 1931. The original lettering system is listed opposite.

The style of the original timetable hand bills did not lend the design to the additional information required by the cross-London routes and a folded leaflet gradually became standard. This leaflet was produced for the extension of route T from Tring to Aylesbury on 18th February 1931. The extension fell foul of the traffic commissioner and had to be withdrawn after 31st March.

				No. of coaches		
Letter	Route	Frequency	Garage	MF	Sat	Sun
A	Ascot or Sunningdale – Great Scotland Yard – Dartford	30 mins	Staines	7	7	7
			Swanley	5	5	5
B	Brentwood – Charing Cross	12/15 mins (1)	Romford	18	18	16
C	Chertsey – Poland Street Coach Station	30 mins	Addlestone	7	7	7
D	Dorking – Poland Street Coach Station	30 mins	Leatherhead	7	7	7
E	Crawley – Redhill – Oxford Circus – Bushey	30 mins (2)	Crawley	3	3	3
			Reigate	4	4	4
			Watford	4	4	4
F	Hertford – Poland Street Coach Station	30 mins	Ware	7	7	7
G	Guildford – Poland Street Coach Station	30 mins	Guildford	8	8	8
H	Harpenden – Oxford Circus – Great Bookham	30 mins	Harpenden	6	6	5
			Leatherhead	6	6	6
I	Farningham – Poland Street Coach Station	60 mins	Swanley	3	3	3
J	Edenbridge – Chelsham – Poland Street Coach Stn	30 mins (3)	Chelsham	6	6	6
K	Hemel Hempstead – Oxford Circus – Caterham	60 mins	Watford	4	4	4
			Godstone	2	2	2
L	Tunbridge Wells – Poland Street Coach Station	30 mins	Tunbridge Wells	9	9	9
M	Maidenhead – Poland Street Coach Station	30 mins	Slough	6	6	6
N	Windsor – Staines – Poland Street Coach Stn	30 mins	Staines	7	7	6
O	Bishop's Stortford – Charing Cross	30 mins	Bishop's Stortford	8	8	8
P	Rickmansworth – Poland Street Coach Station	30 mins	Watford	6	6	6
Q	Uxbridge – Poland Street Coach Station	30 mins	Southall	4	4	4
R	Reigate – Oxford Circus – Hitchin	30 mins	Reigate	6	6	6
			Hitchin	9	9	9
S	Sunbury Common – Poland Street Coach Stn	30 mins	Sunbury	6	6	5
T	Aylesbury – Oxford Circus – Godstone Green	60 mins	Aylesbury	4	4	4
			Watford	1	1	1
			Godstone	3	3	3
U	East Grinstead – Poland Street Coach Station	60 mins	East Grinstead	4	4	4
V	Watford – Golders Green	30 mins	Watford	3	3	3
AV	Upminster – Barking – Charing Cross	60 mins	Romford	3	3	3
W	Watford – Charing Cross	30 mins	Watford	5	5	5
X	Sevenoaks – Westerham – Poland Street Coach Stn	60 mins	Dunton Green	4	4	4
Y	West Byfleet – Poland Street Coach Station	30 mins	Addlestone	6	6	6
Z	Windsor – Slough – Charing Cross	30 mins (4)	Slough	10	11	6

Notes: (1) Every 6 minutes Romford – London during peak hours.
(2) Crawley – Redhill every 60 minutes.
(3) Edenbridge – Chelsham every 120 minutes.
(4) Peak hours and Saturday afternoon every 10/20 minutes.

The scheduled coach requirement at this stage was 201 Monday to Friday, 202 Saturday and 192 Sunday and these figures increased by two daily when the AV was increased to 30 minutes from 28th February. The enforced withdrawals after 31st March saw the daily requirement fall by six coaches to a maximum of 196 on Saturday. These figures exclude the daily requirement of four coaches for the Amersham & District route.

After 1st April operators could not vary their services without the approval of the traffic commissioners so the suburban coaching scene entered a short-lived period of stability. Apart from some minor intermediate diversions the only significant change came on 20th May when route Z was increased to a summer frequency of 10 or 20 minutes daily thus providing a 10-minute headway between London and Slough with route M.

The licence applications of Green Line and the independents came before the traffic commissioners in late autumn 1931. At this time the Metropolitan Traffic Commissioner covered the Metropolitan Police area so similar hearings had to be held by the relevant traffic commissioners for the adjoining areas into which the coach services operated. This led to bizarre situations, for example, the two Watford services passed out of the

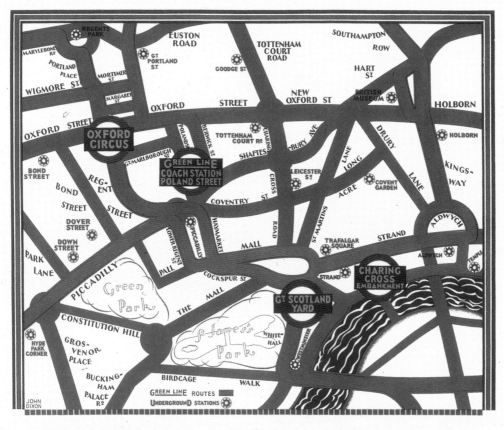

The introduction of route letters on 21st February 1931 made route identification somewhat easier. This poster, by John Dixon and dating from the summer of 1931, shows the main central London stopping places for the routes but it must be remembered coaches could be hailed at any point. *London's Transport Museum*

GREEN·LINE COACH SERVICES

From GREEN·LINE Coach Station (Poland St. - Near Oxford Circus)

Route				Route			
C	-	CHERTSEY	Every 30 Mins.	M	-	MAIDENHEAD	Every 30 Mins.
D	-	DORKING	Every 30 Mins.	N	-	WINDSOR (VIA STAINES)	Every 30 Mins.
F	-	HERTFORD	Every 30 Mins.	P	-	RICKMANSWORTH	Every 30 Mins.
G	-	GUILDFORD	Every 30 Mins.	Q	-	UXBRIDGE	Every 30 Mins.
I	-	FARNINGHAM	Every 60 Mins.	S	-	SUNBURY COMMON	Every 30 Mins.
J	-	EDENBRIDGE	Every 120 Mins.	U	-	EAST GRINSTEAD	Every 60 Mins.
J	-	CHELSHAM	Every 30 Mins.	X	-	SEVENOAKS (VIA WESTERHAM)	Every 60 Mins.
L	-	TUNBRIDGE WELLS (VIA SEVENOAKS)	Every 30 Mins.	Y	-	BYFLEET	Every 30 Mins.

From Oxford Circus (District Messenger & Theatre Ticket Co. Ltd. 279 REGENT STREET, W.)

Route				Route			
E. K. T or W	-	BUSHEY	Every 10 Mins.	K	-	HEMEL HEMPSTEAD	Every 60 Mins.
E	-	REDHILL	Every 30 Mins.	K	-	CATERHAM	Every 60 Mins.
E	-	CRAWLEY	Every 60 Mins.	R	-	HITCHIN	Every 30 Mins.
H	-	HARPENDEN	Every 30 Mins.	R	-	REIGATE	Every 30 Mins.
H	-	GREAT BOOKHAM	Every 30 Mins.	T	-	TRING	Every 60 Mins.

T or U - GODSTONE GREEN - Every 30 Mins.

From Charing Cross UNDERGROUND Station (Embankment)

Route				Route			
B	-	BRENTWOOD	Every 15 Mins.	W	-	WATFORD	Every 30 Mins.
O	-	BISHOPS STORTFORD	Every 30 Mins.	Z	-	WINDSOR (VIA SLOUGH)	Every 15 Mins.

From Great Scotland Yard (Whitehall)

Route				Route			
A	-	ASCOT	Every 60 Mins.	A	-	SUNNINGDALE	Every 60 Mins.
				A	-	DARTFORD - Every 30 Mins.	

(1640-350-14.7.31)

(1509-2000-7.7.31)

WATERLOW & SONS LTD LONDON, DUNSTABLE & WATFORD

Metropolitan area at the River Colne bridge in Watford Lower High Street so the hearing for the backing licences involved all interested parties travelling to Cambridge to be heard before the Eastern Area Traffic Commissioner.

The transcripts of the hearings provide an interesting account of operational practices at the time. The independent operators which were objecting to Green Line's applications claimed that the latter had flooded the road with coaches thus making their services less remunerative. Jean Pierre Hensman, the proprietor of Sunset Pullman Coaches, referred to Green Line as the 'Green Monster'! On routes where they were engaged in competition it was alleged that Green Line were operating duplicate coaches to act as chasers to the independents' coaches rather than due to any traffic demand. Green Line were also accused of timing their coaches to run immediately prior to those of their competitors. Evidence was often presented to show that Green Line loadings were poor especially towards the terminals of some routes with the assertion that they should be curtailed well short of their existing destinations. For example the Rickmansworth route had an average loading beyond Batchworth Heath of only 2.9 passengers per coach. The average loadings at Harlow on a given day for the Bishop's Stortford service were just two passengers per coach against Acme's figure of nine. Bucks Express claimed that their half-hourly service (fifteen minutes at peak times) from Watford was adequate to cater for demand but that in addition to this Green Line were providing some 122 daily journeys from Bushey Station to London. Green Line were accused of advertising impossibly tight journey times where they were in competition necessitating the speed limit to be broken. This certainly seems to be the case with 45 minutes from Bishop's Stortford to Loughton requiring an average speed of 22.5 miles per hour, 52 minutes from Windsor to Hammersmith necessitating an average speed of 23.5 mph, 65 minutes from Guildford to Hammersmith requiring 25.7 mph and 62 minutes from Tunbridge Wells to Bromley requiring an average of 25.8 mph. These timings may have been achievable with a full coach from the terminal with no intermediate riders but would be virtually impossible with the need to make a number of stops to pick up passengers. The early coach drivers were certainly expected to put their foot down at all times!

Allegations were made that short distance passengers were sometimes carried at fares less than those advertised by the practice of issuing child's tickets. Some independent operators clearly regarded the fare chart as submitted to the traffic commissioners as no more than a rough guide. Anecdotal evidence tells the story of a lady travelling on a Hillman's coach who on stating her destination was asked by the conductor how much General charged. Upon receiving the reply 'fourpence halfpenny' he promptly issued a 4d ticket. Redcar alleged that Green Line were running an unauthorised service as it had become custom and practice to operate certain duplicates from London to Tunbridge Wells via Westerham which was a linking between routes L and X. To this end a surviving destination blind record reveals that a 'Tunbridge Wells via Westerham' display was actually provided.

As might be expected the solicitor representing General and Green Line at the hearings, Mr King-Hamilton, presented a rather different view of things. He claimed that General, National or East Surrey were the first operator on the road with ordinary bus services and that Green Line was merely an enhancement of their services in the light of coach competition in their area. It was claimed that in 1929 General had lost some five million passengers paying a fare of 7d or more compared with 1928 and in 1930 had lost a further 3.5 million. General's policy was stated to be to provide transport facilities in every part of the Metropolitan area or within 25 miles of Charing Cross. Green Line was claimed to be fulfilling a public demand and that in many cases the capacity of their competitors' coaches was inadequate to meet such demand. Green Line's operating costs were stated to be 8d per car mile and that it had taken some time to work up the receipts to an acceptable level but it was claimed that by mid 1931 their operations were broadly covering costs.

The first Traffic Commissioner for the Metropolis was Gleeson Edward Robinson (1881–1978), an experienced solicitor and barrister-at-law. Robinson considered his decisions in the light of the Minister's directive, previously stated, that restrictions should be applied to motor coach operation within six miles of Charing Cross. The commissioner favoured terminal locations away from the central area of London examples being Harewood Avenue at the side of Marylebone station, Lancaster Street at Elephant & Castle and Buckingham Palace Road near the junction with Pimlico Road. Many applications of both Green Line and the independents were refused and where they were granted the picking up points within the Metropolitan Police area were severely restricted. A licence was granted for the

Tunbridge Wells was always a popular destination with Green Line travellers. Due to the intensive competition between Green Line and Red Car the return fare cost just 4d more than the single. Return fares were normally fifty per cent higher than singles which would indicate that under normal circumstances the return fare to Tunbridge Wells should have cost 5/3d. The 78-mile round trip cost just over an old halfpenny per mile – bargain travel! Verney L. Danvers designed this poster in 1931. *London's Transport Museum*

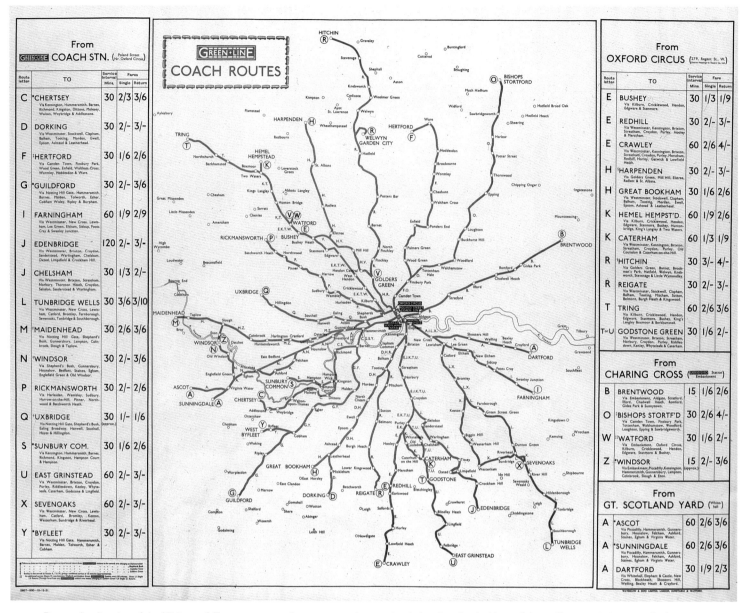

Route letter	TO	Service Interval Mins.	Fares Single	Return
C	CHERTSEY Via Kensington, Hammersmith, Barnes, Richmond, Kingston, Dittons, Molesey, Walton, Weybridge & Addlestone.	30	2/3	3/6
D	DORKING Via Westminster, Stockwell, Clapham, Balham, Tooting, Morden, Ewell, Epsom, Ashtead & Leatherhead.	30	2/-	3/-
F	HERTFORD Via Camden Town, Finsbury Park, Wood Green, Enfield, Waltham Cross, Wormley, Hoddesdon & Ware.	30	1/6	2/6
G	GUILDFORD Via Notting Hill Gate, Hammersmith, Barnes, Malden, Tolworth, Esher, Cobham Wisley, Ripley & Burpham.	30	2/-	3/6
I	FARNINGHAM Via Westminster, New Cross, Lewisham, Lee Green, Eltham, Sidcup, Foots Cray & Swanley Junction.	60	1/9	2/9
J	EDENBRIDGE Via Westminster, Brixton, Croydon, Sanderstead, Warlingham, Chelsham, Oxted, Limpsfield & Crockham Hill.	120	2/-	3/-
J	CHELSHAM Via Westminster, Brixton, Streatham, Norbury, Thornton Heath, Croydon, Selsdon, Sanderstead & Warlingham.	30	1/3	2/-
L	TUNBRIDGE WELLS Via Westminster, New Cross, Lewisham, Catford, Bromley, Farnborough, Sevenoaks, Tonbridge & Southborough.	30	3/6	3/10
M	MAIDENHEAD Via Notting Hill Gate, Shepherd's Bush, Gunnersbury, Brentford, Colnbrook, Slough & Taplow.	30	2/6	3/6
N	WINDSOR Via Shepherd's Bush, Gunnersbury, Hounslow, Bedfont, Staines, Egham, Englefield Green & Old Windsor.	30	2/-	3/6
P	RICKMANSWORTH Via Harlesden, Wembley, Sudbury, Harrow-on-the-Hill, Pinner, Northwood & Batchworth Heath.	30	2/-	2/6
Q	UXBRIDGE Via Notting Hill Gate, Shepherd's Bush, Ealing Broadway, Hanwell, Southall, Hayes & Hillingdon.	30 (approx.)	1/-	1/6
S	SUNBURY COM. Via Kensington, Hammersmith, Barnes, Richmond, Kingston, Hampton Court & Hampton.	30	1/6	2/6
U	EAST GRINSTEAD Via Westminster, Brixton, Croydon, Purley, Riddlesdown, Kenley, Whyteleafe, Caterham, Godstone & Lingfield.	60	2/-	3/-
X	SEVENOAKS Via Westminster, New Cross, Lewisham, Catford, Bromley, Keston, Westerham, Sundridge & Riverhead.	60	2/-	3/-
Y	BYFLEET Via Notting Hill Gate, Hammersmith, Barnes, Malden, Tolworth, Esher & Cobham.	30	2/-	3/-

From OXFORD CIRCUS (279, Regent St., W.)

Route letter	TO	Service Interval Mins.	Fare Single	Return
E	BUSHEY Via Kilburn, Cricklewood, Hendon, Edgware & Stanmore.	30	1/3	1/9
E	REDHILL Via Westminster, Kennington, Brixton, Streatham, Croydon, Purley, Merstham & Merstham.	30	2/-	3/-
E	CRAWLEY Via Westminster, Kennington, Brixton, Streatham, Croydon, Purley, Merstham, Redhill, Horley, Gatwick & Lowfield	60	2/6	4/-
H	HARPENDEN Via Golders Green, Mill Hill, Elstree, Radlett & St. Albans.	30	2/-	3/-
H	GREAT BOOKHAM Via Westminster, Stockwell, Clapham, Balham, Tooting, Morden, Ewell, Epsom, Ashtead & Leatherhead.	30	1/6	2/6
K	HEMEL HEMPST'D. Via Kilburn, Cricklewood, Hendon, Edgware, Stanmore, Bushey, Hemelbridge, King's Langley & Two Waters.	60	1/9	2/6
K	CATERHAM Via Westminster, Kennington, Brixton, Streatham, Croydon, Purley, Old Coulsdon & Caterham-on-the-Hill.	60	1/3	1/9
R	HITCHIN Via Golders Green, Barnet, Brookman's Park, Hatfield, Welwyn, Knebworth, Stevenage & Little Wymondley.	30	3/-	4/-
R	REIGATE Via Westminster, Stockwell, Clapham, Balham, Tooting, Mitcham, Sutton, Belmont, Burgh Heath & Kingswood	30	2/-	3/-
T	TRING Via Kilburn, Cricklewood, Hendon, Edgware, Stanmore, King's Langley Boxmoor & Berkhamsted.	60	2/6	3/6
T or U	GODSTONE GREEN Via Westminster, Brixton, Streatham, Norbury, Croydon, Purley, Riddlesdown, Kenley, Whyteleafe & Caterham.	30	1/6	2/-

From CHARING CROSS (Underground Station Embankment)

B	BRENTWOOD Via Embankment, Aldgate, Stratford, Ilford, Chadwell Heath, Romford, Gidea Park & Sunnytown.	15	1/6	2/6
O	BISHOPS STORTF'D Via Camden Town, Finsbury Park, Tottenham, Walthamstow, Woodford, Loughton, Epping & Sawbridgeworth.	30	2/6	4/-
W	WATFORD Via Embankment, Oxford Circus, Kilburn, Cricklewood, Hendon, Edgware, Stanmore & Bushey.	30	1/6	2/-
Z	WINDSOR Via Embankment, Piccadilly, Kensington, Hammersmith, Gunnersbury, Lampton, Colnbrook, Slough & Eton.	15 (approx.)	2/-	3/6

From GT. SCOTLAND YARD (Whitehall)

A	ASCOT Via Embankment, Hammersmith, Gunnersbury, Hounslow, Feltham, Ashford, Staines, Egham & Virginia Water.	60	2/6	3/6
A	SUNNINGDALE Via Piccadilly, Hammersmith, Gunnersbury, Hounslow, Feltham, Ashford, Staines, Egham & Virginia Water.	60	2/6	3/6
A	DARTFORD Via Whitehall, Elephant & Castle, New Cross, Blackheath, Shooters. Hill, Welling, Bexley Heath & Crayford.	30	1/9	2/3

Due to the directive of the Minister of Transport concerning motor coach operation in London, the decisions of the traffic commissioner on the licence applications and the ensuing inquiry the system was to remain static for nearly a year. This poster map shows the system in 1931 before the acquisition of any independent operators. *London's Transport Museum*

Ascot and Sunningdale services. Starting from Harewood Avenue the route was via Westbourne Grove to the next picking up point at Shepherds Bush The Lawn after which coaches could pick up at Chiswick Heathfield Terrace, Hounslow Alcazar Cinema, East Bedfont The Bell and Staines Police Station.

It was hardly surprising that the operators lodged appeals to the Minister of Transport either over the failure to be granted a licence or the terms of their licence, namely the unsuitable terminal points and severely restricted boarding points. Inundated with appeals the Minister of Transport decided to set up a Committee of Inquiry into London motor coach services. The chairman was

Lord Amulree (1860–1942), born William Warrander MacKenzie. He was an experienced lawyer who served as President of the Industrial Court from 1919 to 1926 and, among other duties, chaired a Royal Commission on licensing laws. He had been Minister for Air in the MacDonald government but had resigned in August 1931.

The inquiry opened at Middlesex Guildhall on 18th April 1932 and among those heard Frank Pick gave evidence at considerable length. The first report was published on 18th June and dealt with the exclusion of motor coaches from the central area and the limitation of picking up points within the entire Metropolitan Police Area and recommended that all coach services should terminate off of the public highway.

The second report, issued on 2nd August, dealt with some 35 appeals of which it was recommended that Green Line be allowed to operate some 13 routes refused by the Traffic Commissioner. The minister accepted the findings and announced that the new arrangements should apply from 19th September. There was a great deal at stake within the industry and protests were considerable from the operators who among other actions petitioned the King. Action was taken in the High Court and a 'rule nisi' was granted against the Traffic Commissioner which resulted in the minister suspending his decision to accept the Amulree recommendations thus allowing the services to continue unchanged for a further period.

The use of double-deck vehicles on Green Line offered certain advantages as the larger seating capacity could negate the need for a duplicate vehicle at busy times and on the more frequent routes would permit a reduction in frequency thereby achieving cost savings. Over the years four such experimental vehicles were produced. The first, LT 1137, appeared in 1931. It was fitted out to full coach standards and, curiously, had a front entrance and a rear staircase. A section of the roof could be folded back when the weather permitted. It ran initially on route E from Bushey to Crawley and, after the October 1933 revisions, on route J from Watford to Reigate. It was displaced from Green Line work in 1935 to be used as a Country Area bus and was rebuilt in 1937 with the staircase at the front. *London's Transport Museum*

Left A view of the upper deck when new. *London's Transport Museum*

ACQUISITION
1932–1934

As if the uncertainty of the situation following the Amulree Inquiry did not cause enough trouble for the independent coach operators, even blacker clouds were on the horizon. In December 1929 Herbert Morrison, the Minister of Transport, had stated in the House of Commons that it was his government's view that common management had to be established for London's passenger transport through public ownership. Work on the bill advanced but was interrupted by the fall of the government in August 1931. Work was restarted on the London Transport Bill in early 1932 by Percy Pybus, the new minister in MacDonald's national government. It was in this period of a somewhat unclear future that a number of the independents decided to offer their businesses to the Combine rather than to await their fate under the proposed legislation.

The existing route licences could not be varied thus Green Line, when acquiring an independent's route, were obliged to run to the existing times and to charge the existing fares. On certain routes return and season tickets eventually became inter-available with existing Green Line services but passengers using the acquired services were never allowed the established facility of transferring to the Underground.

The first to be acquired was the Skylark Motor Coach Co. Ltd on 6th February 1932 which by this time was running three routes – Hertford Heath to Oxford Circus, designated AF by Green Line, Guildford to Oxford Circus (BG) and High Wycombe to Oxford Circus (AQ). It was noted that the Skylark fleet was in poor condition and the

coaches would require overhauls and repainting and it was decided to paint them into green livery but they could not carry the Green Line fleet name until the vehicle licences had been transferred. Skylark's garage facilities were used for a short time but from 2nd March AF was transferred to the National garage at Ware. On 2nd April a new permanent garage in Leas Road, Guildford was opened to replace the temporary Green Line premises at Rice and Harpers and, in addition, the coaches for BG were worked from this site. In the case of High Wycombe the coaches were transferred to the Amersham & District garage in that town. In common with other acquired operators London based coaches were required which Skylark garaged in Thackray's premises in Ledbury Mews. It is believed that these coaches were transferred to the former General, now Green Line, private hire garage at Brixton Hill at an early opportunity. The conductors, however, were instructed that they must pay in at Poland Street Coach Station. Skylark received £32,117 for its business and some 19 Gilford coaches came into the Green Line fleet.

On 20th February Bucks Expresses was acquired with its Watford to Oxford Circus service becoming AW. The fleet consisted of three Maudslays, five Gilfords and two AEC Regals and the garage in Watford Parade continued to be used until the coaches were transferred to Leavesden Road on 18th May. The business had been sold for £21,677 and the petrol and service station was sold by General as soon as practicable.

With the demise of Skylark it was only a matter of time before the same fate befell Regent Motor Services which shared garage facilities with Skylark at Hertford Heath. The company acquired on 2nd March had a fleet of four Gilfords which operated its Hertford to Oxford Circus service which Green Line designated CF. One of the smaller concerns, the business fetched just £5,239.

The operation of coach services to Ongar had a rather complex ancestry with many operators trying their luck on a variety of intermediate routeings. Curtis and Thompson had commenced operation in November 1929 running to Liverpool Street via Epping New Road, Chingford and Dalston. They sold out to Associated Coaches (Ongar) Ltd in June 1930 and it was this company which, in turn, sold out on 31st March 1932. An intensive service, now designated AO, was operated with coaches running at 20-minute intervals at busy times and short-stage fares were charged between Epping and Ongar. As there was no convenient garage in the area the existing premises at Ongar continued to be used and seven Gilfords and three Leylands were taken over. The business was sold for £20,286.

With the acquisition of Associated Coaches (Ongar) Ltd the garage in Ongar passed to Green Line. Coaches stand on the forecourt of the so-called Bridge Garage in Ongar in April 1932. *London's Transport Museum*

GREEN LINE — ROUTE D

Operated by
EAST SURREY TRACTION CO., LTD.,
Bell Street, Reigate ('Phone: Reigate 593),

DORKING EPSOM & LONDON

(GREEN LINE COACH STATION)
(Poland Street - Near Oxford Circus)

Via Leatherhead, Epsom, Morden, Tooting,
Balham, Clapham Common, Kennington,
Westminster, Regent Street

DAILY EVERY 30 MINS.

LEATHERHEAD EPSOM AND LONDON EVERY 15 MINUTES

(See time-table of Route H Harpenden and Gt. Bookham
for additional times).

To London

Departure Points	WEEKDAYS			SUNDAYS		
	First Coach	Then at mins. past each hour	Last Coach	First Coach	Then at mins. past each hour	Last Coach
	a.m.		p.m.	a.m.		p.m.
Dorking (Falkland Arms) ... dep.	7 12	42 12	9 42	7 42	12 42	9 42
Dorking (White Horse) ,,	7 15	45 15	9 45	7 45	15 45	9 45
Leatherhead (Institute) ,,	7 31	1 31	10 1	8 1	1 31	10 1
Epsom (Clock Tower) ,,	7 41	11 41	10 11	8 11	41 11	10 11
Ewell (Post Office) ... ,,	7 47	17 47	10 17	8 17	47 17	10 17
Morden Station (Und.) ,,	8 1	31 1	10 31	8 31	1 31	10 31
Tooting (38, Tooting High St.) ,,	8 11	41 11	10 41	8 41	11 41	10 41
LONDON (Poland Street Coach Stn.) arr.	8 51	21 51	11 21	9 21	51 21	11 21

Late Coaches to Leatherhead from Dorking on Weekdays & Sundays at 10.3, 10.33, 11.3, 11.33 p.m., 12.3, 12.33, 1.9 a.m.

To Dorking

Departure Points	WEEKDAYS			SUNDAYS		
	First Coach	Then at Minutes past each hour	Last Coaches	First Coach	Then at Minutes past each hour	Last Coaches
	a.m.		p.m. p.m.	a.m.		p.m. p.m.
LONDON (Poland Street Coach Stn.) dep.	8 54	24 54	10 54 11 30	9 24	54 24	10 54 11 30
London (Gt. Scotland Yard) ,,	9 5	35 5	11 5 11 41	9 35	5 35	11 5 11 41
Kennington (The Horns) ,,	9 14	44 14	11 14 11 50	9 44	14 44	11 14 11 50
Stockwell (231, Clapham Rd.) ,,	9 18	48 18	11 18 11 54	9 48	18 48	11 18 11 54
Clapham Com. (9, South Side) ,,	9 22	52 22	11 22 11 58	9 52	22 52	11 22 11 58
Balham (1, Station Parade) ,,	9 28	58 28	11 28 12 4	9 58	28 58	11 28 12 4
Tooting (38, Tooting High St.) ,,	9 34	4 34	11 34 12 10	10 4	34 4	11 34 12 10
Morden Station (Und.) ,,	9 44	14 44	11 44 12 20	10 14	44 14	11 44 12 20
Ewell (Post Office) ... ,,	9 58	28 58	11 58 12 34	10 28	58 28	11 58 12 34
Epsom (Clock Tower) ,,	10 4	34 4	12 4 12 40	10 34	4 34	12 4 12 40
Leatherhead (Institute) ,,	10 14	44 14	12 14 12 50	10 44	14 44	12 14 12 50
Dorking (Falkland Arms) arr.	10 33	3 33	12 33 1 9	11 3	33 3	12 33 1 9

Early Coaches to Dorking from Leatherhead on Weekdays at 6.53, 7.23, 7.53, 8.23, 8.53, 9.23, 9.53 a.m.
Sundays at 7.23, 7.53, 8.23, 8.53, 9.23, 9.53, 10.23 a.m.

Fares

Fare stages	LONDON (Poland St. Coach Stn.)		BALHAM (Bailey's Kiosk).		NORTH CHEAM (Jerrold Parade).		EPSOM (Railway Bridge).		ASH-TEAD (Rectory Lane).		LEATHER-HEAD (The Swan).	
	Sin.	Ret.	Sin.	Ret.	Sin.	Ret.	Sin.	Ret.	Sin.	Ret.	Sin.	Ret.
Epsom (Marquis of Granby)	1/-	1/6	1/-	1/6	...	...	...	...	...	...	...	...
Ashtead (Rectory Lane)	1/3	2/-	1/-	1/6	1/-	1/6	1/-	1/6	...	...	...	...
Leatherhead (The Swan)	1/6	2/6	1/3	2/-	1/-	1/6	1/-	1/6	1/-	1/6	...	...
Dorking (Falkland Arms)	2/-	3/-	1/9	2/6	1/6	2/-	1/-	1/6	1/-	1/6	1/-	1/6

Return Tickets are available for return on any day but the whole ticket must be retained for the return journey.

CHILDREN'S FARES.—Children under 3 years of age, when accompanied by a fare paying passenger
and not occupying a seat, may be carried free. Children of 3 years and under 14 years of age are
carried at half the ordinary fare, fractions of 3d. being charged as 3d.

PASSENGERS MAY HAIL, OR ALIGHT FROM, GREEN LINE COACHES ANYWHERE EN ROUTE

TICKETS ARE OBTAINABLE ON THE COACHES OR AT AGENTS' OFFICES

Light hand luggage may be carried at the discretion of the Conductor and at owner's risk, and the Company shall not be responsible for any loss or injury thereto, however caused. Such luggage must remain in the passenger's own charge and not occupy a seat, nor obstruct the platform or gangways. Articles which are likely to interfere with the comfort of other passengers are not allowed on the coach and the conductor has authority to refuse to carry passengers having such articles. Lap dogs only carried at the discretion of the conductor.

NOTE.—The Company, or its Agents, cannot be held responsible for failure to adhere to the scheduled times of the coaches nor can they guarantee the running of the services to be as stated, though every effort will be made to maintain them.

GREEN LINE COACHES LTD.
66, Broadway, Westminster, S.W.1.

VICTORIA 6800.

GREEN LINE — ROUTE M & Z

MAIDENHEAD, WINDSOR & LONDON

(GREEN LINE COACH STATION)
Poland St. - Near Oxford Circus)

DAILY EVERY 30 MINUTES (Slough - London every 15 mins.)

TO LONDON.

(Detailed timetable — MONDAYS TO FRIDAYS, SATURDAYS, SUNDAYS — for stops including Maidenhead (Bridge Av.), Windsor (Lord Raglan), Slough (Public Hall), Colnbrook (George), "Peggy Bedford," Langton (Wilson's Corner), Shepherds Bush (Und. Stn.), Hammersmith Broadway, Oxford Circus (D.M. Office), LONDON (Poland St. & Charing X Emb.).)

Later night coaches leave Maidenhead for Slough on Mondays to Fridays at 10.28 p.m., 11.8 p.m., 12.8 a.m. ; Saturdays 10.28 p.m., 11.8 p.m., 11.38 p.m., 12.8 a.m. ; and on Sundays at 10.28 p.m., 11.8 p.m., 11.38 p.m., 12.8 a.m.
Later night coaches leave Windsor (Lord Raglan) for Slough at 10.50 p.m., 11.20 p.m., 11.50 p.m., 12.20 a.m., 12.50 a.m.

TO MAIDENHEAD & WINDSOR.

(Detailed timetable — MONDAYS TO FRIDAYS, SATURDAYS, SUNDAYS — for stops including LONDON (Charing X Emb. & Poland St.), Oxford Circus (D.M. Office), Hyde Park Corner, Hammersmith Broadway, Shepherds Bush (Und. Stn.), Langton (Wilson's Corner), "Peggy Bedford," Colnbrook (George), Slough (Public Hall), Windsor (Lord Raglan), Maidenhead (Bridge Av.).)

Earlier morning coaches leave Slough for Maidenhead on Weekdays at 7.3 a.m., 7.36 a.m., 8.3 a.m., 8.2 a.m., and on Sundays at 9.3 a.m. and 9.33 a.m.
Earlier morning coaches leave Slough for Windsor (Lord Raglan) on Weekdays at 7.59 a.m., 7.59 a.m., 8.29 a.m., 8.53 a.m., and on Sundays at 9.29 a.m., 9.50 a.m., 9.52 a.m. and 9.50 a.m.

FARES.

	Maidenhead.	Taplow Station (G.W.R.)	Windsor Lane.	Windsor (Lord Raglan)	Slough (Public Hall)	Colnbrook.	Harlington Corner.
	S. R.	S. R.	S. R.	S. R.	S. R.	S. R.	S. R.

S—SINGLE. R.—RETURN.

(Fare stages listed: Windsor Lane, Slough (Public Hall), Colnbrook, "Peggy Bedford," Cranford, Osterly, Thornbury Road, Gunnersbury Station, Gunnersbury, Shepherds Bush, Hammersmith, London.)

CHILDREN'S FARES.—Children under 3 years of age, when accompanied by a fare-paying passenger and not occupying a seat, may be carried free. Children of 3 years and under 14 years of age are carried at half the ordinary fare, fractions of 3d. being charged as 3d.
RETURN TICKETS.—Return Tickets are available for return on any day, but the interchange facility with the Underground Railway can only be used in accordance with the route shown on the ticket.
TICKETS.—Tickets are issued on the coaches.

PASSENGERS MAY HAIL, OR ALIGHT FROM, GREEN LINE COACHES ANYWHERE EN ROUTE

SERVICE.—The Company or its Agents, cannot be held responsible for failure to adhere to the scheduled times of the coaches nor can they guarantee the running of the services to be as stated, though every effort will be made to maintain them.

GREEN LINE COACHES LTD. Chief Office—55, Broadway, S.W.1. Victoria 6800.
Local Enquiry Offices :
Green Line Coach Station (Poland St., Near Oxford Circus). Gerrard 3101.
Alpha Str., Slough. Slough 806.

The early Green Line panel timetables were all produced to 23-inch depth irrespective of the information content, had distinctive curved corners and were, of course, printed in green ink.

Upon acquisition the independents' coaches were withdrawn from service pending examination, overhaul and re-painting into Green Line colours. When returned to service some coaches were employed on other services. Due to a technicality they could not carry the Green Line fleet name until the vehicle licences had been transferred.

Ex Skylark Gilford originally numbered GF 18, later GF 129, lays over outside Poland Street coach station while working on Green Line route S to Sunbury Common. The coaches tended to cause their own congestion and at busy times it was sometimes impossible for them to enter the coach station. Under such circumstances one member of the crew was instructed to report to the inspector on duty. *J.F. Higham collection*

Ex Regent Motor Services Gilford GF 19 (later to be renumbered GF 23) stands outside the coach station working the former Skylark service to Guildford, lettered BG. The coach carries no fleet name. *J.F. Higham*

Ex Blue Belle T 350 is seen in Kingsbury Square, Aylesbury before working to London on the former Red Rover service. *J.F. Higham*

T 351, one of the ex Blue Belle Regals, is seen in Green Line livery working on the former Blue Belle route from Paddington to East Grinstead, designated AU by Green Line. *E.G.P. Masterman*

On 20th July 1932 the service of Blue Belle Motors Ltd was acquired, running from East Grinstead to Paddington Spring Street via Croydon Aerodrome, and became designated AU. Six AEC Regal coaches joined the Green Line fleet but Blue Belle continued running its coastal services.

The next independent to sell out was Acme Pullman Services Ltd on 22nd September 1932 which ran from Charing Cross to Bishop's Stortford with projec-

tions to Stansted and Newmarket. In this case the company continued to trade as part of the Combine and the route was not allocated letters in the Green Line series but was shown in publicity as ACME. The Acme fleet consisted of 15 Gilfords which continued to operate from the company's premises in South Street, Bishop's Stortford. An important condition of the sale was that all staff should retain their Acme seniority dates with Green Line.

Below The publicity produced for the acquired services continued to feature the names of the independent operators.

Red Rover's coach service from Aylesbury to Seymour Street near Marble Arch was acquired on 30th November 1932 with the coaches, designated AT, running out of Tofelds Garage in Park Street, Aylesbury until 15th August 1933. As far as can be established, on the following day they were transferred to the former Chiltern garage at Tring. The Red Rover company continued to operate local buses in the Aylesbury area for many years.

ASSOCIATED
COACHES (ONGAR) LTD

ROUTE AO
ONGAR &
LONDON
(BISHOPSGATE)
VIA EPPING & CHINGFORD

SEASON TICKET RATES

For all enquiries:
Chief Office:
55, Broadway, S.W.1.   Victoria 6800
Local Enquiry Offices:
Green Line Coach Station, Poland Street
(near Oxford Circus)   Gerrard 2101
Divisional Office, L.G.O.C., Kingsland Road,
Dalston   Clissold 4608
Bridge Garage, High St., Ongar   Ongar 77

1237—10,000— 6-5-32.

WATERLOW & SONS LIMITED, LONDON, DUNSTABLE & WATFORD.

SKYLARK
MOTOR COACH Co., LTD.

ROUTE AF
HERTFORD HEATH
& LONDON (OXFORD CIRCUS)

ROUTE AG
HIGH WYCOMBE
& LONDON (OXFORD CIRCUS)

ROUTE BC
GUILDFORD &
LONDON (OXFORD CIRCUS)

DAILY
Every 60 Minutes

Passengers may hail or alight from the coaches anywhere en route.

For all Enquiries :
55, Broadway, S.W.1., or 'Phone - Gerrard 2101.

907—10000—29-4-32 R. WATERLOW & SONS LIMITED, LONDON WALL, LONDON.

ACME
PULLMAN SERVICES LTD.

NEWMARKET,
BISHOP'S STORTFORD &
LONDON
(CHARING CROSS UND. STATION)

DAILY SERVICE

Via
Saffron Walden
Newport
Stansted
Sawbridgeworth
Harlow
Epping
Woodford
Leytonstone
Stratford
Bishopsgate

For all enquiries :
55, Broadway, S.W.1.   Victoria 6800
Bell St., Reigate, Surrey.   Reigate 1200
Green Line Coach Station,
Poland St. (near Oxford Circus). Gerrard 2101
South St., Bishop's Stortford. B. Stortford 172
951—10,000—11-4-33 (R).

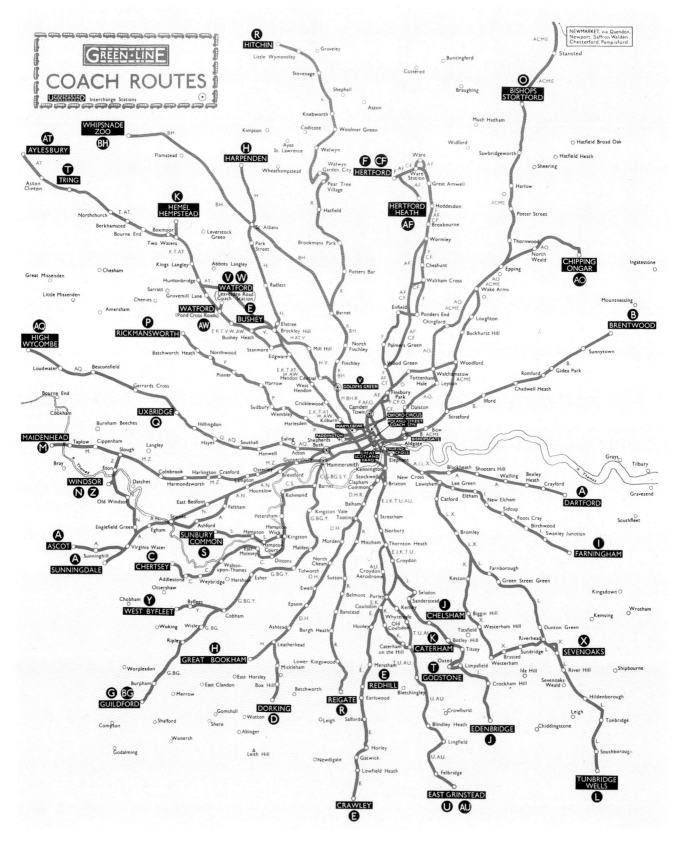

Following the acquisition of various independent operators, the Green Line map was revised to include new services. Only the former ACME route to Newmarket wandered off the edge of the map. This version dates from early 1933 before the acquisition of the Queen Line service to Baldock. *London's Transport Museum*

Following accident damage in April 1933, T 232 was rebuilt using a Weymann 35-seat metal body which was 9 inches longer than the one it replaced. It was unique to the Green Line fleet and was eventually fitted with conventional side route boards. *Capital Transport*

The final acquisition before the formation of the London Passenger Transport Board came on 26th April 1933 when the Queen Line Coaches service from Baldock to Kings Cross Coach Station became Green Line route AK. With the service, which was sold for £18,500, came six AEC Regal coaches and a garage in Baldock High Street. It is uncertain whether these premises continued to house the coaches or if they were transferred to the Green Line premises in Queen Street, Hitchin. However, by December 1933 a new garage in Bridge Street, Hitchin came into use replacing the Queen Street premises.

Other events had taken place during this period when route development was suspended due to protests over the decisions of the Traffic Commissioner and the subsequent inquiry. The most significant was the decision to transfer responsibility for operating the National bus services, which were run on behalf of General to the north of London, to the East Surrey Traction Company. Clearly the name East Surrey would be inappropriate and at an extraordinary general meeting of that company on 20th January 1932, the decision was made to change the name to London General Country Services Ltd. The licences for the 315 Green Line and private hire coaches were transferred to the new company with effect from 11th May 1932 and comprised:

AEC Regal T 38, 51–149, 155, 157–306	251
AEC Regal private hire T 150–154	5
AEC Reliance	25
Daimler all-weather 419 type	33
AEC Renown double deck LT 1137	1

In addition East Surrey had a fleet of 25 coaches plus seven acquired from the Great Western Railway.

A new garage opened in Dorking on 16th March 1932 which incorporated a bus station frontage for buses and coaches to stand. Route D was altered to terminate there instead of at the Falkland Arms and the allocation of coaches for the route was transferred from Leatherhead to the new garage.

With the development of both bus and coach services some of the existing LGCS garages were becoming inadequate and a number of proposed sites were examined including Brentwood, Chertsey, Hertford, St Albans and Tonbridge but with the impending London Passenger Transport Act, the policy was to defer any major expenditure until the new organisation had taken over. A garage at Windsor originally proposed to accommodate 100 vehicles was scaled down to house half that number and opened operationally on 1st March 1933 although the coach station facilities at the front of the building came into operation on 18th January.

The only new route to be granted a licence at this time was designated BH and commenced operation on 24th March 1932 from Marylebone Station Harewood Avenue to Whipsnade Zoo, a new attraction which had opened the previous summer. Passengers were conveyed to and from Whipsnade only and could board intermediately at Golders Green Underground Station and Barnet, New Road, Christ Church. It was also possible for passengers to transfer to or from the Underground at Golders Green. The coaches were allocated to Southall but it is probable that at busy times other garages helped out. Publicity initially defined the terminal as Baker Street Station Melcombe Street but, just five days later, it was altered to Marylebone Station so it seems highly probable that the latter point was used from the start.

The London Passenger Transport Bill received royal assent on 13th April 1933 with the new authority, the London Passenger Transport Board, taking over from 1st July. Lord Ashfield was appointed Chairman with Frank Pick as Vice Chairman and Chief Executive Officer. The new Board comprised the Underground Group companies, the municipal tramways, the Metropolitan Railway, the London business of Thomas Tilling Ltd and the London operations of Tilling and British Automobile Traction. The Board's defined area extended approximately 25 to 30 miles from Charing Cross encompassing almost 2,000 square miles. Much of the boundary was based on the former East Surrey and National operating boundaries but in the south east where General had an agreed boundary with Maidstone & District, the area was extended to include Gravesend and Wrotham. The Board had unrestricted monopoly rights within its Special Area and no operator could run a bus service without its permission. If such permission was withheld the Board was required to negotiate terms for the takeover of the company. In addition the Board was granted running rights to cross the boundary in order to continue serving certain towns such as Aylesbury and Tunbridge Wells. Certain territory both in the north and south lay outside the London Traffic Area and was still subject to application for licences from the area traffic commissioners. Organisationally the London General Country Services operations, including Green Line, became the Country Buses and Coaches operating department of the new Board with Mr Hawkins, the founder of East Surrey, becoming the operating manager. A decision was taken at this time for the LGCS buses to be painted green instead of the existing red livery.

A number of changes to the coach services took place on 1st July 1933 with route A being extended from Dartford to Gravesend, Denton and route I being extended from Farningham to Wrotham. The ACME route north of Bishop's Stortford was well outside the Board's area and was temporarily worked by Eastern National before being sold to Varsity Coaches. Two independent operators were also acquired. First was Lewis's Cream Line Coaches Ltd dating from September 1930 which by this time was running from Brookmans Park to Portman Square. The service was designated BR and was worked from Hatfield Garage. The other acquisition was the Premier Omnibus Company (West Herts) whose operations included a service from Hemel Hempstead to Marylebone via Abbots Langley and Watford By-Pass which became AK.

Following the publication of the Amulree report senior management had been in discussion with the Minister of Transport concerning the operation of Green Line coaches under the new regulations. This involved exclusions within the central area, the limiting of picking up points throughout the Metropolitan Police area and the need for all terminals to be off the public highway. In addition to Green Line, the restrictions also applied to the independent operators and to long-distance services. Clearly the Traffic Commissioner's rulings had been too restrictive and while Amulree had allowed more routes to operate, further negotiations took place in order to ensure that Green Line would have a viable route network. No doubt the proposed

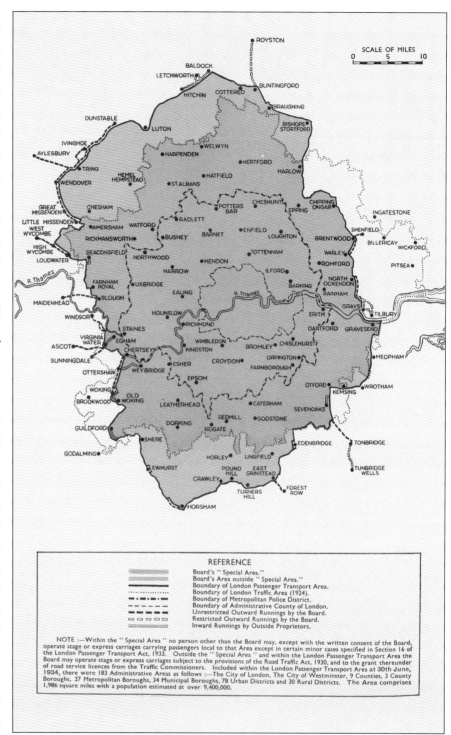

establishment of the LPTB helped Green Line's case and eventually it announced that it accepted the decisions affecting its services. Despite many protests from the coaching industry the Minister of Transport announced that the new regulations applicable to motor coach services would apply from 1st October 1933. Green Line was granted dispensation to defer the changes to Wednesday 4th October in order that the revised arrangements could coincide with the start of the pay week.

The London Passenger Transport Board area from the first annual report.

One of the Cream Line Gilfords is seen in Portman Square just after the takeover by the LPTB. The coach is still in its former owner's livery but carries a new route board with the route letters BR allocated by Green Line. *A.D. Packer*

The major changes to the Green Line system on 4th October 1933 meant that new timetable leaflets had to be printed for all routes. The coaches could now only pick up passengers at defined stopping places within the Metropolitan Police area but after representations by Frank Pick, a number of additional stops were granted during November and the leaflets were overprinted with the details. Some leaflets were quickly reprinted in an attempt to highlight the new stopping arrangements.

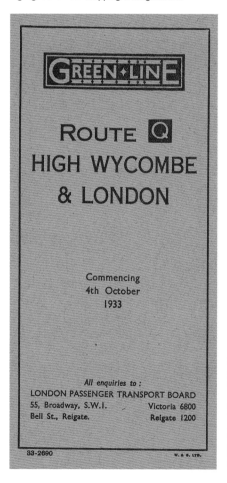

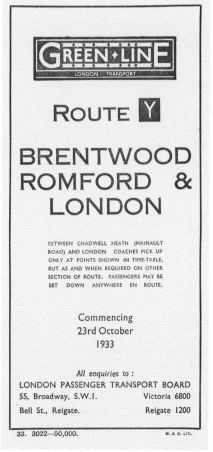

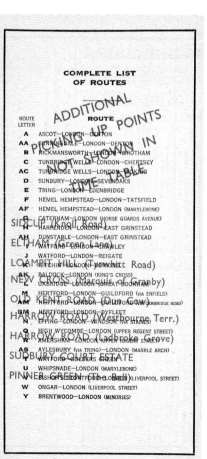

The first Green Line stop sign appeared on 18th August 1933 and following the acceptance of the Amulree recommendations such signs were progressively erected throughout the Metropolitan Police area. This view taken after the 4th October changes shows one of the new stops in Horse Guards Avenue. T 264 is on route D from Sevenoaks to Sunbury prior to the route's extension to Staines on 3rd January 1934. The inspector no doubt intends to have a word with the crew – perhaps they have arrived a little sharp to time!

The new arrangements included the closure of Poland Street Coach Station at the request of both the Metropolitan Police and Westminster City Council after not quite three years. It had proved difficult to work 27 coaches per hour each way, plus duplicates, through the narrow Soho streets and traffic circular references indicated that the coaches sometimes caused their own congestion – staff were instructed that if the coach was unable to enter the coach station one member of the crew had to report to the inspector on duty. The practice of cross-London running was much increased with a number of routes being concentrated at Eccleston Bridge, Victoria. The halcyon days of coaches stopping anywhere within the Metropolitan Police area to pick up passengers were now over as was unrestricted competition and no longer would there be in excess of twelve coaches per hour running along the Great West Road. Boarding points were severely regulated and controlled within the area although coaches could stop anywhere upon request in order to set down passengers. Under the Traffic Commissioner's original proposals six boarding points had been granted between London and Staines where as now 16 such stops were allowed. Similar restrictions applied to those independent operators allowed to continue but in a number of cases the granting of licences proved to be a hollow victory as the new London Passenger Transport Board possessed statutory powers to acquire them. With the exception of new routes T and U all transfer facilities to and from the Underground were withdrawn.

Such major changes required a revised network of routes which were lettered in a more logical sequence based on the country terminals starting at Gravesend and working in a clockwise progression. Plans to acquire the remaining independents had been carefully considered and such routes had been allocated route letters which initially showed up as gaps in the sequence. The details of routes as at 4th October 1933 are listed below together with the frequency and, where known, the garage allocation:

Letter	Route	Frequency	Garage
A	Gravesend (Denton) – Victoria – Ascot	60mins	Crayford
AA	Gravesend (Denton) – Victoria – Sunningdale	60mins	Staines
B	Wrotham – Victoria – Rickmansworth	60mins	Swanley/Leavesden Road
C	Tunbridge Wells – Victoria – Chertsey	60mins (1)	Tunbridge Wells
AC	Tunbridge Wells – Victoria – Woking	60mins (1)	Addlestone
D	Sevenoaks – Westerham – Victoria – Sunbury Cmn.	30mins (2)	Dunton Green/Sunbury
E	Edenbridge – Victoria – Tring	60mins (3)	Chelsham/Tring
F	Tatsfield – Victoria – Hemel Hempstead	60mins (4)	Chelsham/H. Hempstead
AF	Portman Square – Watford By-Pass – H. Hempstead	90mins	Hemel Hempstead
G	Caterham – Horse Guards Avenue	60mins	Godstone Green
H	East Grinstead – Victoria – Harpenden	60mins	East Grinstead
AH	East Grinstead – Victoria – Dunstable	60mins	Harpenden
I	Crawley – Oxford Circus – Watford	30mins (5)	Crawley/Reigate/ Leavesden Road
J	Reigate – Oxford Circus – Watford	30mins	Reigate/Leavesden Road
K	Dorking – Victoria – Potters Bar – Hitchin	30mins (6)	Dorking/Hatfield/Hitchin
AK	Kings Cross – Barnet By-Pass – Baldock	60mins	Hitchin/Romford
L	Great Bookham – Victoria – Uxbridge	30mins	Leatherhead/Southall
M	Guildford – Oxford Circus – Enfield – Hertford	30mins	Guildford/Ware
AM	Guildford – Oxford Circus – Great Cambridge Rd –Hertford	60mins (7)	Guildford/Ware
BM	Byfleet – Oxford Circus – Gt Cambridge Rd – Hertford	60mins	Addlestone/Ware
N	Windsor – Staines – Portman Square – Epping	30mins	Windsor/Ongar
Q	High Wycombe – Oxford Circus	60mins	High Wycombe
R	Amersham – Oxford Circus	60mins	Amersham
AS	Aylesbury – Watford By-Pass – Marble Arch	Irregular (8)	Tring/Brixton
T	Watford – Golders Green	30mins	Leavesden Road
U	Marylebone – Whipsnade Zoo	Irregular (8)	
V	Bishop's Stortford – Liverpool St – Horse Guards Av.	30mins (9)	Bishop's Stortford
W	Ongar – Liverpool Street	30mins	Ongar
Y	Brentwood – Aldgate – Horse Guards Avenue	10mins (10)	Romford

Notes:
(1) Monday to Friday and Saturday am combined 60 min service Tunbridge Wells to Sevenoaks.
(2) 60min service Sevenoaks to Westerham Hill apart from positioning journeys.
(3) 120min service Edenbridge to Chelsham.
(4) 120min service Tatsfield to Chelsham.
(5) 60min service Crawley to Redhill.
(6) 60min service Welwyn Garden City to Hitchin.
(7) Monday to Friday and Saturday am no service Guildford to Esher except positioning journeys.
(8) Limited stop service.
(9) Service extended to Horse Guards Avenue Mon to Fri late evening, Sat pm and Sunday.
(10) 5min service Romford to Aldgate and service extended from Aldgate to Horse Guards Avenue Mon to Fri late evening Sat pm and Sunday.

Such a major change to the network was not without problems with something in excess of 30 fewer coaches being required daily which resulted in some staff redundancies. In other cases drivers and conductors were displaced from their home garages and obliged to transfer to other, often far-removed, locations. For example some staff were transferred from Bishop's Stortford to Ongar while the even less fortunate were offered positions at Romford. In an age when jobs were hard to come by those in good employment such as Green Line crews would have had little alternative but to accept a transfer. A new pay agreement came into force during October 1933 under which Green Line drivers were paid 80/- basic pay for a six day, 48 hour week with 60/- being the corresponding figure for conductors.

The Poland Street premises had now become something of a white elephant and were used for duplicate coaches to lay-over until final closure on 13th February 1934. From this date coaches laying-over went to Chalk Farm Central Omnibuses garage and the Green Line control office was transferred to Cranbourn Chambers above Leicester Square station.

The contentious question of stopping places was still the subject of negotiations between Gleeson Robinson, the Traffic Commissioner, and Messrs Ashfield and Pick and during November a number of additional places were granted with details being over-printed on the timetable leaflets. Restricted boarding arrangements meant that coach stop signs were progressively erected within the entire Metropolitan Police area; the very first example had come into use on 18th August 1933 outside Hyde Park Corner Underground station. The Board continued to make representations to the Traffic Commissioner concerning stopping places and routeings arguing that it had reduced the number of omnibuses running in restricted streets by much greater numbers than the journeys formerly run by the coaches. Green Line was now less attractive to intending passengers as they could not be carried to the heart of the shopping and business centres. Amulree had envisaged this situation and argued that passengers would not be lost to the Board overall as they would switch to other modes but the Board claimed that this was not the case as increasing private car usage was adding to congestion. In spite of representations made by the Board very few further concessions were granted by the unyielding Gleeson Robinson.

As might be expected Lord Ashfield and Frank Pick produced a vast amount of statistical information in support of their case and it would seem that in the year to October 1933 the coaches had carried 27.2 million passengers compared with 20.2 million for the year to October 1934, takings had fallen from £1.16 million to £0.88 mil-

lion and receipts per mile had dropped from 8.47d to 7.12d. It was estimated in October 1934 that earnings of 8.3d per car mile were required to cover all costs including provision for renewals and interest on capital. Unquestionably the revised network was less attractive to passengers and usage had declined, but one point that the Board never advanced in its arguments was that many fares had been adjusted from 4th October 1933. The original fare scale was somewhat coarse and considered major traffic objectives and the fares of Green Line's competitors but under the new arrangements, the base was strictly on mileage which meant that a number of single and return fares increased generally by 3d. For example, from Brentwood to Aldgate (1/3 single, 2/- return) both bookings increased by 3d. In some cases the 1/- single, 1/6 return minimum fares from central London no longer took passengers quite so far, an example being to Purley which was cut back to South Croydon. Some fares actually went down, an incredible example being Pinner to London, 1/9 single, 2/3 return which dropped to 1/3 and 1/9 respectively.

A new route was granted on 25th October 1933 when X was introduced running from Gidea Park to Aldgate via Romford and Eastern Avenue with a Saturday pm and Sunday extension to Horse Guards Avenue. Problems over the number of coaches using Watford High Street had not been overcome by 4th October and routes E and F were diverted away from central Watford via Aldenham Road and Watford By-Pass until 21st February 1934, when apparently, the diffi-

culties were overcome by defining boarding and alighting points within Watford.

Minor changes continued to take place. On 26th November 1933 route AS had stopping restrictions north of Watford lifted and the standard fare scale was applied. The arrangement with Comfy Cars was terminated when their Harpenden garage was used for the last time on Boxing Day 1933 and from the next day the coaches for routes H and AH ran out of the former St Albans & District premises in Hatfield Road, St Albans. On 3rd January 1934 route D was extended from Sunbury Common to Staines with the garage at Sunbury closing in favour of Staines. The garage facilities in the AEC Works at Southall were closed on the same day when the coaches for route L were transferred to Amersham and High Wycombe garages. Positioning journeys were run in service to and from Amersham while the High Wycombe coaches ran dead to and from Beaconsfield. Crayford garage lost its coaches at this date with the allocation for routes A and AA being transferred to the former Maidstone & District garages at Dartford and Northfleet. On 7th February 1934 route V ceased to follow the former Acme route via Epping New Road in order to run via the somewhat more populated areas of Loughton and Buckhurst Hill.

From 4th January 1934 the eastern allocation for routes A and AA was transferred from Crayford to the former Maidstone & District garages in Dartford and Gravesend. Leyland Tiger L 8 was transferred from the M&D fleet and has been repainted into Green Line livery. In 1935 L 8 was renumbered TR 12. *J.F. Higham collection*

The new Board wasted very little time in using its powers to acquire other operators. On 1st December 1933 the business of J. H. Price (Super Services Coaches) was acquired, a small undertaking which operated a 45-minute service from Aveley to East Ham charging 1d bus fares east of Rainham and offering workman's returns before 8am. The route was designated AZ as the letter Z was reserved for the main service in this corridor. The business was sold for £3,800 with three Gilfords passing to the Green Line fleet.

A rather larger concern was swallowed up on 20th December 1933 when the Premier Line together with the Premier Omnibus Company was purchased. Premier Line route A from Windsor and route B from Farnham Common to Trafalgar Square became Green Line routes O and P respectively, with the O running via Colnbrook By-Pass and the P via Colnbrook village. The Premier garage in Bath Road, Slough passed to the Board together with three other services which were handed over to Country Buses. Premier had a fleet of 19 Leyland Titan coaches and 20 Tigers two of which eventually passed to Thames Valley.

Attention turned to east London when Batten's (Amalgamated Omnibus) service from Aldgate to Tilbury Docks Station was taken over on 23rd December 1933 as route Z. A 20-minute service was run to Grays with an hourly projection beyond. Like Price, 1d fares were offered east of Rainham and workman's returns were issued prior to 8am. Batten's Garage at 439 Barking Road, East Ham was used initially but from 6th January 1934 operations joined those of the former Price route in Seabrooke's Brewery Yard at Grays. Tilbury Coaching Services' route from East Ham to Tilbury Docks Station via Purfleet dating from October 1930 was acquired on 23rd March 1934 without any apparent augmentation to route Z, with three Gilfords passing to the Board.

A very small concern, Sunshine Saloon Coaches Ltd, running every 80 minutes except Sunday from Ashford Station to Kingston, was acquired on 30th December 1933. Sunshine had been granted a licence by the traffic commissioner in July 1931 and was sponsored by Bentalls department store in Kingston. The route was transferred to Central Buses as 198 and the only effect on Green Line was the reduction of the Sunbury to Kingston fare on route D from 1/- to 6d.

By far the largest concern to be acquired was that of Hillman's Saloon Coaches and a subsidiary company Upminster Services Ltd. Hillman's ran a very intensive service from its coach station at Bow to Brentwood with projections to Chelmsford and beyond. Upminster Services had been formed on 15th June 1932 following a court case resulting from the failure of Woodgrange Coaches, which had operated an intensive service from Upminster to Aldgate via Ilford. Edward Hillman had worked the service since 12th February 1931 on behalf of Gilfords which had repossessed their coaches. Following appeals in the traffic courts the Minister of Transport imposed certain conditions, including the imposition of a 1/- minimum fare, on Upminster Services from 23rd January 1933. Hillman claimed that traffic had fallen by 75 per cent and was thus keen to get rid of his operations. He virtually demanded that the Board should take over as a result of which both the Upminster and Brentwood services were acquired on 10th January 1934 together with the coach station at Bow and the garage in London Road, Romford. Sixty-five Gilford coaches came into the Green Line fleet which left Hillman with 27 to operate to Chelmsford and beyond.

Premier Line Ltd was acquired on 20th December 1933 and its routes from London to Windsor and Farnham Common became lettered O and P respectively in the Green Line network. This Leyland Titan stands outside Windsor garage shortly after the takeover and is still in the Premier red and cream livery but with LPTB legal lettering and a Green Line sticker over the Premier fleet name. *J.F. Higham*

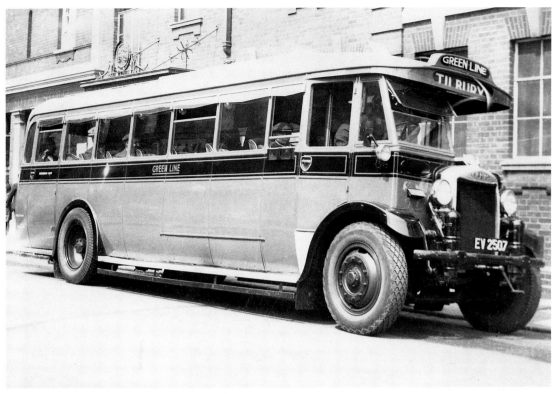

Three Gilfords passed to the Board upon the acquisition of Tilbury Coaching Services on 23rd March 1934. This coach is seen running in Green Line livery and was numbered GF 140 by London Transport.
J.F. Higham

With the acquisition of the routes to Aveley and Tilbury the need to find an operating base was pressing. Accommodation was rented in Seabrooke's Brewery Yard in Grays until the new garage in the town was opened on 25th February 1935. T 83 stands nearer to the camera in the somewhat primitive surroundings. *London's Transport Museum*

An agreement was then made with Eastern National to take over the Bow to Chelmsford service with restrictions on local carriage between Bow and Brentwood, together with nine coaches. The remaining 18 coaches passed to the Board which eventually agreed a price of £168,000. The Brentwood route was absorbed into route Y and the Upminster route became AY. The latter was unusual in that virtually an all-night service was provided. Due to the intensity of the services Green Line retained their garage in North Street which had opened on 4th December 1931 together with the London Road premises.

Two further acquisitions tidied up the Romford services when the Sunset Pullman Coaches Ltd service from Brentwood to Aldgate (curtailed from Charing Cross on 1st October 1933) passed to the Board on 25th January 1934. Thirteen coaches were transferred and the service absorbed into route Y which continued the Sunday afternoon extension to Highwood Hospital in Brentwood which had been established by Sunset. Jean Pierre Hensman, the owner, could not agree with the Board on the price offered and engaged the solicitor J. Cort Bathurst who specialised in such cases. In the event the parties settled out of court for £19,800

The acquisition of Hillman's on 10th January 1934 saw some 83 Gilfords eventually passing into the LPTB fleet. GF 62, ex Hillman's, sets down passengers at the Yorkshire Grey terminus in Brentwood. The coach carries a slightly revised livery with a prominent London Transport fleet name and the Green Line wording positioned above on the black band.
Laurie Akehurst collection

Hillman's large garage in London Road Romford also passed to London Transport. This view taken in 1936 shows a splendid line up of coaches – the larger profile of the Regals when compared with the Gilfords is readily apparent.
London's Transport Museum

This Duple bodied Saurer XY5337 passed to Green Line with the acquisition of West London Coaches on 17th January 1934. It was normally used to provide the connecting shuttle between Amersham and Chesham. Although repainted into Green Line livery it was never allocated a fleet number and was withdrawn in 1935.
Laurie Akehurst collection

in March 1936 which was £5,000 more than Board originally wished to pay. The other acquisition on 21st February was that of Fleet Transport Services which used two coaches to provide an all-night service from Romford to Aldgate. An approximately 45-minute service was provided for the benefit of market porters and other night workers and an ideal arrangement had existed whereby Fleet and Sunset honoured each others' return tickets. The night journeys were provided on route Y initially but from 13th June 1934 they were transferred to Central Bus route 617. The business had fetched some £2,750.

The long established service of West London Coaches to Aylesbury via Rickmansworth and Amersham with a connecting shuttle to Chesham passed to the Board on 17th January 1934. The service had originally started from the Coastal Coaches coach station in Lupus Street but when Victoria Coach station opened on 10th March 1932, the terminus was transferred there. It became Green Line route S and was the only such service to use Victoria Coach Station during the period covered by this book. An irregular service was operated and on Sunday evening the last two journeys from London ran via Halton RAF Camp. Initially the coaches continued to be based in County Garage, Aylesbury but it is not known how long this arrangement lasted.

Green Line finally achieved its desire to get to Luton when on 1st February 1934 the business of Harry Hill, Strawhatter Coaches, was acquired. The route from Luton to Kings Cross Coach Station ran via London Colney, Barnet and Highgate on an hourly headway increased to 30 minutes at busy times. Strawhatter's fleet consisted of 24 Gilfords which were also used on its coastal coach services which London Transport sold on to Eastern National together with eight of the Gilfords. After much negotiation the business eventually fetched some £97,500 which was a vast improvement on the original offer of £57,000.

The garage in Park Street West, Luton passed to the Board which not only continued to operate the coach service (designated BH) therefrom but transferred the country buses from the Eastern National garage in Castle Street on 11th April.

The service of Beaumont Safeway coaches from Leighton Buzzard to Kings Cross via Dunstable and London Colney had suffered following the introduction of Green Line route AH to Dunstable on 4th October 1933, but London Transport formally granted permission for the service to continue. Beyond Dunstable, outside the Board's area, the route was not well used and Eastern National showed no interest in a joint purchase. Mr Beaumont, the proprietor, was eventually forced to approach the Board who offered a mere £1,250 and even after the intervention of Cort Bathurst the price was only increased by a further £100. The business was acquired on 27th April 1934 with three Gilfords being transferred but no strengthening of the service on route AH.

The Board had now acquired all suburban coach operations running solely within its area but many longer-distance operators continued to offer fares on their services for journeys purely within the area.

Strawhatter Gilford MJ75, which eventually became GF 163 in the LPTB fleet, stands in Park Square, Luton prior to running to Kings Cross.
J.F. Higham collection – Omnibus Society

CONSOLIDATION
1934–1939

The London Passenger Transport Board had before it the task of consolidating its organisation under one corporate entity. As far as Green Line was concerned, this was the integration of the acquired services into the established network so as to achieve a more economic operation and the concentration of the various non-standard coaches to garages by type so as to keep maintenance costs to manageable proportions. Acquired vehicles had to be examined and any necessary maintenance work, which often entailed a complete overhaul, carried out. The process of providing coach stop signs at all authorised boarding points within the Metropolitan Police area had already commenced. In some areas garage facilities were inadequate and a programme of providing new garages and rebuilding at some existing sites was undertaken. Such changes could not be made overnight and the speed at which the various improvements were made was a great credit to the new organisation.

One economy measure was the reduction or withdrawal of parallel Country bus routes in districts where passengers were scarce. In compensation for the loss of the bus services, bus fares with the 1d minimum were charged over the sections of coach routes concerned. The coaches were fitted with slip boards advertising '1d fares on this coach' which the conductors were to ensure were displayed on the appropriate section of route. Bus fares had been inherited on the Rainham to Grays section of route Z and were extended to the Wrotham to Farningham section of route B on 16th May 1934, and to the Epping to

Bishop's Stortford and Ongar sections of routes V and W from 5th September, the St Albans to Dunstable section on route AH from 5th December and the Edenbridge to Oxted section on route F from 19th December. A similar initiative involved the progressive provision of 3d, 6d and 9d fares in country districts to offer a faster means of travel than the existing Country bus routes. Routes with no fares below one shilling had been licensed as express carriages and from 1934 with one exception they were relicensed as stage carriages in order that fares below one shilling could apply in country districts. The exception was route U to Whipsnade which was to remain an express carriage as the traffic commissioner refused to approve a 9d booking from Kensworth to the zoo.

Improvements and alterations were made to the route network on a continuing basis, minor examples being the diversion of route H away from Lingfield via Eastbourne Road and the diversion of companion route AH between Lingfield and East Grinstead via Baldwins Hill on 25th April 1934. A much larger alteration, the North-West London coach scheme, was advertised to start on 11th July but internal sources indicate that it was deferred until 14th July. Acquired services AF, S and AS were withdrawn with routes B, E, F and I being revised as follows. The B was extended from Rickmansworth via Amersham with alternate hourly journeys extended to either Chesham or Aylesbury replacing route S. The northern allocation for route B was transferred from Watford Leavesden Road to Amersham. Route E

(Edenbridge to Tring) was curtailed to start from Chelsham, apart from early and late journeys to and from Tatsfield, with alternate coaches extended from Tring to give a 120-minute service to Aylesbury replacing the AS. Route F was revised to run from Edenbridge (120 minutes) and Tatsfield (120 minutes) to give a combined 60-minute service to Hemel Hempstead. Route I was extended from Leavesden Road Garage to Abbots Langley replacing part of route AF. The 30-minute service to Abbots Langley proved excessive and from 5th September alternate coaches were curtailed at Leavesden Road. One week later route E was adjusted to give Aylesbury a 60-minute service on Saturday pm and Sunday pm. On 18th July route Z was revised to absorb route AZ and extended in Tilbury to Feenan Highway. At the same time the workman's return facilities on this route were withdrawn being replaced by workman's weekly tickets – the only such facility on Green Line.

Above This photograph of May 1934 has been composed by superimposition in order to promote the delights of Green Line travel. The coach, its passengers and crew look genuine enough however. Route B was extended to Aylesbury in July 1934 to cover the former West London service. Leyland Tiger L 4 passed to London General Country Services from the Chiltern Omnibus Service. The authorities at Reigate numbered the Leylands in the L series but when Chiswick Works assumed control of the fleet in 1935 they were reclassified TD (Titans) and TR (Tigers). L 4 became TR 8. *London's Transport Museum*

Epping, the first of the new garages to be provided by the Board, opened on 5th September 1934 with the coaches for routes N and W being transferred from Ongar garage, which was closed, together with those for route V from Bishop's Stortford garage. Prior to October 1933 the Green Line coaches had run out of the National garage and the former Acme coaches had ran from the Acme premises, both in South Street, Bishop's Stortford. After the 4th October changes it is believed that the former Acme premises were used for route V. Ownership of the former National garage was transferred from the Board to Eastern National on 20th June 1935.

Minor adjustments continued with route H being extended from Harpenden to Luton on 19th September 1934 when it was also diverted away from Borehamwood between Allum Lane Corner and Apex Corner to run via Elstree Village and Watford Way offering 3d fares over that section. One week later routes A and AA were curtailed from the Board's boundary at Denton to terminate at Gravesend Clock Tower. On 5th December route O was reduced in frequency on Monday to Friday and Saturday am to 20 minutes and diverted via Colnbrook Village. Companion route P was reduced to 60 minutes but additional coaches were provided on route O between Slough and London in rush-hours.

In April 1934 it was planned to extend the long established LGOC practice of using garage code letters and running numbers to the Country buses and coaches. The Romford coach routes were the first to be so equipped which, in view of the intensive service was quite understandable, and the use spread to the remainder of the fleet during the summer and autumn of 1934.

Dating from Green Line's earliest days weekly, monthly and quarterly tickets had only been issued where there had been competition with other operators but from 18th November 1934, with the exception of six-day tickets issued on routes BH and T, all previous arrangements were superseded. Under the new system weekly tickets

Above Garage codes and running numbers were introduced to the Country Buses and Coaches department of London Transport on a progressive basis from April 1934. T 310 is seen adjacent to one of the new coach stop signs at Oxford Circus and carries the WE code which was for the former Peoples Motor Services garage at Park Road, Ware. The coach was a former East Surrey touring coach and was renumbered T 394 in 1935.
London's Transport Museum

Left Route O was diverted away from Colnbrook By-Pass to run through Colnbrook village on 5th December 1934. Ex Premier Line Leyland Titan TD 183 stands outside Windsor garage. Note the very comprehensive route board information. *J.F. Higham collection*

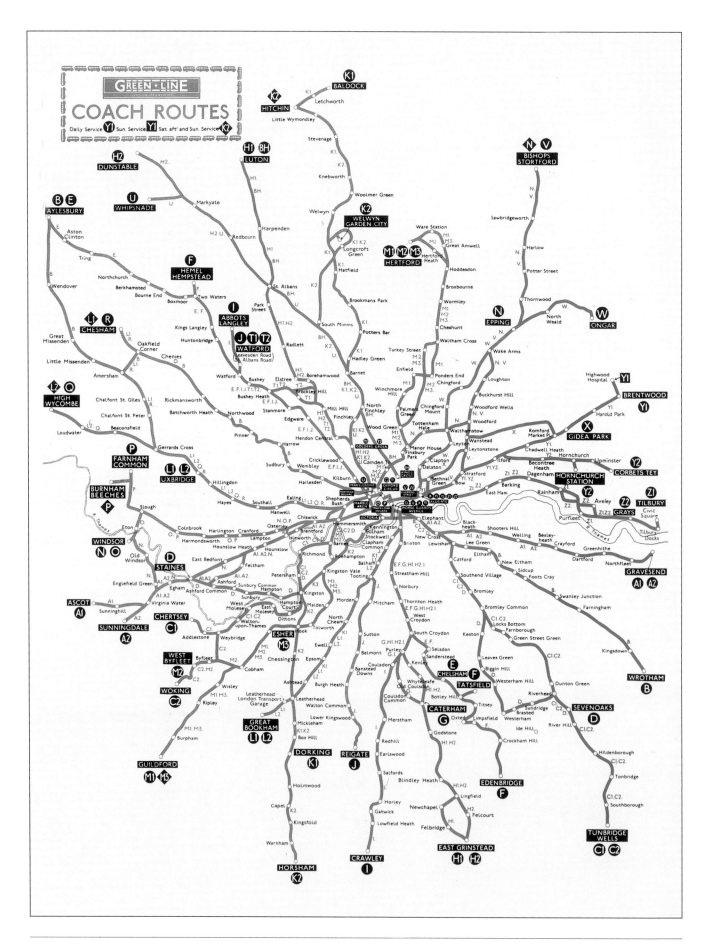

obtainable from conductors and 4-weekly tickets obtainable from offices became generally available.

A new garage was opened in Fairfax Road, Hertford on 2nd January 1935, to replace the former National and Peoples Motor Services garages both located in Ware. The latter had been acquired on 1st December 1933 and either at that time or subsequently the ex Peoples buses had been transferred to the National garage and the coaches were re-allocated to the former Peoples premises.

Although the year 1935 saw few changes to Green Line a number of improvements to the services did take place. Terminal facilities in the centre of Upminster had long caused problems which were solved on 8th May when route AY was extended to Corbets Tey. On 5th June a revised system of route designation first appeared when route Z became Z1 and a new route Z2 running from Aldgate to Grays via Aveley every 60 minutes was introduced. Bus fares were charged between Rainham and Stonehouse Corner. On 26th June route Y became Y1 and AY became Y2 with part of the service being re-routed to Hornchurch Station.

On 3rd July routes A and AA became A1 and A2 respectively and from 6th July route P was increased to a 30-minute frequency on Summer Saturday pm and Sunday and extended to Burnham Beeches. On 31st July the former Redcar service which had been acquired by Maidstone & District was transferred to London Transport and ran as an additional 60-minute service on route C between Tunbridge Wells and Victoria.

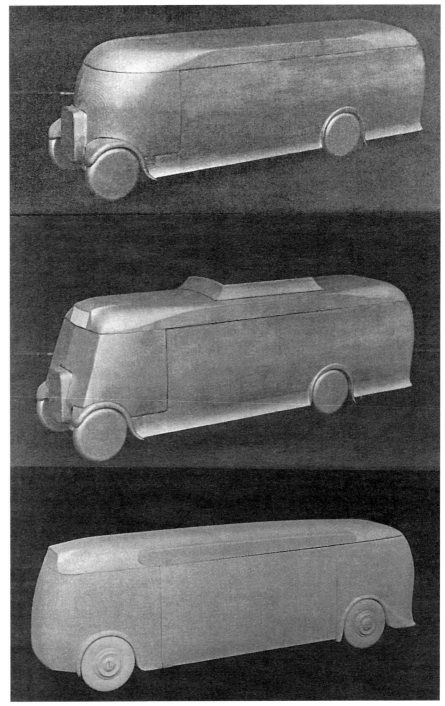

Left The former independent operators' services were integrated into the system which is depicted here at the beginning of 1936. *London's Transport Museum*

Top The Maidstone & District (ex-Redcar) service from Tunbridge Wells to Victoria passed to London Transport on 31st July 1935. This is one of five Leyland Tigers that were transferred to the LPTB fleet. The coach is still in Maidstone & District colours and it can clearly be seen that the M&D fleet name has been painted out and replaced by the new owner's identity. *D.W.K. Jones*

Right The mid-1930s was the era of streamlining. These carved wooden wind-tunnel models show some of the ideas for Green Line vehicle styling being considered by London Transport. The bottom example has some similarity to the 4Q4's outline. *TfL Archives*

The needs of passengers returning to London at the weekends were often difficult to predict. If the weather was fine people would stay in the countryside for as long as possible and duplicates would have to be operated to supplement the normal services. However, the vagaries of the English climate often led to situations when during inclement or unseasonably cold weather passengers would make an earlier return to London thus resulting in service inadequacies. To overcome this difficult situation agreement was reached with the main line railways whereby from 3rd August passengers holding return coach tickets from central London could return to London by train or Underground after 4pm on Saturday and Sunday. A supplement listing approved railway routes was published with the Green Line Coach Guide.

The coach service to Hertford Heath which had been lost in October 1933 was restored on 14th August 1935 when route BM was diverted away from Ware. Bus fares were charged between Hertford and Hoddesdon. To supplement route V alternate coaches on route N were extended from Epping to Bishop's Stortford on Saturday pm and Sunday from 19th September. Dartford garage lost its allocation of coaches on routes A1 and A2 when they were transferred to Northfleet from 20th November.

During this period London Transport's programme of garage improvements in the Country area was in full swing with new premises in London Road, Grays, which replaced the brewery yard, opening on 25th February 1935. This was quickly followed by Two Waters which opened on 10th April replacing the former National garage in Bury Road, Hemel Hempstead. A new garage adjacent to the former Amersham & District shed at Amersham opened on 14th August with the former remaining in use while at Tring a new building on the existing site was finished in October. Staines Garage was temporarily closed after 8th October to allow a new structure to be built with the vehicles being located in The Avenue, Egham until the new garage opened on 3rd June 1936. New premises in Station Road, Addlestone came into operation on 24th June 1936 replacing facilities in Hamm Moor Lane dating from November 1932 which in turn had superseded facilities in Weymann's Works. On 26th August it was the turn of St Albans with a new building in St Peter's Street replacing the so-called Drill Hall site in Hatfield Road. Slough Bath Road garage was used for the last time on 15th December after which the allocation was transferred to an enlarged Windsor.

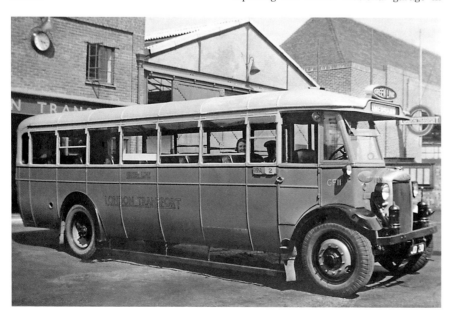

Above London Transport's new garages allowed the engineering staff to perform their duties in a good working environment in contrast to some of the open muddy yards that had previously sufficed. T 56 receives some attention in Two Waters garage at Hemel Hempstead which opened on 10th April 1935.
London's Transport Museum

Left Ex Upminster Services Gilford GF 11 stands outside the former Amersham & District garage at Amersham. The new garage which opened on 14th August 1935 can be seen in the background. The old A&D shed continued in use as part of the garage for some years.
A.D. Packer

Significant alterations to coach services took place on 8th January 1936 when route B ceased to serve Chesham with the alternate hourly journeys being projected over the main route as far as Wendover leaving a two hourly headway onwards to Aylesbury. Route R was extended from Amersham garage to Chesham to cover the loss. The former Redcar service on route C was withdrawn with the main route C becoming C1 and AC becoming C2 with the Sevenoaks journeys being projected to Tunbridge Wells. Routes H and AH were redesignated H1 and H2 respectively and the former was diverted between Blindley Heath and Newchapel to run via Lingfield and also diverted between Apex Corner and Allum Lane Corner away from Watford Way to run via Borehamwood. To compensate for the loss of route H from Elstree Village, route T was split as T1 and T2 with the latter running from Bushey Heath via Elstree, Barnet Lane and Stirling Corner to join the original route at Apex Corner. Both routes provided a combined 30-minute service from Watford to Golders Green. The former Queen Line route AK running from Baldock to Kings Cross was withdrawn in favour of a revised route K, redesignated K1 which now ran in two sections – Baldock to Leatherhead Garage (projected to Dorking on Summer Sunday) every 60 minutes and Welwyn Garden City, Longcroft Green to Dorking, also every

On 8th January 1936 alternate coaches on route B were revised to terminate at Wendover. An unidentified T carrying the new fleet name pauses at Eccleston Bridge. *J. Bonell – LCC Tramway Trust*

Route T was revised to become T1 on 8th January 1936 when alternate journeys, designated T2, were diverted away from Watford By-Pass to serve Elstree and Barnet Lane. Ex Batten's Reliance R 38 is seen on route T2 in Mill Hill stopping at one of London Transport's new shelters. From 1935 the Country Buses and Coaches fleet carried the suffix letters B for bus or C for coach. *Laurie Akehurst collection*

Below The former Queen Line route AK from Kings Cross to Baldock was replaced by routes K1 and K2 on 8th January 1936. Ex Queen Line T 354 stops at Stevenage before the change. London Transport, keen to promote its corporate image, erected shelters throughout the system. The seat, Green Line map, panel timetable and prominent bullseyes enhance the pleasing appearance. *London's Transport Museum*

T 187 is seen in Tilbury at the start of the run to Aldgate. A new London Transport shelter has been erected but the scene is not enhanced by the provincial-style bus stop sign. A weight limit imposed on a bridge in Loop Road, Purfleet meant that from 27th July 1938 the coaches ran via Purfleet By-Pass. *London's Transport Museum*

60 minutes. Fairways Coaches' service from Kings Cross to Worthing was acquired by Southdown but London Transport bought the goodwill for the Horsham to London section. Thus Green Line now reached Horsham with route K2 running from there to Welwyn Garden City Station via Kingston, Putney, Victoria, Barnet, South Mimms and Barnet By-Pass. Coaches were two-hourly from Horsham on Monday to Friday, hourly from Dorking, but hourly from Horsham on Saturday and Sunday. At the northern end of the route the service was projected from Welwyn Garden City to Hitchin during Saturday pm and Sunday pm. Horsham to Hitchin became the

longest Green Line route at something in the region of 80 miles with a running time of four hours and seven minutes. With the exception of Saturday pm and Sunday alternate coaches on route L were curtailed at Leatherhead garage rather than continuing to Great Bookham. The final alteration on this date was the redesignation of the M group with M becoming M1, AM becoming M3 and BM becoming M2.

Minor changes took place on 5th February 1936 when Z1 was revised to terminate at Tilbury Civic Square instead of Feenan Highway and short-workings were provided on Z2 between Aveley and Grays in lieu of bus 371. On 30th May a new

summer service enhancement took place when on Saturday pm and Sunday route L was extended from Uxbridge to Chesham as L1 and High Wycombe as L2. Route L was further altered on 15th July when the High Wycombe allocation was transferred to Amersham which saw the end of the Beaconsfield 'when working' journeys. The last of the old system of using two route letters disappeared from 29th July when BH became H3. From the same day passengers returning from Whipsnade could use bus 368 to St Albans City station thence by LMS train to St Pancras in order to alleviate any temporary inadequacies on route U.

NO DISTANCE BY GREEN LINE

FELTHAM TO WELLING

GRAVESEND COACH (A1 or A2)
via Hounslow, Brentford, Hammersmith, Hyde Pk. Corner
Daily every 30 minutes   Return fare 3/-

FINCHLEY TO EWELL

DORKING COACH (K1)
via Golders Green, Hyde Park Corner, Victoria, Lambeth
Daily every 30 minutes   Return fare 3/-

ENFIELD TO TOLWORTH

GUILDFORD COACH (M1)
via Wood Green, Finsbury Park, Hammersmith, Barnes
Daily every 30 minutes   Return fare 3/-

The majority of Green Line passengers travelled either to or from central London or the country terminal towns. This poster by Laurence Bradshaw attempts to promote the use of Green Line for three cross-London journeys.
London's Transport Museum

The Romford routes required considerable augmentation during the Monday to
Saturday rush-hours which resulted in
spare coaches being available at other
times. London Road garage had a hand in
the Whipsnade service and also supplied
Sunday duplicates for route H3. From 2nd
August summer Sunday route Y3 was
introduced from Brentwood running via
the Y1 to Mansion House then Ludgate
Hill and Strand to Trafalgar Square
whence it continued via route O to
Windsor. A 30-minute service was projected
to Brentwood Highwood Hospital on
Sunday afternoon. The use of restricted
streets in the City was authorised by the
traffic commissioner in conjunction with
the City of London police for operation on
Sunday. A further change in Romford took
place from 19th August when route X was
curtailed from Gidea Park to Romford
Market Place.

New coaches were required to replace
the inherited fleet and 50 front entrance
thirty-seat Weymann bodied Regals classified 9T9 (T 403–452) were purchased with
the first examples entering service in June
1936. Mechanically they had oil engines,
preselective gear boxes and fluid flywheels
and were fitted out to Green Line specification with deep seats, luggage racks,
heaters, wind-down windows and ash trays
on the seat backs. They were put to work
on routes I, J, K1 and K2.

Top On 19th August 1936 route X was
withdrawn between Gidea Park and Romford
Market Place. T 277 operates a busy journey
after the change. Note the rear boards carried
by the early T type coaches. *The Omnibus Society*

Right and facing page The Underground Group
and London Transport were very aware of the
power of the poster to promote their services.
Comparatively few posters actually featured the
vehicles themselves but this pair by Percy Drake
Brookshaw of 1936 depict the rear entrance T
type. A journey from London's countryside
where unrestricted stopping applies to the very
heart of the West End is depicted. The coach has
stopped at one of the new Terrazzo stop posts
and a police constable is reassuringly on hand to
direct passengers to their theatre.
London's Transport Museum

Above left and above By 1936 new coaches were needed to replace those inherited from the many independent operators, notably the Gilfords which incurred high maintenance costs. Fifty of these thirty-seat Weymann bodied Regals entered service on routes I, J, K1 and K2 from June 1936. Classified 9T9 they had a very attractive appearance as depicted by T 405 posing for the official photographer. T 449 is seen at Tally Ho! Corner, North Finchley on route K1 heading for Leatherhead. Note the different liveries – T 449 has a Lincoln green roof and different treatment of that colour below the headlights. *London's Transport Museum, Photomatic Ltd.*

GREEN LINE
AT ALL TIMES
Green Line Guide 2ᵈ at all bookstalls

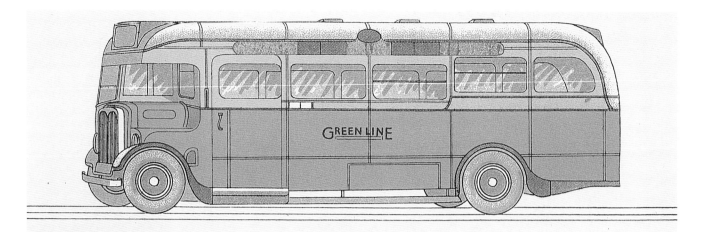

Green Line Coach, Type 9T9. Introduced in 1936

This colour drawing of a 9T9 coach appeared in issue 3 of the 1937 Green Line Guide. One issue of the Green Line Guide appeared in 1933 and several issues were produced in each year from 1936 to 1939 and 1948 to 1969. The guides contained full timetables of all routes, fare tables, diagrams showing boarding points at key locations and a map.

Left Towards the end of 1936 a batch of fifty 32-seat Park Royal bodied Q type coaches with an offside engine began to enter service. Q 217 passes Marble Arch en route to Byfleet on route M2. *London's Transport Museum*

The revolutionary side-engine AEC Q-type single-decker whose prototype dated from 1932, had been developed as both Country area and Central area buses, when a batch of 50 coaches with a long wheelbase and a 32-seat central entrance Park Royal body completed to full Green Line standards was ordered. Classified 6Q6 and numbered Q 189–238 they entered service between November 1936 and the following January. They were allocated to routes H3, M1/2/3, Q and R and were joined at Amersham on the latter route by four 9T9 coaches for comparison purposes.

There was still a need to replace the remaining Gilford coaches which incurred high maintenance costs so 27 of the 4Q4 Country buses (Q 81–105, 186/7) were upgraded to coaches, albeit retaining their 35 bus seats, and placed in service at Amersham, Leatherhead, Northfleet and Staines from 27th March 1937.

A revision of fares took place on 2nd May 1937 providing for fare stages more closely spaced which resulted in more variable fares. The 1/- minimum in the London area was retained but many 6d fares were introduced in country districts with single fares in 3d progressions. Cheaper fares became available on all routes except the east London services and T and U.

A major revision of services also took place on that day principally designed to increase the service to Windsor during Coronation year. Route L was withdrawn altogether and covered south of London by an extension of route O. In its new form the O now ran between Windsor and Great Bookham via Trafalgar Square with odd shorts from Windsor projected to Horse Guards Avenue which also became the terminal for route P. The basic service between Windsor and Leatherhead was 30 minutes with alternate coaches projected to Great Bookham except on Saturday pm and Sunday when all coaches served Great Bookham. Route G from Caterham to Horse Guards Avenue was doubled to every 30 minutes, diverted to run via Purley Way to serve Croydon Airport, and extended via

route O to Windsor. North of London the L was replaced by short journeys on route R from Oxford Circus to Uxbridge. On summer Saturday pm and summer Sunday route R became a 30-minute service from London to Amersham with alternate journeys projected to Chesham, and Q became half hourly throughout between London and High Wycombe. Other adjustments involved the withdrawal of route T2 with all coaches running as route T over the original, pre-January 1936 routeing. The operation of two coaches per hour via Great Cambridge Road by the M group resulted in an uneven service interval between Waltham Cross and Hertford so the situation was overcome by re-routeing the M1 away from Ponders End to run via Great Cambridge Road and Bullsmoor Lane with M2 and M3 now running via Great Cambridge Road and Ponders End. As a precursor to the opening of the new Northfleet Garage on 7th July routes A1 and A2 were re-routed away from Dover Road to run past the new garage.

Five experimental double deck versions of the Q type were built for London Transport including Q 188, a 51-seater with a Park Royal body. Delivered in February 1937, it was intended to be the prototype for a fleet of such vehicles for use on the busy routes serving the Romford area. There had been a previous unaccepted proposal to use 50 front-entrance STLs on the routes concerned in 1936. The intention was that a larger capacity vehicle would enable headways to be reduced. Fewer staff would have been required to work the services and this point was not lost on the Transport & General Workers' Union. Agreement could not be reached between the management and trade union and Q 188 never ran in Green Line Service. *London's Transport Museum/Capital Transport collection*

Letter	Route	Garages	Type	No of coaches MF	Sat	Sun
A1	Gravesend – Ascot	⎱ Northfleet (NF)	4Q4	7	6	6
A2	Gravesend – Sunningdale	⎰ Staines (ST)	4Q4	7	7	7
B	Wrotham – Aylesbury	Amersham (MA)	9T9	4	4	4
	Wrotham – Wendover	Amersham (MA)	T(27)	1	1	1
		Swanley (SJ)	T(30)	3	3	3
C1	Tunbridge Wells – Chertsey	Addlestone (WY)	T(27)	8	8	8
C2	Tunbridge Wells – Woking	Tunbridge Wells (TW)	T(30)	6	6	6
		Tunbridge Wells (TW)	T(29)	3	3	3
D	Staines – Sevenoaks	Dunton Green (DG)	T(30)	4	4	4
	Staines – Westerham Hill	Dunton Green (DG)	TR(30)	3	3	3
		Staines (ST)	TD(26)	6	6	6
E	Aylesbury – Chelsham	Chelsham (CM)	T(30)	7	7	7
	Tring – Chelsham	Hemel Hempstead (HH)	T(30)	3	3	3
F	Hemel Hempstead – Tatsfield	Tring (TG)	T(30)	3	3	3
	Hemel Hempstead – Edenbridge	Tring (TG)	T(27)	2	2	1
G	Windsor – Caterham	Godstone (GD)	TR(*)	6	6	5
		Windsor (WR)	TD(26)	6	6	6
H1	Luton – East Grinstead	East Grinstead (EG)	T(30)	8	8	8
H2	Dunstable – East Grinstead	St Albans (SA)	T(30)	3	3	3
		Luton (LS)	T(30)	5	5	5
H3	Luton – Kings Cross	Luton (LS)	6Q6	7	7	7
I	Abbots Langley – Crawley	Reigate (RG)	9T9	4	4	4
		Crawley (CY)	9T9	3	3	3
		Watford Leavesden Rd (WT)	9T9	6	6	6
J	Watford – Reigate	Reigate (RG)	9T9	5	5	5
		Watford Leavesden Rd (WT)	9T9	6	6	6
K1	Dorking – Welwyn Gdn City	Dorking (DS)	9T9	4	4	4
	Leatherhead – Baldock	Leatherhead (LH)	9T9	3	3	2
	Dorking – Baldock (Summer Sun)	Hatfield (HF)	9T9	3	3	3
		Hitchin (HN)	9T9	6	6	5
K2	Horsham – Welwyn Gdn City	Dorking (DS)	T(30)	5	5	5
	Dorking – Welwyn Gdn City	Hatfield (HF)	T(30)	3	5	5
	Horsham – Hitchin (Sat & Sun)					
M1	Hertford – Guildford	Addlestone (WY)	6Q6	3	3	3
M2	Hertford – Byfleet	Guildford (GF)	6Q6	9	10	11
M3	Hertford – Esher (Guildford Sat/Sun)	Hertford (HG)	6Q6	16	16	13
N	Windsor – Epping (Bishop's	Epping (EP)	T(30)	5	6	6
	Stortford Sat, Sun)	Windsor (WR)	T(30)	6	6	6
O	Windsor – Great Bookham	Leatherhead (LH)	TR(26)	6	6	5
	Windsor – Leatherhead (Mon	Windsor (WR)	TD(26)	4	3	5
	to Fri and Sat am)	Windsor (WR)	TR(26)	3	3	3
P	Farnham Cmn (Burnham Beeches	Windsor (WR)	T(27)	5	7	7
	Sat & Sun)– Horse Guards Av.					
Q	High Wycombe – Oxford Circus	High Wycombe (HE)	6Q6	4	4	4
R	Chesham – Oxford Circus	Amersham (MA)	6Q6	4	5	5
	Uxbridge – Oxford Circus	Amersham (MA)	4Q4	4	5	5
	Amersham – Oxford Cir (Sat/Sun)	Amersham (MA)	T(27)	1	1	1
T	Watford – Golders Green	Watford Leavesden Rd (WT)	4Q4	3	3	3
		Watford Leavesden Rd (WT)	T(27)	1	1	1
U	Marylebone – Whipsnade	Romford London Rd (RE)	T(27)	2	3	5
V	Bishop's Stortford – Eldon Street/	Epping (EP)	T(27)	7	7	5
	Horse Guard's Avenue	Epping (EP)	T(30)	4	4	4
W	Ongar – Eldon Street	Epping (EP)	T(27)	3	3	3
		Epping (EP)	T(30)	4	4	4
X	Romford – Aldgate/Horse Guards	Romford North Street (RF)	T(30)	13	14	10
Y1	Brentwood – Aldgate/Horse Guards	Romford London Rd (RE)	T(27)	44	44	42
Y3	Brentwood – Windsor (Sun)					
Y2	Upminster/Hornchurch – Aldgate	Romford London Rd (RE)	T(27)	34	34	25
Z1	Tilbury/Grays – Aldgate	Grays (GY)	T(30)	13	13	13
Z2	Grays – Aldgate	Grays (GY)	T(27)	1	2	3

Notes: (*) 26 seaters plus one 31 seater.
The figures in brackets after the vehicle type indicate the seating capacity.
The 27 seater Green Line Ts were now classified 7T7 and the 30 seater version 1/7T7/1.

The Central bus practice of producing periodic allocation books showing vehicle requirements by garage and type was extended to the Country Buses and Coaches operating department with the first issue appearing on 7th July 1937. The Green Line details are shown here.

The requirement for service coaches was 349 on Monday to Friday, 358 on Saturday and 339 on Sunday plus a maximum of 26 duplicates on Monday to Friday, 49 on Saturday and an amazing 141 on Sunday which brought the totals to 375, 407 and 480 respectively. The Summer Sunday duplication figure gives some indication of the heavy demand put upon the system. While routine maintenance would be kept to a minimum on Sunday and a limited number of single-deck Country buses could be used it was necessary to have vehicles in the fleet which were nominally only required on one or two days in the week. Routes C1 and C2 required some 13 duplicates on Sunday with routes E and F, H1 and H2 and the M group each requiring 12. This led to a situation where other garages provided duplicates at weekends – Romford London Road worked on route H3, Watford Leavesden Road worked on routes E and F, Dunton Green could be found on routes C1 and C2 and Dartford helped out on routes A1 and A2. Under an agreement with the Transport and General Workers' Union made in pre-London Transport days double-deck buses could only be used as Green Line duplicates on journeys towards London. It was not until May 1938 that agreement was reached that they could be worked in service from London subject to a payment of 1/- per journey to both the driver and conductor.

Twenty-seven 4Q4 Country buses were upgraded to Green Line work from 27th March 1937. Q 103 arrives at Eccleston Bridge, Victoria, en route for Sunningdale on route A2.

Eccleston Bridge had become established as the focal point of the Green Line system and attractive shelters were provided for waiting passengers. Proposals to provide waiting rooms were considered but were not pursued. In this view, T 210 on route E to Aylesbury arrives to help deal with holiday crowds during the summer of 1937. Inspectors move forward to supervise alighting and boarding and a good range of London Transport publicity material is on display. *London's Transport Museum*

Above A selection of Green Line posters as displayed on vehicles during 1936 and 1937. *London's Transport Museum*

Right In contrast to T 210 on the previous page, a modern image is represented by the arrival of T 452, then just under a year old, on route K1 bound for Baldock. Both this and the previous view offer interesting studies of 1930s fashions. *London's Transport Museum*

DINING OUT   YOUR CAR— GREEN·LINE

OUT AND ABOUT

BY GREEN LINE

Green Line was particularly popular on summer Sundays and bank holidays. About 150 extra vehicles would be operated and some would be temporarily loaned from one garage to another as required. Ex Blue Belle T 351 fitted with a new Weymann body stands at Eccleston Bridge prior to working a relief to Dunstable. Frank Pick, the vice-chairman, had noted coaches running without correct destination blinds and directed that paper labels be provided. Following negotiations with the trade union, from May 1938 agreement was reached for the greater use of double-deck Country area buses on Green Line relief work. Hatfield garage's STL 1512 has been loaned to Hitchin. Although the destination blinds are unclear, Hitchin garage worked only Green Line at the time.
J. Bonell, Laurie Akehurst collection

The last major revision to services before the Second World War occurred on 9th February 1938 when route D was withdrawn between Westerham and Sevenoaks. Coaches ran every 30 minutes between Staines and Westerham Hill with alternate journeys continuing to Westerham. Garage journeys, on which through bookings were available, worked in service to and from Dunton Green garage via Riverhead. Route O from Windsor to Great Bookham was withdrawn completely resulting in the latter place no longer being served by Green Line. In compensation route G was strengthened between Windsor and Horse Guards Avenue by one coach per hour which was increased to two per hour during Saturday pm and Sunday pm. Route K1

was rerouted in Hatfield away from Great North Road to run via New Hatfield and companion route K2 was revised to run from Dorking to Welwyn Garden City via Epsom, Potters Bar, South Mimms and Barnet By-Pass. This compensated in part for the loss of route O as there were now three coaches per hour between London and Leatherhead via Epsom but the Saturday and Sunday projections to Hitchin were lost. Horsham was served by a new K3 two-hourly Monday to Friday (hourly from Dorking) hourly on Saturday and Sunday to Marylebone Station via Kingston and Putney. The coaches stood in Harewood Avenue and started the southbound journey from Baker Street Station.

On 6th October 1937 the practice of extending routes V, X and Y1 from Aldgate to Horse Guards Avenue at certain times was discontinued. T 207 awaits departure from Horse Guards Avenue to Bishop's Stortford before the change. The conductor was instructed to reverse the 'via Stratford' slip board, the other side of which read '1d fares on this coach' on reaching Epping where bus fares were charged over the section therefrom to Bishop's Stortford *Laurie Akehurst collection*

Facing page The style of the individual route time and fare tables varied during the mid-1930s. From 2nd May 1937 a larger sized leaflet was introduced which, as an economy measure, used the printing plates created for the Green Line Guide. By this time a Plain English style had been adopted for conditions of travel.

ROUTES A AND AA

ROUTE A
GRAVESEND,
DARTFORD,
LONDON &
ASCOT

ROUTE AA
GRAVESEND,
DARTFORD,
LONDON &
SUNNINGDALE

Commencing 3rd January, 1934

All enquiries to:
LONDON TRANSPORT
55 Broadway, S.W.1.   Victoria 6800
Bell St., Reigate.   Reigate 1200

33 3668 10000   W. & S. LTD.

ROUTES O & P

WINDSOR
FARNHAM
COMMON
AND
LONDON

Time-table and particulars
from 17th February, 1935

All enquiries to:
LONDON TRANSPORT
Bell Street, Reigate   Reigate 1200

GREEN LINE
ROUTE
K2
TIME TABLE

Hitchin
Welwyn
Garden City
London
Dorking
Horsham

All enquiries to:
LONDON TRANSPORT
55 BROADWAY, S.W.1   VIC. 6800

Ordinary Tickets. When you travel by Green Line you can take a single or a return ticket : in any case it must be bought on the coach. If you are coming back you need not hurry : you can use your return ticket within a month but not to make two journeys in the same direction ; you must go there and back.

Children's Fares. If Baby is under 3 he rides for nothing, but must be carried and not occupy a seat ; and there may be only one baby per passenger. For children between 3 and 14 the fare is halved : fractions of 3d. are charged in full except on some country stretches where odd halfpennies are reckoned as pennies.

Return Tickets. You can return to the place where your ticket was issued from any place on any route (except T and U) where the fare is the same or less. If it is more, you pay the difference between the single fares with a minimum of 3d.

Railway Routes Back. If you have a return ticket for 1/6 or more which was issued at Oxford Circus, Victoria, Horse Guards Avenue, Marble Arch, Trafalgar Square or Northumberland Avenue, and you want to go back after 4 p.m. on Sat. or Sun. you may return by main line train instead, from any station near the coach route on which the ticket was issued. Hand your Green Line ticket intact to the ticket office clerk, and he will give you in exchange a special railway ticket to the London station. If the railway fare is less than the coach fare you can't have the difference back, or if you spend money getting from the London railway station to the coach point in London, London Transport can't give it back.

Season Tickets. With a Season you may make an unlimited number of journeys. A weekly ticket will last from Sunday morning to the following Saturday night. A four-weekly ticket will last for 28 days from any Sunday morning. *Scholar's Season Tickets.* If you are

TIMETABLE FOR
GREEN LINE
Route W
ONGAR
LONDON
(LIVERPOOL STREET)

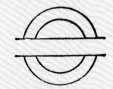

On and after May 2, 1937

ALL ENQUIRIES TO
LONDON TRANSPORT
55 Broadway, S.W.1 VICtoria 6800

under 18 and still at school you can have a season ticket for your school term (if it is not less than 8 weeks) at roughly half the ordinary season rates. But you can't use your half season ticket on Sundays and public holidays. For particulars apply to 75A Bell Street, Reigate : tel. Reigate 2400. You can get scholar's tickets at the same places as the four-weekly season tickets.

Standing Passengers. Five of you may stand during peak hours or " in circumstances in which undue hardship would be caused " if you were left behind. Please do not argue with the conductor. His decision is final.

Dogs. It is for the conductor to say whether your dog can be taken. If he is a small dog London Transport will carry him free but at your own risk.

Luggage. It is for the conductor to say, too, whether you can bring luggage. It must be light hand baggage, and you bring it at your own risk. Whatever happens London Transport accepts no responsibility even if it is lost. Don't bring anything which would make the journey unpleasant for other people.

Lost Property. If you leave articles in the vehicles, ask for them at the Lost Property Office, 200 Baker Street, London, N.W.1 (adjoining Baker Street Station), any time between 10 a.m. and 7 p.m., from Monday to Friday inclusive : on Saturday and Sunday the office is closed. Or, if you prefer, you can write. Or, within 24 hours you can go and claim at the nearest garage.

Service. If the coaches do not run strictly to programme you cannot hold London Transport responsible. If you take a return ticket London Transport is not liable to you for any loss, damage, inconvenience or delay which you may suffer through any failure of the service or lack of accommodation.

In February 1938 delivery commenced of a new design of Regal designated 10T10, in a move to replace all pre-1936 coaches. The first batch of 10T10s to be delivered went into service on routes G and P. T 506 was new in May 1938 and is seen standing outside Windsor garage on route G.
J.F. Higham collection

Below Routes K1 and K2 were revised on 9th February 1938 and new route K3 was introduced between Baker Street station and Horsham. T 558 arrives back at Dorking garage on route K3 one evening in August 1938. During 1938 the destination blinds began to carry the route identification.
London's Transport Museum

Green Line reliability was of a very high standard in a period where public transport was considered essential and the concept of cancellations due to either staff shortage or vehicle shortage was totally unknown. Organisations were adequately resourced and spare staff and adequate numbers of reliable vehicles were always available. Traffic congestion in central and inner London did exist but it did not assume anywhere near the proportions that were to become regarded as normal during the 1960s. Both management and staff had a far more responsible attitude to timekeeping and punctuality checks were regularly undertaken with explanations being given in all cases where lateness was in excess of 10 minutes. Surviving records from Tuesday 22nd February 1938 show

that of 1,594 journeys noted at their respective central London points, 1,264 (79.3 per cent) were on time or slightly early as allowed for terminating services, 288 (18.1 per cent) were from 2 to 6 minutes late, 31 (1.9 per cent) were between 7 and 10 minutes late and just 11 (0.7 per cent) were in excess of 10 minutes late. The 11 incidents of lateness in excess of 10 minutes were analysed as six due to traffic congestion, three due to mechanical problems and two of 'driving to rule book'! Regrettably no further information was given.

As part of a vehicle replacement programme it was decided that all pre-1936 coaches should be displaced and an order was placed for 266 AEC Regals designated 10T10 (T 453–718). They had a shorter

wheelbase than the 9T9 and differed by having an external sliding door and a revised front end design. The first 150 seated 30 passengers but the remaining 116 were modified to seat 34. Delivery commenced in February 1938 and was completed in March 1939 with the first examples being placed on routes G and P. The provision of 34 seaters on the busy routes Y1 and Y2 meant that headway reductions could be achieved and the reduced numbers resulted in Romford London Road garage being able to accommodate all the coaches; accordingly North Street garage closed after 29th November.

A completely new design of coach with an underfloor engine was evolved by London Transport and Leyland Motors Ltd with the prototype vehicle TF 1 being

delivered in July 1937. It went into service at Tunbridge Wells garage on routes C1 and C2 later in that year and was subsequently transferred to Romford London Road garage. TF 2 to 13 were private hire coaches and the next 75 vehicles (TF 14–88) were Green Line coaches with Chiswick 34-seat bodywork; they were the first London Transport vehicles to have air operated brakes and gears, both new developments. They were delivered between February and August 1939 all going to Romford London Road. The provision of so many new coaches meant that in addition to all pre-1936 vehicles, the 27 upgraded 4Q4s and the 9T9s could now be demoted to Country bus work.

Prior to the outbreak of the Second World War the year 1939 saw little change to the Green Line network. Route P's summer extension to Burnham Beeches did not operate on Saturday but continued to do so on Sunday. On 27th August a major fares revision took place on all routes except those in east London with many additional fare stages being inserted which necessitated completely revised tickets.

Passenger traffic had been increasing year by year since the drop following the implementation of the Amulree Inquiry's proposals in October 1933. In the year ended 30th June 1934 Green Line had carried some 17.4 million passengers which had increased to 24.3 million for the year ended 30th June 1939. The receipts had risen from £807,000 in 1934 to £981,000 in 1939 and car miles operated had only increased from 26.4 million to 27.6 million.

London Transport did not publish separate financial and statistical information for Green Line but to put the operation in perspective, the passenger usage figure for 1939 represented just in excess of one per cent of the total passenger journeys for all bus and coach services and just 0.6 per cent of the total number of passengers carried on all London Transport services. The receipts of £981,000 represented approximately six per cent of the entire receipts for bus and coach services. In the year ended 30th June 1939 London Transport made a surplus of £4.8 million which was broadly in line with the figures for the five previous years of the Board's existence.

Above London Transport and Leyland Motors Ltd worked on a completely new design of under-floor engined coach and a prototype vehicle TF 1 was delivered in July 1937. From 1st December 1937 it was allocated to Tunbridge Wells garage for work on routes C1 and C2. Note the unusual glass house style cab and the very high driving position. *A. D. Packer*

Left The front end design on the production batch of the TF class was improved to give the vehicle a more conventional appearance. All 75 of the 34-seat coaches were allocated to Romford London Road to work on the busy east London routes. The TF class were finished in the darker Lincoln green livery – TF 16 was delivered in February 1939 and was chosen to pose for the official photographer. *London's Transport Museum*

WARTIME
1939–1942

The worsening diplomatic situation in the late 1930s caused the government to envisage a time when war would break out between the United Kingdom and Germany and plans were drawn up in July 1938 for the conversion of Green Line coaches into public ambulances at 24 hours' notice. It was feared that upon declaration of war, London would be subjected to massive aerial bombardment and gas attacks and that casualties would be considerable. In the event war was declared on Sunday 3rd September 1939 but the coaches were requisitioned on the preceding Friday. Official London Transport sources state that the coaches were withdrawn after 31st August but three quite separate instances of anecdotal evidence indicate that a service was started on the Friday morning with the coaches being run in to their garages during the day. Such information as available and written accounts are sometimes contradictory but it seems that the Romford routes continued for a further day. In the event places such as Baldock, Byfleet, Edenbridge, Horsham and Ongar would never be served again by a London Transport Green Line coach.

The withdrawal of the coach services caused particular hardship to passengers on those sections where the coaches were offering 1d fares without alternative facilities and also in the Romford area where the loss of such high frequency routes caused inadequacies on other services. It would seem that the 1d fare sections were covered by local arrangement using available buses some of which were transferred from the Central area. Anecdotal evidence says that a Leyland Cub initially operated between St Albans and Dunstable while red STLs provided a service from Epping to Bishop's Stortford and Ongar and a red ST ran from Amersham to Great Missenden. The 'Sevenoaks News' reported that red double-decker buses were operating between Tunbridge Wells and Sevenoaks. It was just three weeks before these temporary arrangements were made formal with the following Country Bus routes starting on 25th September:

Route	Terminals	Replacing
369	St Albans – Dunstable	H2
371	Grays – Aveley – East Ham	Z2
371A	Grays – Purfleet By-Pass – East Ham	Z1
380A	Hertford – Broxbourne	M2
392	Woodford Wells – Epping – Ongar	W
393	Amersham – Great Missenden	B
396	Epping – Bishop's Stortford	V
403C	Warlingham – Tatsfield	F
403D	Tunbridge Wells – Sevenoaks	C1/2
465	Warlingham – Edenbridge	F
478	Swanley – Wrotham	B

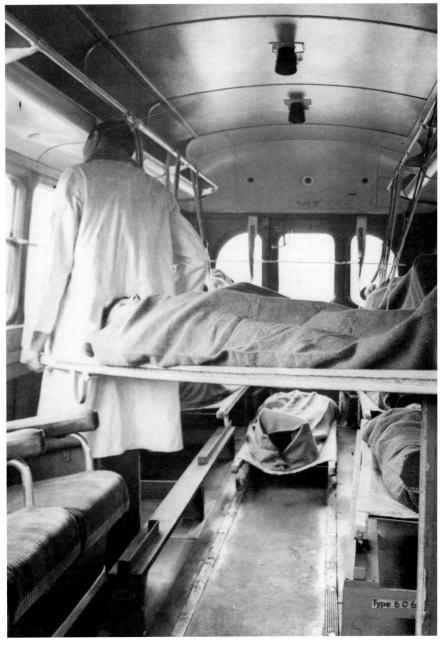

Opposite Route H1 resumed on 7th February 1940 between Luton and Victoria and was extended to East Grinstead and redesignated route H on 13th March. In this view, northbound and southbound 10T10 coaches on the route call at Eccleston Bridge. The destination blind has been amended to show route H by blacking out the 'I'. The driver of the southbound coach has taken the opportunity to check the radiator water level. *Charles F. Klapper*

Opposite below Immediately prior to the outbreak of the Second World War Green Line services were withdrawn and the coaches were converted into public ambulances. T 539 has been suitably adapted and awaits its new duties. *Laurie Akehurst collection*

Right A stretcher case is loaded into a 6Q6 which has been equipped for ambulance duties. Blackout precautions have been observed, most of the light bulbs have been removed and the centre lights have been heavily shaded. *London's Transport Museum*

Some of the routes proved to be short lived and were absorbed into other routes with some sections being withdrawn altogether. As a result of the withdrawal of the coaches, Hitchin and Romford London Road garages, both of which did not operate Country Buses, were closed. Some of the surplus staff were transferred to other Country Area garages and in some cases to the Central Buses or Trolleybuses and Trams operating departments. Very little is known about such transfers which had implications concerning rates of pay and the arrangements for eventually returning staff back to their home garages. It is also recorded that some conductors, recently promoted to drivers, were obliged to cover conductors' duties.

There was public complaint at the loss of the coaches particularly in the Romford area where the local press campaigned for the reintroduction of an express bus service. It seems that some former coach passengers were hard-hit as those travelling to London were obliged to use the already overcrowded rail services which also put pressure on local bus services feeding railway stations. Visitors to Highwood Hospital were obliged to use the train to and from Brentwood but at the start of the war the railways had withdrawn cheap day return fares thus they were forced to pay considerably more.

The war caused an increased demand for public transport, not least because of the imposition of petrol rationing, and the government authorised the restoration of certain routes and the release of some 160 coaches that had been converted to ambu-

lances. No doubt the reintroduction of some of the east London routes on 1st November eased the situation considerably. Country Area front entrance STLs were used to restart route Y1 complete with the Sunday afternoon extension to Highwood Hospital, and rear entrance examples were used on routes Z1 and Z2 but with no service between Grays and Tilbury. The use of double-deckers enabled the frequency of Y1 to be reduced with Brentwood receiving a 30-minute service on Monday to Friday Saturday am and Sunday am, 20 minutes Saturday pm and 10 or 15 minutes on Sunday pm. Additional journeys were run between Romford and Aldgate at certain times. The Z1 and Z2 generally provided a joint 15-minute service from Aldgate to Grays and buses 371 and 371A were with-

drawn. On 13th December route Y2 reappeared using some of the released 10T10 coaches. A 30-minute service (18 minutes at rush-hours) from Corbets Tey was supplemented to give a 10-minute service (6 minutes during rush-hours) from Hornchurch garage, not Hornchurch station as under the pre-war arrangements.

On 17th January 1940 routes A1 and A2 (Gravesend–Ascot/Sunningdale) were reintroduced running at half of the pre-war frequency with each route on a 120-minute headway. Routes Q (High Wycombe–Oxford Circus) and R (Chesham–Oxford Circus) recommenced with both routes on a 60-minute headway. Just four daily journeys on route R were projected beyond Amersham to Chesham. Further routes reappeared on 7th February with a 30-

minute service between Luton and Victoria on route H1 together with the same frequency of service being provided on the northern section of route M1. The severe terminal and stand arrangements imposed on Green Line in 1933 continued to apply. The M1 therefore ran from Hertford to Shepherds Bush on Monday to Saturday where the coaches stood in the Central area garage. The Traffic Commissioner agreed to the route terminating at Oxford Circus on Sunday but no stand time was allowed.

Further restorations took place on 13th March with route C running every 30 minutes from Tunbridge Wells to Weybridge and alternate coaches continuing to Chertsey. The northern sections of routes E and F provided a combined 30-minute service from Victoria to Two Waters with E continuing to Tring (alternate journeys projected to Aylesbury) and route F continuing to Hemel Hempstead. Route H1 was redesignated H and extended from Victoria to East Grinstead via Felbridge. It had been proposed to operate alternate journeys via Baldwins Hill as H2 but it seems that at short notice this was cancelled.

The last restoration came on 8th May with the northern section of route N from Portman Square to Epping every 30 minutes with the summer projection to Bishop's Stortford (60 minutes Sunday am and 30 minutes Saturday pm and Sunday pm). A half-hourly service to Bishop's Stortford represented an improvement on the pre-war service. With the finish of the summer service route N was destined to run to Bishop's Stortford for the last time on 29th September.

Under arrangements with the fuel control authorities the Board were allowed to run a maximum of 75 per cent of the combined pre-war Country bus and coach mileage. Further proposals to reintroduce routes D, G, H3 and J in their entirety, route V between London and Epping, to extend route M1 to Guildford and to increase routes A1 and A2 to their pre-war frequency were not pursued. It was estimated that the combined mileage would reach 66.9 per cent of the pre-war figure. The margin of 8.1 per cent was held in reserve to allow for summer duplication and to act as a buffer should the allowance be reduced.

Minor adjustments were made to the services with Y2 reaching Hornchurch station on 1st May and route M1 being redesignated M. A coach was saved from 18th June when route M terminated daily at Oxford Circus but no stand time was allowed. This was a very contentious matter as complaints had been received from the Commissioner of Police for the Metropolis that coaches were arriving early at Oxford Circus which resulted in a stand of several minutes at the outward-bound stop. Crews were instructed that in no circumstances must coaches arrive before their scheduled time!

Far left STL 1487 works between Sevenoaks and Tunbridge Wells on route C1 in September 1939. The bus was allocated to Tunbridge Wells garage just four days prior to the introduction of route 403D on 25th September. *J.F. Parke*

Left Route Y2 resumed on 13th December 1939 using 10T10 coaches released from Ambulance duties. T 704 with heavily masked headlights and white wings sets down passengers while en route to Aldgate. *J. Dodkins*

This view of Golders Green taken in May 1940 shows the measures taken to cope with blackout conditions. Street furniture has been painted with white bands; the kerb has been painted with white sections, a solid white strip has been applied across the road to guide pedestrians where to cross and sand-bags are in evidence. A 10T10 on route H is captured heading into Golders Green Road bound for Luton. The conductor has the door open and the white paint applied around the entrance can be seen. Central buses, trolleybuses and 1938 tube stock complete the scene. *London's Transport Museum*

During the war-time operation the panel bill timetables were folded and issued to the public. The Green Line Guide, pocket maps and other publicity material were withdrawn. This is the panel bill for the resumption of routes Z1 and Z2 on 1st November 1939.

Routes Z1 & Z2

To GRAYS

Daily

P.M. times are in heavy figures

	✕X	✕X	✕X	✕X	✕X	✕X	✕X	✕X	✕X	✕X	✕X	✕X	✕X
ALDGATE High Street *U-D Station*	....	....	....	....	....	....	6 29	6 44	6 59	7 14	7 29	7 44	7 59
Stepney East *Station*	..	..	..	..	..	..	6 36	6 51	7 6	7 21	7 36	7 51	8 6
Blackwall Tunnel	....	....	....	....	....	....	6 42	6 57	7 12	7 27	7 42	7 57	8 12
East Ham *Town Hall*	5 15	5 38	5 53	6 8	6 23	6 38	6 53	7 8	7 23	7 38	7 53	8 8	8 23
Ripple Road *Barking Public Library*	5 19	5 42	5 57	6 12	6 27	6 42	6 57	7 12	7 27	7 42	7 57	8 12	8 27
Dagenham *Chequers*	5 31	5 54	6 9	6 24	6 39	6 54	7 9	7 24	7 39	7 54	8 9	8 24	8 39
Rainham *Clock Tower*	5 38	6 1	6 16	6 31	6 46	7 1	7 16	7 31	7 46	8 1	8 16	8 31	8 46
Rainham *Chandlers Corner*	↓	6 4	↓	6 34	↓	7 4	↓	7 34	↓	8 4	↓	8 34	↓
Wennington *Post Office*	5 43	↓	6 21	↓	6 51	↓	7 21	↓	7 51	↓	8 21	↓	8 51
Wennington *Lennard Arms*	5 45	6 8	6 23	6 38	6 53	7 8	7 23	7 38	7 53	8 8	8 23	8 38	8 53
Aveley Road *Purfleet Road*	5 48	6 11	6 26	6 41	6 56	7 11	7 26	7 41	7 56	8 11	8 26	8 41	8 56
Aveley *Old Ship*	5 53	↓	6 31	↓	7 1	↓	7 31	↓	8 1	↓	8 31	↓	9 1
Purfleet *Stonehouse Corner*	5 58	6 16	6 36	6 46	7 6	7 16	7 36	7 46	8 6	8 16	8 36	8 46	9 6
GRAYS *War Memorial*	6 8	6 26	6 46	6 56	7 16	7 26	7 46	7 56	8 16	8 26	8 46	8 56	9 16

		Then at these minutes past each hour									
ALDGATE High Street *U-D Station*	8 14		29	44	59	14		3 59	4 14	4 29	4 44	4 59
Stepney East *Station*	8 21		36	51	6	21		4 6	4 25	4 40	4 55	5 10
Blackwall Tunnel	8 27		42	57	12	27		4 12	4 35	4 50	5 5	5 20
East Ham *Town Hall*	8 38		53	8	23	38		4 23	4 49	5 4	5 19	5 34
Ripple Road *Barking Public Library*	8 42	Then	57	12	27	42		4 27	4 53	5 8	5 23	5 38
Dagenham *Chequers*	8 54	at these	9	24	39	54		4 39	5 5	5 20	5 35	5 50
Rainham *Clock Tower*	9 1	minutes	16	31	46	1	UNTIL	4 46	5 12	5 27	5 42	5 57
Rainham *Chandlers Corner*	9 4	past	↓	34	↓	4			5 15		5 45	↓
Wennington *Post Office*	↓	each	21	↓	51	↓		4 51	↓	5 32	↓	6 2
Wennington *Lennard Arms*	9 8	hour	23	38	53	8		4 53	5 19	5 34	5 49	6 4
Aveley Road *Purfleet Road*	9 11		26	41	56	11		4 56	5 22	5 37	5 52	6 7
Aveley *Old Ship*	↓		31	↓	1	↓		5 1	↓	5 42	↓	6 12
Purfleet *Stonehouse Corner*	9 16		36	46	6	16		5 6	5 27	5 47	5 57	6 17
GRAYS *War Memorial*	9 26		46	56	16	26		5 16	5 37	5 57	6 7	6 27

		Then at these minutes past each hour									
ALDGATE High Street *U-D Station*	5 14		29	44	59	14		9 29	....	10 4	....	10 29
Stepney East *Station*	5 25		40	55	10	25		9 40	..	10 15	..	10 40
Blackwall Tunnel	5 35		50	5	20	35		9 50	....	10 25	....	10 50
East Ham *Town Hall*	5 49		4	19	34	49		10 4	10 31	10 39	10 56	11 4
Ripple Road *Barking Public Library*	5 53	Then	8	23	38	53		10 8	10 35	10 43	11 0	11 8
Dagenham *Chequers*	6 5	at these	20	35	50	5		10 20	10 47	10 55	11 12	11 20
Rainham *Clock Tower*	6 12	minutes	27	42	57	12	UNTIL	10 27	10 54	11 2	11 19	11 27
Rainham *Chandlers Corner*	6 15	past	↓	45	↓	15			10 57	↓	11 22	↓
Wennington *Post Office*	↓	each	32	↓	2	↓		10 32	↓	11 7	↓	11 32
Wennington *Lennard Arms*	6 19	hour	34	49	4	19		10 34	11 1	11 9	11 26	11 37
Aveley Road *Purfleet Road*	6 22		37	52	7	22		10 37	11 4	11 12	11 29	11 37
Aveley *Old Ship*	↓		42	↓	12	↓		10 42	↓	11 17	↓	11 42
Purfleet *Stonehouse Corner*	6 27		47	57	17	27		10 47	11 9	11 22	11 34	11 47
GRAYS *War Memorial*	6 37		57	7	27	37		10 57	11 19	11 32	11 44	11 57

✕X—Sunday excepted

With increasing numbers of conductors being conscripted into the armed forces women were recruited as conductors in the Country Buses and Coaches operating department from July 1940. A trainee conductress stands by the door of a 10T10 coach. The ticket punch is the type manufactured at the Board's works at Effra Road which came into use on Country Buses and Coaches during the early part of the war. The triangular piece of metal attached to the cash bag strap is for clearing the slot of a clogged ticket punch.
Kosmo Press Bureau

T 589 has come to grief while performing ambulance duties in September 1940. According to the approved caption the driver was proceeding to a call when the coach finished up in the crater of an unexploded bomb. The ambulance was empty and the driver uninjured.
Sunday Express

A fares revision took place on 3rd July when fares increased by an average of 10 per cent on the August 1939 standard with the 1d bus fares being increased to 1½d. The last coaches on the restored routes left central London between 10pm and 10.30pm which was about an hour earlier than in pre-war days. Additional running time was allowed during the black-out hours with, for example the last coach on route C being allowed four hours, eight minutes from Tunbridge Wells to Chertsey against the daytime allowance of three hours 32 minutes. The demand for the coach services was extremely high with much duplication being operated during the summer often using double-deck Country buses. It would seem that due to the black-out conditions many people preferred to return to London on Monday morning rather than on Sunday evening and some routes required Monday morning only duplicates. Tunbridge Wells continued to be a particularly popular destination and on Sundays, the southern section of route C required two duplicates from Tunbridge Wells garage, five from Dunton Green, four from Northfleet and a further four from Swanley.

The demand for duplication caused problems on the northern section of route H and the western section of route C as low railway bridges meant that double-deck vehicles could not initially be employed. From 17th May the Traffic Commissioner permitted the use of double-deck buses on route H by authorising such journeys to run from St Albans via London Colney, South Mimms and Barnet By-Pass to join line of route at Stirling Corner in order to avoid the bridge at Park Street. Conductors were instructed that passengers could not be picked up or set down while on the deviation. A similar arrangement was applied to route C from 1st November when double-deck vehicles were authorised to use Hampton Court Bridge in order to avoid a low bridge at Thames Ditton.

The long expected blitz on London started on 7th September 1940 and consequential delays and disruptions made long cross-London journeys during the hours of darkness particularly arduous. Cases occurred of crews being stranded overnight at the other end of the route to their home garage. Such conditions were not conducive to operation and from 23rd October the cross London routes A1, A2, C and H were all split into two sections both terminating at Victoria. Revised timetables came into operation on all routes at this date with last coaches departing from central London generally between 8pm and 8.30pm. A further fares revision, in line with the increase imposed on the railways, took place on 1st December with fares being increased 16⅔ per cent over the August 1939 standard.

By this time the bombing of the railway system was causing difficulties and the

Government authorised the restoration of much of the Green Line network in December 1940. The new routes, which all terminated in central London, were numbered in a clockwise progression by country terminal commencing with Gravesend. Certain numbers were not used so as to avoid sections of route where Green Line would be running parallel to a Central Bus route with the same number. Where Green Line routes had not been reintroduced suitable numbers had obviously been reserved to permit further expansion of the network, which, in the event, was destined never to come. The revised network was introduced in two phases on 4th and 18th December, the latter indicated thus *:

Green Line
Route 9
CRAWLEY, REDHILL and OXFORD CIRCUS
Route 40B
WATFORD and VICTORIA
(formerly Route I)

No.	Ex	Route	Coaches per hour	Allocation	Type	No of coaches			Note
						MF	Sat	Sun	
2	A1/2	Gravesend – Victoria	2	Northfleet	10T10	6	6	6	
3	B	Wrotham – Victoria	1	Swanley	10T10	3	3	3	
5	C	Tunbridge Wells – Victoria	2	Tunbridge Wells	10T10	9	9	9	
8	H	East Grinstead – Victoria	2	East Grinstead	10T10	8	8	8	
9	I	{ Crawley – Oxford Circus	1 }	Crawley	11T11	3	3	3	(1)
		{ Redhill – Oxford Circus	1 }	Reigate	11T11	4	4	4	(1)
10	J	Reigate – Oxford Circus	2	Reigate	7T7	6	6	6	(1)
14*	K1/2	Dorking – Epsom – Victoria	2	Dorking	10T10	6	6	6	
15*	K3	Dorking – Kingston – Victoria	2	Leatherhead	10T10	6	6	6	
18	M1	Guildford – Oxford Circus	2	Guildford	10T10	7	7	7	
20	C	Chertsey – Victoria	2	Addlestone	10T10	7	7	7	
21*	D	Staines – Kingston – Victoria	2	Staines	10T10	6	6	6	(2)
23	A1	Ascot – Victoria	1 }	Staines	10T10	7	7	7	
23A	A2	Sunningdale – Victoria	1 }						
26*	G	Windsor – Slough – Victoria	3 }	Windsor	7T7	12	12	12	
26A*	P	Farnham Common – Victoria	1 }						
33	Q	High Wycombe – Oxford Circus	2	High Wycombe	4Q4	7	7	7	(3)
34	R	{ Chesham – Oxford Circus	1 }	Amersham	4Q4	8	8	8	(3)
		{ Amersham – Oxford Circus	1 }						
35	B	Aylesbury – Amersham – Victoria	1	Amersham	7T7	5	5	5	
40	E	Aylesbury – Tring – Victoria	2	Tring	10T10	9	9	9	(4)
40A	F	Hemel Hempstead – Victoria	2	H. Hempstead	10T10	6	6	6	(4)
40B	I	Watford (L. Rd) – Victoria	2	Watford (L. Rd)	ST	5	5	5	(5)
45	H	Luton – Radlett – Victoria	2	Luton	10T10	7	7	7	
46	H3	Luton – Barnet – Victoria	2	Luton	ST	7	7	7	(6)
47*	K1	Hitchin – Victoria	1	Hitchin	10T10	4	4	4	
47A*	K2	Welwyn Gdn City – Victoria	1	Hatfield	10T10	3	3	3	
49	M	Hertford – Oxford Circus	3	Hertford	4Q4	10	10	10	
52	N	Epping – Oxford Circus	2	Epping	10T10	5	5	5	
53	V	Bishop's Stortford – Aldgate	2	Epping	10T10	8	8	8	
54*	X	Romford – Eastern Av – Aldgate	2/4	Romford (L. Rd)	STL	6	6	4	
55	Y1	Brentwood – Aldgate	2/6	Romford (L. Rd)	STL	18	19	16	(7)
58*	Y2	{ Upminster – Aldgate	2/3 }	Romford (L. Rd)	STL	14	14	14	(8)
		{ Hornchurch Stn – Aldgate	2/3 }						
59	Z1	Grays – Purfleet New Rd – Aldgate	2/3 }	Grays	STL	17	18	18	
59A	Z2	Grays – Aveley – Aldgate	2/3 }						

Notes (1) 11T11 classification were former R class 1935 Weymann bodies mounted on T type chassis
   Routes 9 and 10 were converted to 10T10 on 18.12.40
(2) Route 21 was originally advertised as 25.
(3) Route 33 and 34 were converted to ST on 18.12.40 and STL on 8.1.41
(4) Routes 40 and 40A were converted to STL on 18.12.40
(5) Route 40B was withdrawn after 17.12.40
(6) Route 46 was converted to STL on 3.3.41
(7) Route 55 was extended to Highwood Hospital on Sunday afternoons
(8) Route 58 was originally planned as 56 which clashed with a central bus route, thus Y2
   continued until it was redesignated 58 on 18.12.40

Timetable leaflets based on panel bills continued to be issued to the public for the numbered routes. Route 40B from Victoria to Watford Leavesden Road lasted for just two weeks from 4th December 1940.

Right This view of Eccleston Bridge taken after the introduction of the numbered routes in December 1940 shows that the stops have been segregated and the elegant glass shelters have been replaced by crude wooden structures. *London's Transport Museum*

Far right, upper At Victoria routes from the south stood in Buckingham Palace Road. T 711 lays over before returning to Dorking on route 14. *Laurie Akehurst collection*

Far right, lower STL 1274 loads up at Eccleston Bridge for a journey to Ascot on route 23. *Laurie Akehurst collection*

Allowing for the withdrawal of route 40B the requirement on 18th December was for 224 vehicles on Monday to Friday, just two more on Saturday and three fewer on Sunday. Duplication requirements varied according to the time of year and the weather but surviving figures for the spring of 1941 indicate that about 60 duplicates were run on Monday to Friday with some additional needs on Monday morning, 110 on Saturday and a hefty 140 on Sunday. This stretched resources and saw garages not normally working on Green Line helping out – Dartford worked on route 2, Dunton Green on route 5, St Albans on 45 and 46 providing a staggering 13 vehicles on Saturday and Sunday, and Watford Leavesden Road assisted with routes 40 and 40A. The demand for route 46 was so high that Romford provided three vehicles on Saturday and two on Sunday. High Wycombe backed up their seven service coaches on route 33 with 15 double-deck duplicates. Where necessary vehicles were borrowed from other garages and clearly Green Line crews enjoyed very few Sunday rest days! Under the new arrangements first coaches tended to run earlier than they did before the war but last coaches left central London by 8pm in most cases.

With all services terminating in London concessions were granted by the Traffic Commissioner, Gleeson Robinson, but they were allowed strictly as war-time temporary measures and it was made clear to London Transport that they should not be regarded as setting precedents for future operation. At Victoria coaches from the north set down by the Grosvenor Hotel and proceeded via Elizabeth Bridge to stand in Hugh Street before running to the departure stop at Eccleston Bridge. From the south vehicles crossed Eccleston Bridge to set down in Buckingham Palace Road where they stood and then ran via Elizabeth Street, Eccleston Place and Eccleston Street back to Eccleston Bridge. Route 46 from Luton was diverted at North Finchley to run via Golders Green into Victoria rather than observe the pre-war route to Kings Cross. The 53 from Bishop's Stortford deviated from the pre-war route running via Eagle Lane and Hermon Hill in order to avoid the low bridge at Snaresbrook station and was diverted at Mile End to terminate on London Transport property at Aldgate rather than use the former Eldon Street stand. At Oxford Circus coaches set down and stood in Cavendish Square and then ran to the appropriate stop in Upper Regent Street.

It represented a major concession to be allowed to terminate route 52 from Epping at Oxford Circus as the truncated N had used Portman Square. Route 18 from Guildford having reached Oxford Circus via Marble Arch was routed as the High Wycombe and Chesham routes to return via Baker Street Station and Sussex Gardens to Lancaster Gate. Route 8 was diverted at Kennington and route 14 was diverted at Stockwell to run via Vauxhall Bridge to Victoria instead of using Lambeth Bridge. No doubt the Oxford Circus arrangements were under review by the police and Traffic Commissioner as, from 10th February, routes 18, 33, 34, 49 and 52 no longer picked up in Upper Regent Street as passengers were allowed to board in Cavendish Square.

The re-introduction of route 3 to Wrotham meant that bus 478 could be withdrawn but routes 393 and 396 continued to run alongside coach routes 35 and 53 respectively. However, provision of both a bus and coach over the section from Amersham to Great Missenden proved to be excessive and bus 393 ran for the last time on 4th February 1941.

Revised timetables were introduced on all Green Line routes on 9th April as the lighter evenings meant that running times

Route 33 lost its STs in favour of STLs from 8th January 1941. STL 1150 stands at Oxford Circus prior to departure for High Wycombe. *Capital Transport*

Front entrance STL 1497 stands in Park End Road, Romford while working on route 55. Anti-blast netting has been applied to the side windows. The Park End Road stand was used on Wednesday and Saturday when the market was in full swing. *The Omnibus Society*

could be reduced and last coaches could now leave central London between 9pm and 10pm. The Oxford Circus stand arrangements were again revised at this date when routes 9 and 10 were required to set down and stand in Portland Place. They turned by running to Marylebone Road via Park Crescent East, returning via Park Crescent West and Portland Place to the departure stop in Upper Regent Street. Following enemy action on Hatfield garage some vehicles were garaged in de Havilland's Works at New Hatfield from 7th May. Route 35 lost its 7T7s for 10T10s on 28th May and during the middle of June STLs replaced 10T10s on routes 2, 5, 8, 18 and 21 which enabled the latter to be cascaded to routes 26/A releasing 7T7s and to route 49 releasing 4Q4s.

On 8th October 1941 the summer timetables were all superseded with last coaches again leaving central London between 7pm and 8pm. Apart from minor timetable revisions on routes 55 and 58, these timetables were all destined to remain in operation until September 1942. A further vehicle adjustment was made on 8th October when route 21 exchanged its STLs with the 10T10s of routes 23/A. Authority was still being troublesome over the standing arrangements at Oxford Circus. From 28th November staff on routes 18, 33, 34, 49 and 52 were instructed that at times other than when recovery time was allowed for the black-out, they were to leave the country terminal one minute later than scheduled so as not to stand in Cavendish Square for more than four minutes. As fuel rationing had substantially reduced the amount of traffic on the roads it really is questionable as to whether all the fuss raised by the Green Line coaches terminating at Oxford Circus was justified.

The provision of STLs on 16 routes caused the need for duplication to be reduced but in July 1942 there was still a requirement for 46 duplicates on Monday to Friday, 37 on Saturday and a significant 94 on Sunday. Routes 20, 35 and 45 all suffered from low bridge restrictions which meant that only single-deck vehicles could be used. Double-deck duplicates on route 20 were allowed to run via Hampton Court Bridge so as to avoid the low bridge at Thames Ditton, an arrangement established with route C. Some duplicates were required to lay over in London and arrangements were made for them to be parked in Battersea, Holloway, Old Kent Road and Putney Central Area garages.

In the summer of 1942 the government directed that many bus stops be withdrawn and certain traffic lights were switched off in an effort to save fuel, wear and tear on tyres and brake linings. Further savings were sought and with the pending withdrawal of long-distance coach services London Transport announced that all Green Line services would be withdrawn

After the withdrawal of Green Line services in September 1942 six 9T9 and 88 10T10 coaches were loaned to the United States authorities. Fifty-five were used as Red Cross Clubmobiles, nine as coaches and 24 became US army vehicles. These 10T10s have been prepared for the US authorities. T 590 nearest the camera became US no. 1824056 and was transferred on 31st December 1942. *Laurie Akehurst collection*

after Tuesday 29th September. Unlike the 1939 withdrawal this time it was carefully planned with four-weekly tickets being phased out and alterations and augmentations to both Central and Country bus services were made to cover the loss of Green Line facilities. The extreme hardship suffered by some passengers in 1939 was not repeated. This time the withdrawal of Green Line would be for the remainder of the war and as a result Romford London Road and Tunbridge Wells garages closed. Unlike in 1939, Hitchin garage remained open as it had acquired a Country bus allocation from 2nd July 1941. There was a proposal to operate a supplementary service on route 403 from Tunbridge Wells to Sevenoaks but in the event this was not realised. An unusual arrangement concerned the section of route 35 between Amersham and Aylesbury which was covered by new route 359 jointly operated by London Transport and Eastern National.

Green Line was held in high public esteem and it was with much regret that the network was withdrawn and references to the loss were made in the newspapers and on BBC radio. It would be over three years before Londoners would again be able to take a ride on a Green Line coach.

In this propaganda photograph a 10T10 Clubmobile features with aircrew and a plane. The clubmobiles were provided in order to distribute refreshments to members of the United States armed forces. *Alan B. Cross*

RESTORATION

1946–1950

The Board lost no time in planning the post-war network and in so doing devised the following criteria which were to influence the shape of the system that eventually reappeared. Where different routes were common to each other on one side of London forming a joint headway they were to be extended across London to form a joint headway on the other side. The network was to be planned to avoid low bridges and it was claimed that the proposed reintroduction would be with double-deck vehicles. London Transport's post-war vehicle plan provided for the purchase of 386 double deck coaches based on the RT but this provision was, in practice, not realised. It was also proposed that the routes should be numbered in the 700 series starting in a clock-wise progression from Gravesend.

By October 1944 firm proposals were submitted to the Metropolitan Traffic Commissioner, a post still occupied by Gleeson Robinson, and the Metropolitan Police. Disregarding the east London routes the Board proposed to introduce 52 coaches per hour across London compared with 60 per hour pre-war. The proposals were:

701 Gravesend – Victoria – Ascot and *702* Gravesend – Victoria – Sunningdale. Each route to run on a 60-minute interval to give a joint 30-minute service from Gravesend to Virginia Water. Unlike the pre-war A1 and A2 the routes were to run via Bedfont instead of Feltham and Ashford.

703 Wrotham – Victoria – Whipsnade every 60 minutes which was the southern section of route B linked to route U. The

northern section of the B to Amersham and Aylesbury with its low bridge in Amersham was not to be reintroduced and it was felt that Victoria was a better traffic objective for Whipsnade passengers. No further details were given but it seems unlikely that the route north of London would have run all the year round.

704 Tunbridge Wells – Victoria – Windsor (30 minutes) and *705* Westerham (60 minutes) – Westerham Hill (30 minutes) – Victoria – Windsor, thus providing four coaches per hour from Bromley to Windsor. These were the southern sections of routes C1 and C2 and D linked to the western section of the G. Route P to Farnham Common was to be withdrawn and passengers would be required to change to bus 441 at Slough. There would be a reduction in frequency at certain times between London and Slough.

706 Westerham – Victoria – Hemel Hempstead and *707* Oxted – Victoria – Hemel Hempstead both routes every 60 minutes to provide a 30-minute service from Botley Hill to Hemel Hempstead covering routes E and F. Pre-war the F had run alternately to Tatsfield and Edenbridge and the 706 from Westerham covered new ground for Green Line running over bus route 403, while the 707 covered former route F but the section between Edenbridge and Oxted was regarded as withdrawn and left to bus 465. Tatsfield was to be left unserved, again being considered as withdrawn. A low bridge in Selsdon Road was to be avoided by running the coaches via Sussex Road like bus 403. Unlike the pre-war operation

these routes and 708 were to be diverted at Brixton to run via Stockwell and Vauxhall Bridge instead of Kennington and Lambeth Bridge.

708 East Grinstead – Victoria – Aylesbury every 30 minutes covering the southern section of H1 and the northern section of route E. The southern section of H2 via Baldwins Hill was covered by bus 428.

709 Caterham – Oxford Circus – Chesham and *710* Crawley – Oxford Circus – Amersham both routes every 60 minutes to provide two coaches per hour from Coulsdon to Amersham. The gradual rundown of Croydon Aerodrome in favour of Northolt meant that the need for coach G via Purley Way no longer existed. What was effectively proposed was the diversion of the Redhill short-workings on route I to Caterham which were to run via Coulsdon instead of Stoat's Nest Road. North of London the routes would have covered route R.

711 Reigate – Oxford Circus – High Wycombe every 30 minutes covering the southern section of the J and route Q. The Board maintained that with the build up during the war of works services in Watford it could no longer accommodate a Green Line allocation in Leavesden Road garage thus routes 709, 710 and 711 were linked to routes Q and R. The northern sections of I and J would be covered by routes 706, 707 and 708 which would offer double the pre-war frequency provided by routes E and F. The section from Watford to Abbots Langley was officially described as deferred and to be left to bus 318.

Left TF 32 with pale green relief loads up for Dorking at Eccleston Bridge in September 1946. Note the temporary stop sign used prior to the erection of tubular steel shelters.
London's Transport Museum

712 Dorking – Epsom – Victoria – Barnet – Luton every 30 minutes covering K3 and H3. This represented a reduction of one journey per hour via Epsom but a slight increase over the northern section. The Kings Cross to North Finchley section was to be abandoned with the route running as per war-time route 46 from Victoria via Golders Green.

713 and *714* Dorking – Kingston – Marble Arch – Radlett – Luton (713) or Dunstable (714) each route on a 60-minute headway so as to provide a 30-minute joint service between Dorking and St Albans. These routes covered the southern section of K3 with the section between Horsham and Dorking, covered by bus 414, being deferred. The pre-war routeing was diverted at Kingston to run via Richmond instead of Putney and would have offered double the former frequency between Dorking and Kingston. The problem of the low bridge at Park Street was overcome by diverting the routes at Radlett to run to St Albans via Shenley and London Colney. This proposal gave London Colney four coaches per hour with 712 but left the former route to be covered by bus 355. Surviving records offer contrary information concerning the three Dorking routes but it seems that the above proposal eventually emerged from the initial conflicting details.

715 Guildford – Oxford Circus – Hertford every 20 minutes represented a compromise solution to cream-off the best of the pre-war traffic of the four journeys per hour offered by the M group. The section from Byfleet to Cobham was withdrawn together with the operation via Great Cambridge Road (south of Southbury Road) and Ponders End. In order to avoid an uneven service interval with two coaches per hour running via Ware and one via Hertford Heath the latter section was left to bus 342.

716 Chertsey – Marble Arch – Hitchin and *717* Woking – Marble Arch – Welwyn Garden City each route every 60 minutes. This was a linking of the western sections of C1 and C2 with the northern sections of K1 and K2 to give a 30-minute service from Addlestone to Stanborough. The Woking route was diverted via Woodham which left Byfleet unserved by Green Line. From an operational point of view it was obviously more convenient to have the route passing the garage at Addlestone. Both routes would run via the Great North Road to Hatfield leaving bus 340 to serve the section via Barnet By-Pass. The combined service between London and Stanborough represented a reduction of one journey per hour compared with pre-war days. The

section from Hitchin to Baldock was outside the Board's Special Area, although the Board had restricted running powers, and was officially deferred being left to Eastern National. A fundamental flaw in the planning was linking routes entering London via Hammersmith to run through to the north of London as they were unable to serve Victoria. Strictly, in a clockwise numbering scheme, Woking should have been allocated 716 and Chertsey 717 but the numbers seem to have been transposed at an early stage.

718 Windsor – Victoria – Ongar every 30 minutes. The 718 was something of a hotch potch of pre-war routes covering the N from Windsor to Staines then running as D to Kingston and K3 onwards to Victoria. From Victoria the proposed route was via Marble Arch and Oxford Circus to Great Portland Street station from where it then ran as N to Epping and W to Ongar. Both Staines and Epping were to be served by four coaches per hour from London compared with six pre-war. Route W from Liverpool Street running through Dalston and Chingford was officially deferred.

719 Windsor – Uxbridge – Watford – St Albans – Luton (frequency not known). The concept of peripheral Green Line routes had been considered in the early days but in the event time had run out and none could be introduced before the February 1931 deadline. This route was described as an experimental cross-country operation to relieve long-distance traffic on bus routes 457 and 321.

720 Aldgate – Bishop's Stortford every 30 minutes. This was pre-war route V amended to start from Aldgate instead of Liverpool Street and a slight intermediate diversion to avoid the low bridge at Snaresbrook station.

721 Aldgate – Brentwood providing up to eight coaches per hour between London and Romford and six on to Brentwood. The projection to Highwood Hospital was not to be reintroduced and the use of double-deck vehicles permitted a reduction in frequency compared with that on Y1 in 1939.

722 Aldgate – Hornchurch Station or Upminster (Corbets Tey) providing up to four coaches per hour on each leg of the service. The use of double-deck vehicles permitted a reduction on the 1939 frequency of Y2.

723 Aldgate – Grays – Tilbury running as Z1 via Chandlers Corner and Purfleet New Road and *724* Aldgate – Grays running as Z2 via Wennington and Aveley providing a combined service of up to six coaches per hour.

The re-introduction of route T from Watford to Golders Green and route X from Aldgate to Romford via Eastern Avenue were officially deferred but planned enhancements to the Underground would have considerably reduced their value. It seems highly likely that the Board had no intention of ever reintroducing sections of

route defined as being deferred but used this as a ploy to appease the Traffic Commissioner.

These proposals cut very little ice with the uncompromising Gleeson Robinson who felt that the network should be reintroduced exactly as at August 1939. He had previously stated that any concessions granted during the war were to be considered as being strictly of a temporary nature. After consultations with the Metropolitan Police, Robinson did not accept the reduction of eight coaches per hour crossing London as a valid point and opined that double-deck vehicles would require longer times at stops to facilitate boarding and alighting of passengers, many of whom would have luggage. In correspondence to the police, Robinson stated that the revised cross linking of services allowed the Board to "juggle the figures" and concern was expressed over future increases in requirements in the light of proposals to build housing estates on London's outskirts.

The Traffic Commissioner and police objected to the following specific proposals:

Linking the 703 to Whipsnade was felt undesirable and they considered that the route should run through to Aylesbury as pre-war route B. The Whipsnade route should still terminate at Marylebone.

The linking of routes 709, 710 and 711 to Chesham, Amersham and High Wycombe did not find favour and it was considered that they should continue to Watford.

Route 712 which linked Dorking with the pre-war Kings Cross to Luton service was considered completely unacceptable as Kings Cross, where the coaches terminated off of the public highway on the edge of the central area, represented Lord Amulree's textbook example of an ideal arrangement. The proposed diversion to Victoria was not approved.

Operation of route 718 via Oxford Street and Oxford Circus would have meant one additional coach per hour each way along Oxford Street compared with 1939 and was therefore not approved.

The police were against the Board's proposed routeing between Baker Street Station and Marble Arch via Baker Street and Oxford Street and felt that the coaches should run via Marylebone Road and Edgware Road. Pre-war the K1 and K2 had run via the former and H1, H2 and K3 via the latter.

No doubt the proposals were much discussed between the Board, the Traffic Commissioner and Police during 1945 and following the end of the war the actual reintroduction became viable. A statement dated 29th November 1945 shows the reintroduction split into five stages to be introduced between January and July 1946 as vehicles became available and staff were released from the armed forces and included the following amendments. Route 703 would run to Aylesbury via Amersham with the proviso that negotiations with Eastern National would be necessary for the projection beyond Amersham. The 709, 710 and 711 were planned to run through to Watford again with a proviso that until garage space at Watford was available they will have to terminate at Portland Place. Robinson was aghast at this proposal and has written a large "NO!" in the margin of the confidential correspondence. The police comment that "Once the Board, especially the Green Line, get their nose in anywhere, even though it is said to be temporary, they have the bad habit of using their best endeavours to make it permanent and we experience great difficulty in moving them". Operation via the London – Tilbury Road east of Chandlers Corner and Purfleet By-Pass offered minimal intermediate traffic and the proposals for Grays were revised with just one route, 723, running via Wennington and Aveley.

In January 1946 Allsop Place at Baker Street station was accepted to be a suitable stand for routes 709, 710, 711 and the truncated 714. The Dorking group were revised as Dorking – Epsom – Victoria – Radlett – Luton (712) or Dunstable (713) with 714 from Dorking to Baker Street via Kingston. Route 718 was to run via Baker Street station and the projection from Epping to Ongar had been dropped. Pre-war routes Q and R from High Wycombe and Chesham to Oxford Circus reappeared as 724 and 725 respectively. Pre-war route U to Whipsnade became 726 and the H3 from Kings Cross to Luton became 727. The problem of the route between Baker Street station and Marble Arch was compromised with southbound coaches running via Marylebone Road and Edgware Road and northbound via Oxford Street, Portman Square and Baker Street. Other changes before reintroduction were the projection of all journeys on route 705 from Westerham Hill or Westerham to Sevenoaks and the switching of the northern terminals of routes 706 and 707 from Hemel Hempstead to Aylesbury with the 708 now running to Hemel Hempstead.

The Government eased restrictions on coach services which would be in competition with the main line railways on 1st February 1946 and the Board lost no time in introducing the first two routes on 6th February. The proposed five stages of introduction became rather fragmented and it proved too optimistic to introduce all the Aldgate routes on one date.

Stage	Date		Route	Frequency	Allocation	Type	
2	6.2.46	715	Guildford – Oxford Circus – Hertford	30	GF/HG	10T10	(1)
1		720	Bishops Stortford – Aldgate	30	EP	10T10	
3	6.3.46	704	Tunbridge Wells – Victoria – Windsor	30	TW/WR	10T10	
3		709	Caterham – Baker Street	60	GD	6Q6	(1)
3		710	Crawley – Baker Street	60	CY	6Q6	(1)
1		721	Brentwood – Aldgate	10/20	RE	D	(2)
3		723	Tilbury – Grays – Aldgate	15/20	GY	TF	(3)
3	8.3.46	716	Chertsey – Marble Arch – Hitchin	60	WY/HN	10T10	(4)
4	3.4.46	703	Wrotham – Victoria – Amersham	60	SJ/MA	10T10	
4		711	Reigate – Baker Street	30	RG	6Q6	(1)
4		718	Windsor – Victoria – Epping	60	WR/EP	10T10	(5)
1		722	Corbets Tey or Hornchurch Stn – Aldgate	10/15	RE	D	(6)
4		724	High Wycombe – Oxford Circus	60	HE	6Q6	(5)
4	1.5.46	708	East Grinstead – Victoria – Hemel Hempstead	30	EG/HH	10T10	
5		714	Dorking – Kingston – Baker Street	30	DS	TF	
3		717	Woking – Marble Arch – Welwyn Garden City	60	WY/HF	10T10	
5		727	Luton – Barnet – Kings Cross	30	LS	TF	
5	29.5.46	705	Sevenoaks – Westerham – Victoria – Windsor	30	DG/WR	10T10	
4		712	Dorking – Victoria – Luton	60	DS/SA	TF	
4		713	Dorking – Victoria – Dunstable	60	DS/SA	TF	
4		726	Whipsnade Zoo – Marylebone	Irr.	WT	10T10	(7)
5	19.6.46	702	Gravesend – Victoria – Sunningdale	60	NF/ST	10T10	
5		725	Chesham – Amersham – Oxford Circus	30	MA	6Q6	(8)
5	22.6.46	701	Gravesend – Victoria – Ascot	60	NF/ST	10T10	
5	26.6.46	706	Westerham – Victoria – Aylesbury	60	CM/TG	10T10	
5		707	Oxted – Victoria – Aylesbury	60	CM/TG	10T10	

Notes:
(1) Route 715 was increased to every 20 minutes on 17th April and acquired 6Q6 coaches in June with the 10T10s going to routes 709, 710 and 711.
(2) Additional coaches between Aldgate and Romford at certain times.
(3) 60-minute service Tilbury – Grays.
(4) Route 716 was advertised to start on 27th February but the introduction was deferred.
(5) Increased to every 30 minutes on 1st May.
(6) Combined service interval.
(7) Route 726 service was increased for the summer on 17th July with RE providing 10T10s.
(8) 60-minute service Chesham to Amersham.

The first routes to appear on 6th February 1946 were 715 from Guildford to Hertford and 720 from Aldgate to Bishop's Stortford. T 581 on route 715 is seen at Oxford Circus shortly after the reintroduction. The side route boards and destination blinds are in white on black. In contrast to single-deck bus routes at the time the numbers appeared on the right hand side of the destination blinds. *AEC*

THE LIGHTS ARE GREEN

London Transport is taking full advantage of the long-awaited opportunity to restore peace-time services and to start work again on development schemes that were unavoidably held up during the war years. It is good to know, for instance, that GREEN LINE services have been resumed this month on two routes- Bishops Stortford to Aldgate and Hertford to Guildford. This is only a beginning and it is expected that all Green Line services will be running by July

GREEN LINE COACHES ARE RETURNING LONDON TRANSPORT

SHEP

Green Line had been held in high public esteem in pre-war days and the reintroduction of the system was seen by both London Transport and the public as a significant step towards the return to peace-time conditions. Much publicity including some very attractive posters and press advertisements heralded the various stages of the return. This poster of February 1946 by Charles Shepherd (Shep) explains the position.
London's Transport Museum

The first issue of the allocation book produced after the reintroduction of the network on 10th July showed that 248 vehicles (excluding duplicates) were needed for Monday to Friday service composed of 131 10T10, 45 TF, 39 6Q6, 32 D and one RT (RT 97). An extra three vehicles were required on Saturday and three fewer on Sunday. Immediately prior to withdrawal in 1939 some 328 coaches were required on Monday to Friday, thus the 1946 requirement represented a reduction of 24 per cent.

The reintroduction of Green Line meant that Romford London Road and Tunbridge Wells garages were to be re-opened, both on 6th March. Proposed peripheral route 719 between Windsor and Luton, which was planned to be introduced in July, did not materialise and research has been unable to find any reason for this.

A number of differences were to be found compared with pre-war operation. Thirty-seven brand new double-deck utility Daimlers with 56-seat Duple bodies were used on routes 721 and 722 and were very spartan by Green Line standards. They compared poorly with the TFs that had been introduced on the routes' predecessors in 1939. Apart from the Romford and Grays garages' routes the first coaches generally ran about one hour earlier and last coaches were generally just after 11pm from central London. From the early days of Green Line variable running times had been allowed according to day of the week and time of the day but running times were now consistent right across the week. The duty schedules were arranged slightly differently with the practice of crews changing over with those running in the opposite direction at certain locations being abandoned. Sunday coaches tended to start one hour later than Monday to Saturday and this necessitated the practice of one or two crews travelling in one direction as passengers.

Upper Route 710 was introduced on 6th March 1946 and in common with route 709 used 6Q6 coaches. Q 234 is seen on the stand in Allsop Place at the side of Baker Street station which was considered as an acceptable terminus by the traffic commissioner. *Alan B. Cross*

Lower A batch of 37 new utility Daimler 56-seat double-deckers were allocated to Romford London Road garage for busy routes 721 and 722. They were finished in Green Line livery but were not fitted out to Green Line standards and must have compared unfavourably with the TFs of 1939. D 159 stands on the cobbles of Aldgate bus station. *Laurie Akehurst collection*

A series of 'Pay as you board' experiments began in 1944 using specially rebuilt vehicles with a seated conductor near the entrance. The intention was possibly to employ disabled ex-servicemen as conductors. RT 97 rebuilt as a 50-seater entered service on route 721 on 18th April 1946 for a ten-week trial. The bus, which was fitted with platform doors, was the first to appear with the pale green relief used on Green Line in the post-war period, the use of which was gradually extended across the Green Line fleet. Frustrated passengers, denied the convenience of boarding during the stand time, are finally allowed to board at Aldgate. Inside, the conductor, who is proudly wearing his war service medal ribbons, issues tickets from a National Cash Register machine. The experiment was not considered a success and 'Pay as you board' was not perpetuated.
London's Transport Museum

As more routes were introduced the publicity was constantly updated – this poster by Wiseman sets out the position on 1st May 1946. *London's Transport Museum*

GREEN LINE COACHES

NOW RUNNING

703 **Wrotham & Amersham**
via Farningham, Sidcup, Victoria, Rickmansworth

704 **Tunbridge Wells & Windsor**
via Sevenoaks, Bromley, Victoria, Colnbrook, Slough

708 **East Grinstead & Hemel Hempstead**
via Godstone, Caterham, Croydon, Victoria, Bushey, Watford

709 **Caterham & London** (Baker Street)
via Coulsdon, Croydon, Streatham, Oxford Circus

710 **Crawley & London** (Baker Street)
via Horley, Redhill, Coulsdon, Croydon, Oxford Circus

711 **Reigate & London** (Baker Street)
via Lower Kingswood, Sutton, Tooting, Oxford Circus

714 **Dorking & London** (Baker Street)
via Leatherhead, Surbiton, Kingston, Richmond, Hammersmith

715 **Guildford & Hertford**
via Esher, Oxford Circus, Enfield, Waltham Cross

716 **Chertsey & Hitchin**
via Weybridge, Kingston, Baker Street, Barnet, Hatfield

717 **Woking & Welwyn Garden City**
via Weybridge, Kingston, Marble Arch, Barnet, Hatfield

718 **Windsor & Epping**
via Staines, Kingston, Baker Street, Woodford, Loughton

720 **Bishops Stortford & Aldgate**
via Epping, Loughton, Woodford, Leytonstone, Stratford

721 **Brentwood & Aldgate**
via Romford, Seven Kings, Ilford, Stratford

722 **Upminster & Aldgate**
via Hornchurch, Ilford, Stratford

723 **Tilbury & Aldgate**
via Grays, Rainham, Dagenham, Barking

724 **High Wycombe & London** (Oxford Circus)
via Beaconsfield, Gerrards Cross, Uxbridge, Southall

727 **Luton & London** (Kings Cross)
via Harpenden, St. Albans, Barnet, North Finchley, Highgate

GREEN·LINE

WISEMAN

Some garage allocations were revised with all the Dorking routes being allocated to Dorking garage, leaving Leatherhead garage never again to work coaches in London Transport days. The Luton and Dunstable joint service was allocated to St Albans with Luton garage suffering a reduction in coaches compared with pre-war. Interestingly having advised the Traffic Commissioner that an allocation of coaches could no longer be accommodated at Watford Leavesden Road, that garage provided five coaches for route 726. The original intention was to 'when work' the coaches in service from Leavesden Road, to Marylebone via route 708 to Edgware Road station and a faretable is known to exist but problems with route 726 being licensed as an express carriage service caused complications.

Prior to its withdrawal in September 1942, Green Line had been held in high public esteem and its restoration was welcomed by Londoners as a major step in the country's long path in returning to normality. Traffic circulars appealed to every member of staff to "give of his or her best" to ensure that the new services were successful in regaining their pre-war popularity. Green Line was now entering a period of stability and some of the timetables were destined to remain virtually unchanged until the 1960s. The initial timetable for routes 701 and 702 did not receive even a slight adjustment until 1953 – a feat almost unimaginable by today's standards.

Above left The routes introduced on 1st May 1946 were equipped with a revised layout of destination blind in black and white. TF 50 on route 727 stops at the bus and coach compulsory stop opposite St. Albans garage. *Laurie Akehurst collection*

Left On 29th May 1946 new destination blinds officially described as black and amber came into use on all coaches. These blinds made the coaches readily discernible from buses at a considerable distance. Note that the London display carries no route number. *London's Transport Museum*

Below The stop signs in central London and at certain other points listed the route numbers and destinations as depicted by this example at Hyde Park Corner. *London's Transport Museum*

While the network was fairly static once re-introduced the fares certainly were not. Initially only single fares were available and the fares were set at 16⅔ per cent above the August 1939 standard so as to fall into line with railway fares rather than to attempt to undercut them. The central London minimum fare was 1/2d compared with the pre-war 1/- and the country minimum was generally 7d. Hardly had the complete network reappeared when on 1st July 1946 fares were increased to 33⅓ per cent above the pre-war level in line with the railways which meant the London minimum increased to 1/4d with the country minimum now 8d. Weekly tickets reappeared on 30th September 1946 and from 1st October 1946 cheap day returns were reintroduced on a very restricted basis. They were available to or from Central London on Tuesdays to Thursdays only with restrictions on use in the rush-hours whereas pre-war returns were available for any journey every day subject to a general minimum of 1/6d. Because of increased traffic in the country area the introduction of the coaches did not enable any parallel Country bus routes to be withdrawn although in some cases headways were cut. Bus fares did not apply on the coaches in the country districts and the only concession was the provision of 4d fares between Northwood Hills and Rickmansworth on route 703 where no local bus service was provided. From 28th October the fare from Botley Hill to Oxted on 707 was reduced to 4d.

Top Victory Day was celebrated on 8th June 1946 and marches and parades in central London caused many Green Line services to be diverted from their normal route. Route 714 was unable to reach Baker Street and was altered to terminate at Victoria. The route was normally worked by TF coaches but on this occasion Q 237 is seen standing on Eccleston Bridge. The coach still carries the white relief but the boards are now produced in gold on green. The war-time rear target was carried for some considerable time after the end of hostilities. *Alan B. Cross*

Centre and bottom During June 1946 the 6Q6 coaches running on routes 709, 710 and 711 were exchanged with the 10T10s operating on route 715. T 543 leaves the stand at Allsop Place, Baker Street bound for Caterham and Q 199 turns right at Manor House station passing the LT style lightbox signpost. *Alan B. Cross, Laurie Akehurst collection*

Right This poster map shows the completed post-war network which was achieved from 26th June 1946. *London's Transport Museum*

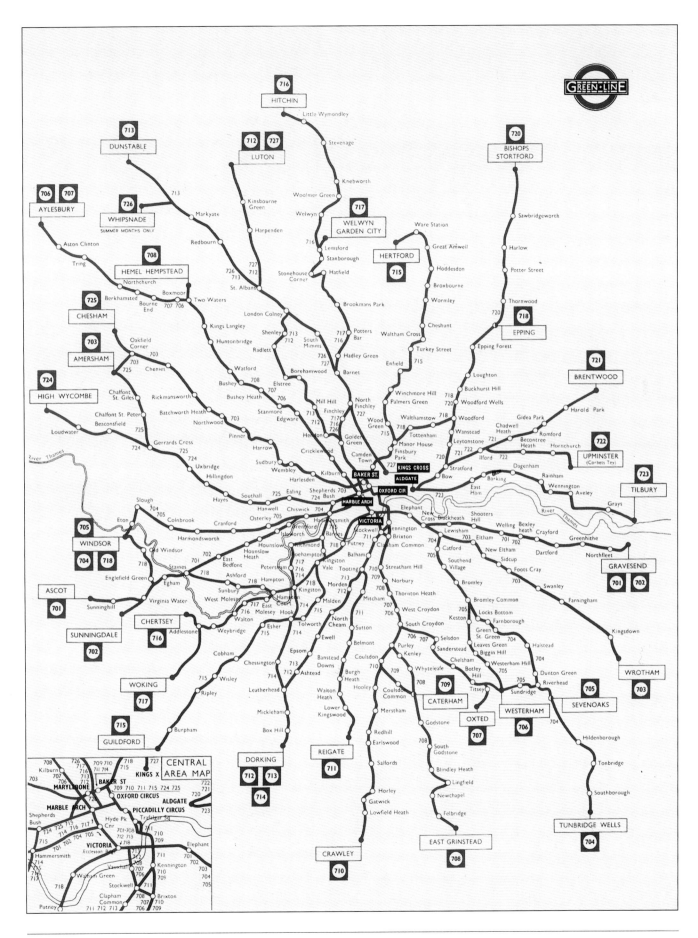

GREEN·LINE

716 HITCHIN

713 DUNSTABLE

712 727 LUTON

720 BISHOPS STORTFORD

706 707 AYLESBURY

726 WHIPSNADE
SUMMER MONTHS ONLY

717 WELWYN GARDEN CITY

708 HEMEL HEMPSTEAD

715 HERTFORD

725 CHESHAM

718 EPPING

703 AMERSHAM

721 BRENTWOOD

724 HIGH WYCOMBE

722 UPMINSTER
(Corbets Tey)

723 TILBURY

705 WINDSOR

704 718

GRAVESEND

701 702

701 ASCOT

702 SUNNINGDALE

716 CHERTSEY

717 WOKING

705 703

WROTHAM

715 GUILDFORD

707 WESTERHAM

706 SEVENOAKS

709 CATERHAM

707 OXTED

712 713 DORKING

714

711 REIGATE

704 TUNBRIDGE WELLS

710 CRAWLEY

708 EAST GRINSTEAD

CENTRAL AREA MAP

91

The arrangements concerning stops were revised and the pre-war practice of passengers being able to hail coaches at any point outside the Metropolitan Police Area and to alight at any point en route was discontinued. Initially passengers could board within the Metropolitan Police Area at defined coach stops but, in country districts, passengers could board, by request, at any bus or coach stop. Passengers could alight at any bus or coach stop over the entire route the only exception being the Polytechnic in Upper Regent Street where passengers were conveyed to Portland Place.

From 30th September some 65 additional stops were provided within the Metropolitan Police Area and passengers could only board or alight within the area at defined coach stops. From 11th May 1947 this practice was extended to country districts and the coaches would only observe coach stop signs. The Traffic Commissioner had allowed two additional restricted boarding points from the start at Piccadilly Circus on routes 709, 710 and 711 and at Selfridge's on route 715, but passengers could only board on Monday to Friday after 7.30pm, Saturdays after 2pm and all day Sundays and Bank Holidays.

An STL presence was maintained at Romford London Road garage from September 1946 until May 1950. STL 2528 was one of the first to be transferred in and is seen at Aldgate together with D 136, a TF on route 723 and 10T10 on route 720. *James H. Aston*

Route 726 ran during the summer season only and was withdrawn for the winter after 1st October 1946. There was the problem of how to employ the Watford Leavesden Road Green Line crews and from 2nd October a supplementary 30-minute service was run on route 708 between Watford Parade and Victoria. Two versions of the timetable were tried but the service did not fit in well with the combined 15-minute service provided by routes 706, 707 and 708 and the service ran for the last time on 16th February 1947. From the 1947 summer season Romford London Road worked route 726 with Daimlers supplemented by some STLs. Adjustments to the service were few during this period but from 2nd October 1946, when working, journeys on route 709 ran in service between Godstone garage and Caterham station. From 29th September 1947 route 727 was diverted at Kings Cross away from the coach station in Birkenhead Street to a temporary open air site in Judd Street.

A further fares revision took place on 1st November 1947 when the single fares were increased to a staggering 55 per cent above the 1939 standard. Cheap Day returns were increased to 1½ times the single fare and weekly tickets to nine times the single fare. This increase did not apply on the western sections of routes 701, 702, 704 and 705, the northern sections of routes 716 and 717 and the Brentwood to Romford section of the 721 where other operators' fare scales continued to apply. From 4th June 1948 cheap day tickets were also issued on Mondays and Fridays and this facility was extended to Saturdays and Sundays and Bank Holidays from 11th June 1949. The evening rush-hour restrictions were removed at this time and the former practice of allowing passengers to return to London by train after 4pm on Saturdays, Sundays and Bank Holidays was again permitted.

Top From the 1947 summer season route 726 was worked by Daimlers from Romford London Road garage. D 135 is seen at Golders Green with day-trippers returning from Whipsnade.
Alan B. Cross

Centre On 29th September 1947 the Kings Cross terminus of route 727 was changed from the coach station in Birkenhead Street to a temporary open-air site in Judd Street. TF 39 stands amongst the somewhat primitive facilities.
Robert F. Mack

Some of London Transport's original proposals for the post-war system were realised on 12th November 1947 when routes 709, 710 and 711 were extended through London to take over routes 724 and 725. T 617 stops at Oxford Circus en route from Crawley to Amersham.
Alan B. Cross

A major change in working conditions for operating staff which involved a reduction in the working week from 48 hours to 44 hours had been subject of negotiation between the Board and the Transport and General Workers' Union during 1947. New conditions of service meant that some routes had to be re-scheduled and the following changes involving Green Line applied from 12th November, having been deferred from 29th October. The Board achieved one of its 1944 proposals when routes 724 and 725 were withdrawn to be covered by extensions of routes 709, 710 and 711. Gleeson Robinson had vacated the post of traffic commissioner in 1946 and it seems that the relationship with London Transport was now a little more amicable. Under the new arrangements 709 ran from Godstone (when working) or Caterham-on-the-Hill to Chesham every 60 minutes, 710 ran from Crawley to Amersham every 60 minutes and 711 from Reigate to High Wycombe every 30 minutes. On the same date route 714 was reduced to an hourly service on Monday to Saturday evenings and Sunday mornings.

On 1st January 1948 large parts of the transport industry were nationalised and a new body, the British Transport Commission, entered into ownership and control of a significant part of inland transport operation. The new organisation consisted, by the end of 1948, of five Executives of which London Transport was one. Lord Ashfield had stepped down as Chairman in 1947 to be replaced by Lord Latham.

The Green Line network continued to remain fairly static with only a few changes taking place. With the re-introduction of 726 on 26th March 1948 the terminal was changed from Marylebone station to Allsop Place at Baker Street station. From 19th May 1948 two daily journeys in each direction on route 708 were diverted away from Lingfield to run direct via the Eastbourne Road but from 2nd March 1949 all journeys ran again via Lingfield.

During 1949 passenger usage declined on route 722 and from 5th October the service to Hornchurch Station was reduced to Monday to Saturday rush-hours only with the combined service being reduced at off peak times from 15 minutes to 20 minutes with all journeys running to Corbets Tey. Reductions applied to routes 721 and 722 following the electrification of the Liverpool Street to Shenfield train service on 7th November. The new electric trains were everything that the old, dirty, un-reliable steam trains were not and large numbers of passengers deserted Green Line in favour of the trains. Weekly tickets issued on route 721 declined by 25 per cent as a result and the management decided that action had to be taken. On 1st March 1950 headway reductions took place on route 721 with the basic 10-minute fre-

quency being widened to 12 minutes except during Monday to Friday rush-hours. From July 1950 new RT buses began to replace the austere Daimlers. Further timetable revisions took place on both routes from 9th August when the 722 was reduced to a 30-minute service on Monday to Friday evenings and all day on Sunday. Petrol for private motorists had come off ration during the spring of 1950 which caused the management to look very carefully at any changes in ridership across the whole system.

In December 1948 five Central Bus Daimlers were repainted in Green Line livery and transferred to Romford London Road garage in exchange for STLs. Unlike the original Green Line vehicles which had Duple bodies the newcomers had Brush bodies which had a number of detail differences including upper deck ventilators above the front windows. D 68 awaits a new crew opposite London Road garage. *Alan B. Cross*

Following a severe delay to Green Line passengers caused by a mechanical breakdown the decision was taken in 1949 to provide a stand-by coach at both Riverside and Victoria (Gillingham Street) garages. Surviving records from 1949 reveal that the two coaches were used on 43 occasions over a 45-day period. T 476 stands in the yard at Gillingham Street. The reduced area blind box enabled all routes and destinations to be accommodated on one blind. *Alan B. Cross*

When planning the post-war network London Transport had stated that it proposed to operate all routes with double-deck vehicles. In the event with the need to renew much of the bus fleet, the resources to develop a new design suitable for Green Line had simply not been available in the early post-war period. The situation eventually improved and the experimental pay-as-you-board bus RT 97 was completely rebuilt and equipped as a 46-seat coach, RTC 1. The front end was re-styled with a full width grille which was achieved by positioning the radiator under the stairs. The interior, with fluorescent lighting, looked quite different from an RT bus. Smoking, which was only allowed on the upper deck of double-deck buses, was permitted on both decks because of the air conditioning system but many public complaints were received about this arrangement. It entered service on route 715 on 6th April 1949 and was subsequently used on routes 711, 708 and 704 before returning to route 715 in July. It was relegated to Country Bus duties in December 1949. A number of mechanical problems had been encountered in service and the suspension caused the vehicle to sway at speed. A major cause of passenger complaint was the lack of luggage racks. Apart from the busy east London routes single-deck vehicles were to remain the mainstay of the Green Line fleet for some years to come.
London's Transport Museum, M. Rooum

The residents of Chingford were not happy about the lack of Green Line facilities in the area after the war as there had been no replacement for the old W route. The steam suburban service to Chingford was not of the best quality with, it was alleged, dirty and antiquated rolling stock so representations to the new Executive were made for the restoration of the Green Line service. The Central Line had been electrified and it was being duplicated by four coaches per hour from Woodford to Epping so from 10th May 1950 route 718 was rerouted between Walthamstow and Woodford Wells away from Gates Corner to run via Chingford Mount and Whitehall Road.

The British Transport Commission was now getting to grips with the business and introduced a passenger charges scheme to bring railway and Green Line fares broadly into line. From 1st October 1950 Green Line single fares were significantly reduced but with the exception of route 726 and a few bookings where other operators' fare scales applied on routes 716, 717 and 721, all return facilities were withdrawn. The London minimum now fell to the pre-war 1/- with an 8d minimum in country districts. Where the fares had previously increased in 3d steps the new scale was calculated on a very fine basis according to distance and now had increments of 1d in many cases. An example of the change can be illustrated by the fare from Dorking to Victoria. Prior to the reduction it was 3/6d single 5/3d return but the new single became 2/9d representing a reduction of 1/6d on two single fares but an increase of 3d if a passenger travelled at times when returns had been available.

Green Line's popularity was quickly regained and the demand for travel was high. Summer weekends and bank holidays saw considerable duplication operated with seemingly all available vehicles and crews employed. Some examples are shown on these two pages.

Above Dorking was a popular destination as demonstrated by this Whitsun Monday scene at Eccleston Bridge with Q 94 and Q 65, the latter in the revised Country area all-green livery. Q 94 still carries clips for side route boards from earlier regular Green Line use. *Alan B. Cross*

Below T 790, a post-war Country area bus classified 15T13 is seen helping out on route 723 at Aldgate in September 1949. A TF on route 720 stands in the background – the route lost its Ts in favour of TFs in May 1949. *Alan B. Cross*

Windsor was the most popular Green Line destination for weekend trips which meant that vast numbers of duplicate journeys had to be operated. Country bus ST 821, dating from 1930 and now preserved in the London's Transport Museum collection, arrives at Eccleston Bridge on 24th August 1948. Crowds wait patiently at Eccleston Bridge on Easter Monday 1949 where an immaculately turned out STL 2327 arrives from Windsor and after turning, will no doubt return with a full load. *Alan B. Cross*

Above left The LTC class, AEC Renowns, dated from 1937 and were designed for use as private hire coaches. In the post-war period some saw occasional use on Green Line work. LTC17 stands at Aldgate prior to working a rush-hour extra to Epping on 5th March 1948. *Alan B. Cross*

Above right T 270, one of the early Green Line coaches, now reduced to Country bus status, is pressed into Green Line use by Windsor garage. *Alan B. Cross*

Left The 9T9 class were not scheduled to be used on Green Line work after the war but could be seen on duplicates as shown by T 416 waiting at Eccleston Bridge before returning to Windsor on route 718. The use of a paper label in the blind box was usual practice. *Alan B. Cross*

From July 1950 the Daimlers were replaced by a batch of 36 brand new 56-seat RTs numbered RT 3224-3259. They were fitted out as standard buses but externally they carried no advertisements and had Green Line metal bullseyes between decks. RT 3224 is seen at Aldgate on route 722 fitted with the original olive green and yellow destination blinds. *Don Jones*

Below It was common practice for the Country Buses & Coaches operating department to borrow Central area buses at summer weekends to supplement their services. As far as possible the red buses were used on Country bus routes releasing green ones for Green Line duties but occasionally red buses turned up on Green Line. STL 836 prepares to leave Eccleston Bridge with a duplicate to East Grinstead on Easter Monday 1949. *Alan B. Cross*

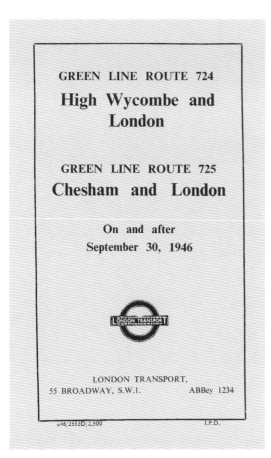

GREEN LINE ROUTE 724
High Wycombe and London

GREEN LINE ROUTE 725
Chesham and London

On and after
September 30, 1946

LONDON TRANSPORT,
55 BROADWAY, S.W.1.   ABBey 1234

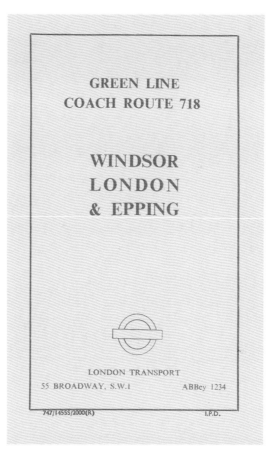

GREEN LINE
COACH ROUTE 718

**WINDSOR
LONDON
& EPPING**

LONDON TRANSPORT
55 BROADWAY, S.W.1   ABBey 1234

From 30th September 1946 the fares were included in the individual route timetable leaflets which went through various cover styles in the late 1940s. The use of green ink enhanced their appearance a little but they continued to be printed on poor quality paper.

GREEN LINE COACHES

ROUTE 721
**Brentwood
Romford
and
London**

On and after May 19, 1948

LONDON TRANSPORT
55 BROADWAY SW1   ABBey 1234

GREEN LINE COACHES

ROUTE 711

**REIGATE
LONDON
HIGH WYCOMBE**

On and after June 11 1949

LONDON TRANSPORT
55 BROADWAY WESTMINSTER S.W.1
ABBey 1234

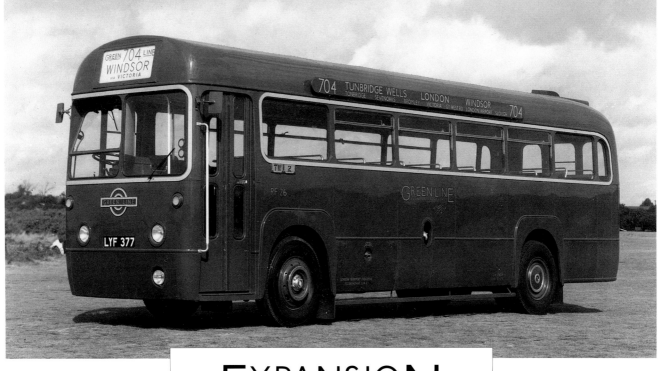

EXPANSION
1951–1957

In 1947 the government took action to resolve the housing crisis in London by introducing the Town and Country Planning Act which established a 'green belt' around London to stop urban sprawl and proposed the building of a number of large new towns outside the green belt. Those to be situated within the London Transport area were located at Crawley, Harlow, Hatfield, Hemel Hempstead, Stevenage and Welwyn Garden City. In addition a number of overspill housing estates were also to be established and many existing towns were to be expanded. London Transport would be called upon to serve these new developments and it was envisaged that the Green Line network would expand.

Work on a London County Council over-spill estate was started at Aveley and from 4th July 1951 alternate 723 journeys were rerouted away from Stonehouse Corner to run via Belhus Park Estate and North Stifford as 723A. Additional coaches were run during Monday to Saturday rush hours.

Another of the 1944 proposals was realised, albeit in modified form, when on 30th September 1951, due to the impending closure of Judd Street Coach Station, route 714 was extended from Baker Street to Kings Cross and thence over the former 727 to Luton. Under the original plans London Transport wanted to run the routes from Dorking and Luton via Golders Green instead of Kings Cross.

Attention now turned to the need to replace the pre-war single-deck fleet and an order was placed for 263 vehicles classified RF. The chassis was an AEC Regal IV and fitted with a 9.6 litre engine similar to that of the RT but modified to a horizontal position. The 30-foot bodies were built by Metropolitan-Cammell of Birmingham and were fitted out to Green Line specification with deep seats, ash-trays and luggage racks. Apart from one seat immediately behind the driver all 39 seats faced forward. RF 1 to 25 were a 27ft 6in version with glazed panels in the roof for the Private Hire fleet so the Green Line fleet was numbered RF 26–288. RF 26 entered service from Tunbridge Wells garage on route 704 on 1st October 1951 to much publicity. The RFs replaced all coaches in the single-deck fleet within a year with many of the existing types being cascaded to bus work to replace older vehicles before they were eventually superseded by RF buses.

The first RF Green Line coach, RF 26, poses in a field for London Transport's photographer. It was delivered on 14th September 1951 and entered service on route 704 from Tunbridge Wells garage on 1st October. All 263 of the Green Line version of the class had been delivered by November 1952. *London's Transport Museum*

Route 723A was introduced on 4th July 1951 to serve new housing at Aveley. TF 77, now preserved in London's Transport Museum, stands in the stark surroundings of the yard at Grays garage together with G28. *Alan B. Cross*

Changes to routes 723 and 723A on 30th April 1952 meant that the former was diverted at Grays to run via Chadwell St Mary and terminate at Tilbury Ferry. RF 120 standing at Aldgate displays the new destination blind that reflects the revised arrangements.
Alan B. Cross

The pleasing interior view of the RF looking towards the emergency door at the rear. The coach seated 39 passengers with all but one facing forward.
London's Transport Museum

On 30th September 1951 route 714 was extended from Baker Street via Kings Cross to Luton to cover withdrawn route 727. TF 43 is seen in St Albans en route from Dorking to Luton. *Alan B. Cross*

Unlike the pre-war period, fares increases were destined to apply with greater frequency and a general revision took place on 2nd March 1952 which involved the Country minimum increasing to 9d. As a prelude to mechanisation, fare stage numbers were introduced to the Green Line faretables at this time. Weekly tickets became available between any two fare stages subject to a minimum single fare of 1/6d whereas previously rates were not quoted for journeys across central London. A further revision took place on 16th August 1953 with most fares being increased by 1d with the London minimum rising to 1/1d and the Country minimum to 10d.

The demand for travel on routes 723 and 723A increased and the routes were revised and increased in frequency from 30th April 1952. Following the adjustment of the London Transport boundary route 723's projection from Grays via Dock Road to Tilbury Civic Square was changed to run via Chadwell St Mary to terminate at Tilbury Ferry and the 723A was extended from Grays to Civic Square to cover the former 723. The combined service gave five coaches per hour from Grays to Aldgate which was enhanced to six during Monday to Friday rush hours, Saturday afternoons and Sunday pm with Aveley Estate being served by three coaches per hour at all times. Both routes had an hourly projection from Grays to Tilbury. A further adjustment was made on 6th May 1953 when route 723A was amended to terminate at Tilbury Ferry. Route 717 was rerouted between Woking and Woodham from 3rd December 1952 in order to serve the L.C.C. estate at Sheerwater.

Peripheral Green Line routes had been planned in the early days but in the event

When women conductors were employed in 1940 it was envisaged that they would step down after the war. In the event London Transport experienced difficulties in recruiting and retaining staff in the post-war period and the women conductors were allowed to remain. It was not until 1951, however, that women conductors in the Country Buses and Coaches department were issued with full green uniforms. In this May 1951 view an immaculately turned out conductress shows the new uniform while standing by the door of a 10T10 coach in Reigate garage. Note the Effra Road type ticket punch and the four digit badge number. *London's Transport Museum*

there was no time to introduce any before the February 1931 Road Traffic Act deadline. The post-war proposal for route 719 from Windsor to Luton did not materialise but the planners were hard at work in 1952 with the idea of both southern and northern peripheral routes. The southern route to be numbered 725 was to link Gravesend and Windsor via Dartford, Sidcup, Bromley, Croydon, Sutton, Kingston then running over the 718 to Windsor. The northern route, numbered 724, was to run from Windsor via route 704 to Harlington Corner thence via Hayes, Hanwell, Greenford, Wembley, Hendon and North Finchley to Wood Green from where it would have run over the City Coach Company's route via Walthamstow, Gants Hill and Romford to terminate at Brentwood. City Coach Company had been acquired by the BTC on 17th February 1952 and allocated to Westcliff-on-Sea Motor Services Ltd. It would seem however that there was a proposal that London Transport would take over some City operations in its special area including the Wood Green to Brentwood section which would have been incorporated into route 724. The basic hourly single-deck operation would have been supplemented by an intensive double-deck service over that section. Apparently London Transport had expressed a previous interest in taking over City and a confidential report produced in 1949 proposed that the Wood Green to Southend operation would become Green Line 719 with some local Brentwood bus operation being retained by L.T. and other routes passing to Eastern National.

The first peripheral Green Line route, 725, was introduced between Gravesend and Windsor via Bromley, Croydon and Kingston on 1st July 1953. RF 246 arrives at Windsor shortly after the route's introduction. *Laurie Akehurst collection*

ROUTE 725
GRAVESEND
BROMLEY · CROYDON
WINDSOR
Starting on July 1, 1953

GREEN LINE

LONDON TRANSPORT
55 BROADWAY
WESTMINSTER S·W·I
ABBey 1234

By 1953 the timetable leaflets had appeared in this attractive style.

After much deliberation route 725 was introduced on an experimental basis on 1st July 1953 with Northfleet and Staines garages providing RFs for the hourly service. So successful was the route that from 28th April 1954 the headway was increased to every 30 minutes between Dartford and Windsor which gave Dartford garage a regular Green Line allocation for the first time since 1935. The 725 proved very popular and much duplication was operated but this did not please the all powerful Central Bus Committee of the Transport and General Workers' Union and Central Bus management both of which saw the route as abstracting traffic from Central Buses. This was indeed the case as the coach offered a faster alternative to Central bus services over a number of sections. For example Sutton to Kingston, some 39 minutes journey time on the bus could be covered on the coach in just 23 minutes. The problem was compounded by the fact that some 11d bus journeys could be done for 10d on the coach. Rates of pay were always a contentious issue with the trade union and as single-deck coach conductors were on a lower rate than Central bus conductors, the trade union saw the situation as a move to undercut rates of pay. Such was its opposition that proposals to further increase the frequency on 725 were withdrawn and route 724 was never introduced.

London Transport embarked on a programme of mechanisation of the ticket system across its fleet in the mid-1950s. Traditionally many thousands of different types of bell punch tickets were required which involved the logistics of ordering, updating ticket details, storing, making up the conductors' ticket boxes and the possibilities of tickets with a stock value being misappropriated, misused or lost.

The standard RF coach weighed 7 tons 17cwt (7cwt heavier than an RT). No doubt with this in mind, during 1953 London Transport borrowed three lightweight vehicles for comparative trial – a Bristol LS, a Leyland Tiger Cub and an AEC Monocoach which were allocated to Reigate garage for use on bus route 447 and Green Line 711. They were subsequently transferred to Dalston garage for use on Central bus route 208.

The Bristol LS, PHW918, was borrowed from Bristol Tramways. It had an ECW body with standard Tilling indicator blind layout and was given Green Line livery. *Alan B. Cross*

The Leyland Tiger Cub, PTE592, was fitted with a Saunders Roe body and was painted in London Transport Country area livery. *Alan B. Cross*

The AEC Monocoach, NLP635, with Park Royal body was a manufacturer's demonstrator and was finished in Green Line livery. The trial finished in April 1954 but the Monocoach returned to Reigate garage for use on routes 447 and 711 for 16 months starting in January 1956. *Laurie Akehurst collection*

Earlier Sunday morning journeys were provided on routes 701, 703, 709, 710, 715 and 716 from the 1954 summer season which reduced the need for crews to travel one way as passengers on certain Sunday duties. This practice became standard but was gradually phased out by timetable revisions, lasting on route 710 until 1968.

The first new route to serve a new town was introduced on 7th July 1954 when route 720A ran between Aldgate and Harlow New Town, The Stow. The new service, worked by Epping garage using RFs, ran every 60 minutes and followed the 720 to First Avenue, just short of Harlow

Post Office, and then ran the short distance to the terminus. On the same date the 723 group was revised and converted to RT operation thus releasing RFs for future Green Line developments. Under the new arrangements route 723 remained unchanged, route 723A was curtailed from Tilbury to Grays and a new 723B ran from Aldgate to Tilbury Ferry via Stonehouse Corner and Dock Road. The double-deck vehicles permitted the headways to be reduced by one journey per hour at certain times with both 723 and 723B running hourly and two journeys per hour on 723A which was increased at busy times.

Conductor Bowden of Epping Garage, equipped with a Setright Speed ticket machine, collects a fare in an RF coach. The introduction of the Setright machines considerably simplified ticket issuing and accounting processes.
David Ruddom collection

In the mid-1950s new Green Line routes were introduced to serve the developing new towns. The first, route 720A, was introduced on 7th July 1954 from Aldgate to Harlow New Town. RF 119 stands at Aldgate shortly after the route's introduction. *Roy Marshall*

Mechanisation simplified the process considerably as the ticket was not produced until it was issued. The machines needed to be maintained but only a supply of blank ticket rolls was required to be topped-up in conductors' ticket boxes. The machine decided on as the most suitable for Green Line was the Setright Speed which was capable of issuing tickets in ½d increments from ½d to 19/11½d. The process of equipping the fleet was a gradual one with the first Setrights being used by Romford London Road garage on 2nd December 1953 and the last conversion being route 711 operated by High Wycombe and Reigate garages on 9th February 1955. A limited use of punch tickets continued for a time on duplicate coaches worked by Country bus conductors, not trained on Setright machines, and also at busy times when there were just not enough Setrights to go round.

When route 726 was reinstated for the summer season on 19th May 1954 the coaches now operated in service from Romford Market Place to Baker Street in order to avoid dead mileage being incurred. Just seven stops were provided between Romford and Aldgate from where the route to Baker Street was via Cheapside, Holborn Viaduct, Grays Inn Road and Kings Cross but without intermediate stops. The 4/3 single fare from Baker Street to Whipsnade applied right through from Romford which offered a bargain to and from east London. The day return fare, however, was withdrawn at this date.

The busy routes between Aldgate and Tilbury were revised on 7th July 1954 and in order to release RFs for future Green Line expansion they were converted to RT operation. Twenty-one new RTs (RT 4489-4509) were turned out in Green Line livery, identical to those used at Romford. RT 4490 working on new route 723B, which ran from Aldgate to Tilbury via Purfleet and Dock Road, leaves Aldgate bus station via the rear exit into Minories. *C. Carter*

Before the war the rates of pay for London Transport's drivers and conductors were considered to be very good and offered secure employment in an age where jobs were very often difficult to come by. London Transport had the pick of would be employees and staff shortage was simply unknown. After the war the position changed. Staff felt that they had lost pay parity when compared with other workers and London Transport experienced difficulties in recruiting and retaining staff. Successive governments wished to keep fare rises to a minimum and would not authorise the increases that would have enabled staff to receive higher wages. Staff shortages became severe in some areas and London Transport was forced to rely on the goodwill of staff working their rest days and overtime to keep services running. In August 1954 matters came to a head and an unofficial ban on rest day and overtime working showed up the serious nature of the situation. London Transport decided to introduce emergency schedules and on 3rd October route 710 was withdrawn and route 705 was amended to run between Sevenoaks and Victoria on a 60-minute headway followed by the withdrawal of route 720A on 13th October. Normal working was resumed on 705 and 720A on 20th October and on 710 one week later.

A fares revision took place on 26th September 1954 with 10d Country minimum fares being increased to 11d and certain local fares of below 1/- being increased by 1d. On 5th June 1955 fares of 1/- and over were increased by 1d but fares of 11d were either increased to 1/- or reduced to 10d which became the new country minimum. A further revision took place on 18th December when fares of 1/1 or over were increased by 1d but the 1/2 fare was increased by 2d. The London minimum was now 1/4 with the country minimum remaining at 10d.

Route 722 underwent some adjustments to its frequency from 5th October 1955 when alternate journeys on Monday to Friday between the peak periods were altered to terminate at Hornchurch Station instead of Corbets Tey. The Monday to Saturday early morning service on route 721 and the Monday to Friday evening service on route 722 were also reduced from three coaches per hour to two. Route 723A was diverted intermediately to serve Mill Road and Sandy Lane between Wennington and Aveley and also in Barking away from Ripple Road via Movers Lane and Barking By-pass in order to avoid a level crossing.

Further service developments for the needs of the new towns applied from this date when route 717 was renumbered 716A and diverted at Valley Road Corner to run to Stevenage White Lion. A temporary garage opened on the same day in Fishers Green Road, Stevenage (coded SV) which provided some of the coaches for the serv-

ice. A revised route 717 ran from Victoria to Welwyn Garden City Station opening up new territory for Green Line with a deviation away from the Great North Road via Brookmans Park and Little Heath. The coaches ran every 60 minutes and were provided by Hatfield Garage. From 18th April the following year the 717 was rerouted at Welham Green to run via new housing development in South Hatfield and from 16th May the 716A was extended to run in service to the temporary Stevenage Garage. From 17th June a Birch Brothers fares revision meant that cheap day returns were withdrawn on route 717 and were now available on route 716 from Hitchin to Hyde Park Corner, High Street Kensington or Barnes but were also available on route 716A if required.

In order to provide the additional vehicles for future expansion some 35 RFs were converted to Green Line coaches. These included RF 16 to 25 from the private hire fleet, former Central area buses RF 289 to 294 and in a complex renumbering scheme 19 former Country buses which became RF 295 to 313. A number of alterations had to be made to the various types in the conversion or at their next overhaul with the ex-buses seating 40 passengers having their seats altered to the Green Line arrangement with the longitudinal seat behind the driver seating two but they were never fitted with the deeper coach type seats. The fittings for the side route boards were different from the original coaches but when the boards were fitted there was no visible difference. These vehicles, known to Green Line staff as 'observation coaches' in the case of the ex-private hire 35 seaters and 'converted buses' in the case of the others, were distributed around the fleet rather than being concentrated at certain garages.

The new coaches were certainly needed

RF 289-294 were Central area buses which were converted for use on Green Line services in 1956. Newly converted RF 289 was allocated to Gillingham Street garage as a stand-by coach on 25th March 1956. By this time the stand-by coaches were fitted with side-boards which simply carried the Green Line fleet name and two slots into which plates carrying the appropriate route number could be inserted. The use of the route number plates and boards on the stand-by coaches gradually fell out of use. *Alan B. Cross*

to cover some of the changes introduced during the summer of 1956. On 11th July routes 712 and 713 were diverted away from Allum Lane Corner via Brook Road and Theobald Street to serve new housing in Borehamwood. Route 718 was extended from Epping to Harlow New Town Centre via Brays Grove and 720A was similarly re-routed and extended. New ground for Green Line was gained when the number 719 was at last used for a route from Hemel Hempstead to Victoria via Leverstock Green, Watford, Honeypot Lane and Willesden. A new garage at Garston which had replaced Leavesden Road in 1952 operated the hourly service. So successful was the 719 that from 29th May 1957 the service had to be increased to every 30 minutes. The residents of Hertford Heath saw their pre-war coach service restored on 8th August 1956 when 715A was introduced from Hertford to Marble Arch running via Edmonton and Tottenham with Hertford Garage providing the vehicles for the 60-minute service. Another inroad against Lord Amulree's severe restrictions was made when a stand was granted for the Marble Arch terminus in Clarendon Place although duplicates on route 715 terminating at Oxford Circus from Hertford were still required to run on to Lancaster Gate.

In the ten years since Green Line had been restored after the war, passenger journeys had increased from 25.3 million in 1947 to 33.6 million in 1956 and traffic was buoyant. The same situation did not apply to Country Buses where on many routes traffic was declining. Where parallel Country Bus services had been reduced there was an increasing trend to introduce fares on the coaches below the usual Country minimum in order to offer facilities for short distance riders. From 17th October 1956 bus fares applied on route 703 between Farningham and Wrotham, 4d minimum fares were available on routes 701 and 702 between Virginia Water and Egham and 6d or 8d fares were available on route 713 over the Markyate to Dunstable section.

Towards the end of 1956 political troubles in the Middle East resulted in the closure of the Suez Canal which reduced the amount of oil available to Great Britain. The situation became so serious that fuel rationing was introduced on 17th December with London Transport being required to reduce consumption by five per cent. As far as Green Line was concerned reductions were made on the following sections of route during the Monday to Friday off-peak period and on both Saturday and Sunday mornings: route 709 Chesham to Amersham; route 712 Luton to St Albans and Leatherhead to Dorking; route 716 Chertsey to Addlestone; route 718 Harlow New Town to Epping; route 722 east of Hornchurch Garage; and route 725 Windsor to Staines and Dartford to Gravesend. These cuts necessitated Leatherhead being added to the destination blinds for route 712. Weekly ticket holders were permitted to change to other coach routes, but not Country buses, to complete their journeys. Private motorists were also rationed which resulted in more passengers using the services and less traffic congestion. The situation eased and the full service was restored from 1st April 1957 but the private motorist was subject to restrictions for a further six weeks.

Some minor adjustments were made in 1957 with route 717 being extended in Welwyn Garden City from the Station to Cole Green Lane from 12th June. A pre-war terminus was again served from 28th July when Sunday afternoon journeys on route 721 were extended to Highwood Hospital in Brentwood. Yet another fares revision applied from 15th September when all fares of 1/5 and over were increased.

The year 1957 represented an all-time peak for Green Line with some 36.7 million passenger journeys being made representing 426 million passenger miles and 25.1 million car miles being operated. This required 270 service coaches on Monday to Friday, 263 on Saturday and 260 on Sunday plus 42 duplicates on Monday to Friday (with 2 extra on Wednesday), 44 on Saturday and 74 on Sunday.

ROUTE ALLOCATIONS AT 16th OCTOBER 1957

No.	Route	Frequency (minutes)	Garage	No. of coaches daily	Type
701	Gravesend – Victoria – Ascot	60	Northfleet	6	RF
702	Gravesend – Victoria – Sunningdale	60	Staines	6	RF
703	Wrotham – Victoria – Amersham	60	Swanley	3	RF
			Amersham	4	RF
704	Tunbridge Wells – Victoria – Windsor	30	Tunbridge Wells	7	RF
			Windsor	7	RF
705	Sevenoaks – Westerham – Victoria – Windsor	30	Dunton Green	7	RF
			Windsor	6	RF
706	Westerham – Victoria – Aylesbury	60	Chelsham	8	RF
707	Oxted – Victoria – Aylesbury	60	Tring	8	RF
708	East Grinstead – Victoria – Hemel Hempstead	30	East Grinstead	7	RF
			H. Hempstead	6	RF
709	Godstone – Oxford Circus – Chesham	60	Godstone	4	RF
			Amersham	3	RF
710	Crawley – Oxford Circus – Amersham	60	Crawley	4	RF
			Amersham	4	RF
711	Reigate – Oxford Circus – High Wycombe	30	Reigate	7	RF
			High Wycombe	7	RF
712	Dorking – Victoria – Luton	60	Dorking	7	RF
713	Dorking – Victoria – Dunstable	60	St Albans	7	RF
714	Dorking – Kings Cross – Luton	30	Dorking	7	RF
			Luton	7	RF
715	Guildford – Oxford Circus – Hertford	20	Guildford	10	RF
			Hertford	10	RF
715A	Hertford – Edmonton – Marble Arch	60	Hertford	4	RF
716	Chertsey – Marble Arch – Hitchin	60	Addlestone	4	RF
			Hitchin	4	RF
716A	Woking – Marble Arch – Stevenage	60	Addlestone	3	RF
			Stevenage	4	RF
717	Welwyn Garden City – Victoria	60	Hatfield	4	RF
718	Windsor – Victoria – Harlow New Town	30	Windsor	7	RF
			Epping	7	RF
719	Hemel Hempstead – Victoria	30	Garston	7	RF
720	Bishop's Stortford – Aldgate	30	Epping	7	RF
720A	Harlow New Town – Aldgate	60	Epping	3	RF
721	Brentwood – Aldgate	10/12/15	Romford	19 (1)	RT
722	Corbets Tey/ Hornchurch Stn – Aldgate	10/20/30	Romford	12 (2)	RT
723	Tilbury Ferry – Grays – Purfleet – Aldgate	60			
723A	Grays – Belhus – Aldgate	10/20/30	Grays	19	RT
723B	Tilbury Ferry – Grays – Purfleet – Aldgate	60			
725	Gravesend – Croydon – Kingston – Windsor	30	Northfleet	4 (3)	RF
			Dartford	3 (4)	RF
			Staines	7 (5)	RF
726	Romford – Baker Street – Whipsnade Zoo	Irregular	Romford	(6)	RT

Notes: (1) Less 4 vehicles on Saturdays, 3 on Sundays.
(2) Less 3 vehicles on Saturdays, 7 on Sundays.
(3) 60 minute service between Gravesend and Dartford.
(4) Plus 1 vehicle on Sundays.
(5) Less 1 vehicle on Sundays.
(6) Route suspended for winter months.

Facing page In 1954 private hire RFs were first used to strengthen the Green Line fleet. RF 9 in the all over green private hire livery with red fleet name serves the coach compulsory stop at Sutton station while running to Reigate on route 711. During 1956 RF 16-25 were permanently allocated to the Green Line fleet. The coaches were fitted with luggage racks and side route boards and finished in Green Line livery. RF 21 was chosen to pose for the official photographs.
Alan B. Cross, London's Transport Museum

GREEN LINE
COACH ROUTE
714
TIMETABLE
AND FARES

With the compliments of
LONDON TRANSPORT
55 Broadway, S.W.1
ABBey 1234

MAY, 1954

CRL 4, one of four prototype Routemaster vehicles was delivered in 1957. The vehicle had Leyland mechanical units and an Eastern Coachworks body and was fitted out to full Green Line standard. Air suspension was used at the rear with front suspension being provided by torsion bar and the vehicle was fitted with folding platform doors. The seats were wider spaced than on the bus versions and as delivered it seated 57 passengers but before entering passenger service the bench seats over the rear wheel arches were modified using bucket type seats which reduced the capacity to 55. The coach entered service on route 721 on 9th October 1957 where it remained until 29th December when it was transferred to route 711. *London's Transport Museum/Alan B. Cross*

USED
TICKETS

CRL·4
578

When new the RF coaches were allocated a book life of 14 years and these drawings of 1957 reveal that London Transport gave some consideration to a mid-life re-styling. In the event no action was taken and apart from some less striking livery experiments in 1960 it was to be a further nine years before some of the class were given a new look. The italicised fleet name was referred to at the time as 'speed-writing'. *Capital Transport*

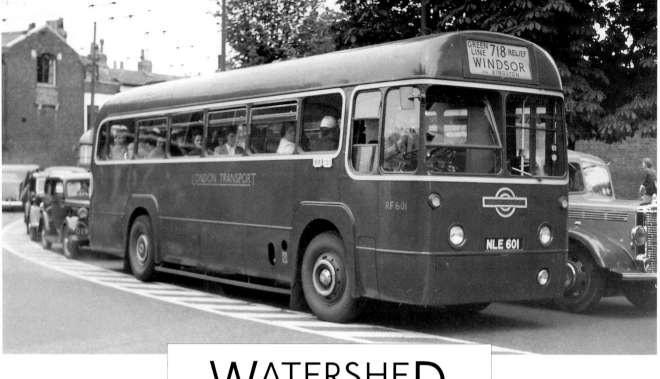

WATERSHED
1958–1964

By 1958 the country had recovered from the immediate post-war period of rationing and austerity, prosperity was rising and private motorcycle and car ownership had progressively increased. Many people preferred to motor to and from work in central London as major parking controls were yet to be introduced resulting in a much greater volume of traffic on the roads, particularly during rush hours. This led to traffic congestion which had an adverse effect on Green Line time keeping. The network, which had run like clockwork some ten years earlier, was now subject to late running and in some cases coaches were curtailed short of their final destinations. In an attempt to overcome these problems, from 22nd January 1958 an experiment was conducted on routes 709, 710 and 711. The overall running times remained unchanged but a number of what London Transport claimed were lightly used request stops in country districts plus a few in the suburbs were withdrawn. The running time was reduced in country districts and consequentially more running time was allowed in the inner London area. Despite some further tinkering with the timetables for routes 709 and 710 on 19th February the experiment was not judged a success. In June the routes reverted to the previous timings but the withdrawn stops were not reinstated. London Transport's argument seemed rather less than robust because if the removed stops were lightly used presumably few journeys would have been required to observe them and thus little time would have been lost.

A minor adjustment was made to route 722 from 8th January 1958 when the route was diverted in Romford to serve Oldchurch Hospital. Cheap day returns were offered as an experiment from central London to Tunbridge Wells (704), Dorking (712/3/4) and Guildford (715) from 8th April until 24th October. They were available on Monday to Friday, except bank holidays, between 9am and 4pm with no restriction on return times.

Industrial relations matters came to the fore during 1958 as in the previous October the Transport and General Workers Union had submitted a claim for a 25/- per week increase for all London Transport staff that it solely represented. This included all drivers and conductors plus some engineering staff. At this time a double-deck coach driver was paid a basic rate of 193/6d and a double-deck coach conductor 189/6d while their single-deck counterparts would be on slightly lesser rates of pay. London Transport stated that it could not possibly justify or afford such an increase and the trade union requested that the matter be referred to the Industrial Court, a course of action to which the management agreed. The Court awarded an increase of 8/6d per week to Central busmen but nothing to Country area or Green Line staff or the engineering workers whereupon the union then demanded 10/6d per week for all staff covered by the claim which was rejected by London Transport. The result was that the trade union called the staff out on strike on 5th May 1958. No L.T. bus or Green Line services at all were run until the strike was called off with services resuming on 21st June. In the event the 8/6d per week was paid to Central Bus drivers and conductors and subject to a joint review, single deck

Green Line drivers were eventually awarded 7/6d per week and the remainder of the staff covered in the dispute to 5/- per week. The strike did irreparable damage to London Transport and resulted in a marked increase in private motoring, a rise in traffic congestion and a consequential spiral of decline in bus usage.

During the strike it was planned to divert certain journeys on route 707 to double run via Tatsfield from 14th May and from 11th June routes 709, 710 and 711 reverted to their old running times. These changes took effect with the resumption of working on 21st June.

Some minor adjustments to the system took place on 15th October 1958 when the 705 was re-routed between Keston and Bromley South Station away from Bromley Common to serve Hayes. Routes 716 and 716A were re-routed in Stevenage to serve the new Bus Station which now became the terminus for the latter route. Route 721 now acquired projections to Brentwood London Hospital Annex/Highwood Hospital every day. With the expansion of bus

Above The derationing of petrol for private motorists in 1950 resulted in a increase in car usage. Later in the decade as private cars were produced for the home market the situation was compounded causing ever-increasing traffic congestion with adverse effects on Green Line timekeeping. Country area bus RF 601 is caught in heavy traffic in Hampton Court Road while working a relief to Windsor on route 718.
Travel Lens Photographic

and coach services, the new towns required improved garage facilities and a new building at Hatfield, virtually opposite the old premises, came in to operation on 18th February 1959. On 29th April a new garage at Stevenage, near to the Bus Station, replaced Hitchin garage and the temporary premises in Fishers Green Road.

When route 726 recommenced for the summer season on 27th May 1959 certain Sunday journeys were extended from Romford to Harold Hill but this innovation only lasted one further season with the last day of operation to Harold Hill being 11th September 1960. On 14th June 1959 route 723B was withdrawn on Sunday leaving no Green Line service to Tilbury via Dock Road. A further Green Line development in Romford was the proposal to run alternate journeys on route 722 to North Romford, Chase Cross as 722A from 14th October 1959. This was cancelled at a late stage, probably due to objections from the Transport and General Workers Union's Central Bus Committee but not before timetables, destination blinds and bus stop enamel plates had been produced.

The increased staff costs resulting from the wage awards after the strike had to be paid for and on 1st November 1959 Green Line fares of 8d and over increased by amounts from 1d to 8d which brought the London minimum up to 1/5 and the Country minimum to 11d.

On 29th April 1959 when the new garage at Stevenage opened, route 716A was revised to terminate at the nearby Bus Station. RF 140 leaves Stevenage bus station at the start of its long journey to Woking. *Alan B. Cross*

From 27th September 1959 Eccleston Bridge was closed for reconstruction and the coaches were diverted to stop on Elizabeth Bridge. Ex-private hire RF 23 stands on Elizabeth Bridge while working on route 719. The absence of the side route board shows the different arrangement of brackets fitted to the coaches converted for Green Line work in 1956. *Vectis Transport Publications*

After the strike in 1958 patronage on many Country area routes declined and a number were converted to one-man operation. To release further Country bus RFs in 1959 a number of RTs were employed on Green Line relief work and the displaced Green Line RFs were used on remaining crew operated single-deck Country routes 391/A, 447 and 458. The RTs that worked on Green Line relief duties were ordinary Country buses but during the latter half of 1960 some 28 were fitted with saloon heaters and repainted in Green Line livery in order to improve the image. Unlike the RTs operating from Romford and Grays garages they were fitted with a transfer bullseye between decks rather than a metal one.

On 23rd November 1960 the residents of Park Street had their Green Line service restored for the first time since 1942 when route 712 was re-routed at Radlett to run via Park Street, North Orbital Road and Chiswell Green to St Albans. Route 716 was re-routed at Stanborough to run via Welwyn Garden City and route 717 was revised between Hatfield and Welwyn Garden City to run via Mill Green Road and Cole Green Lane to terminate at Welwyn Garden City Station.

RT 3656 returned from overhaul in October 1960, one of the 28 turned out in Green Line livery and fitted with saloon heaters for working on relief duties, and was allocated to Guildford for route 715. Subsequently between decks Green Line bullseye transfers were fitted. The bus is seen passing Selfridges while working an evening peak hour relief from Oxford Circus to Guildford but due to the Amulree restrictions imposed in 1933 was not permitted to pick up passengers at the nearby coach stop. *Fred Ivey*

Despite the problems of traffic congestion passenger usage recovered virtually to the 1957 levels during 1960 with some 36.0 million passenger journeys being made and 25.1 million car miles being operated. Green Line receipts for the year totalled some £3.2 million. During the summer 267 service coaches had been required on Monday to Friday supplemented by a further 42 duplicates. In many cases these extras, mostly RT operated, were scheduled to layover in Central Area garages between the peaks. Not all could be accommodated at Victoria Garage so others were parked at Chalk Farm, New Cross, Riverside, and Stockwell. The crews working "spread-over" duties were permitted to travel back to and return from their home garages by Green Line but in practice some preferred to spend the day in London. Saturday saw 22 duplicates provided but Sunday still put the most demands on the system when, typically, some 65 duplicates were required. Apart from the traditionally popular destinations such as Dorking, St Albans, Tunbridge Wells and Windsor, the new towns brought much additional business on Sundays when friends and relations of their residents who still lived in London chose to visit. Everyone wanted to return to London on Sunday evenings and much duplication would be needed.

One of the after-effects of the 1958 strike was a considerable loss of bus and trolleybus passengers and a consequential upsurge in private motoring which despite parking controls being introduced in central London during 1959 brought about ever increasing traffic congestion. Throughout the 1960s so-called road improvement schemes were introduced both in central London and in the suburbs. The works were extremely complex, continuing over a long period of time and involving numerous diversions both short and long-term. In addition one-way street schemes were also introduced throughout the decade. The construction work caused further traffic congestion and when completed many, if not all schemes, had little or no regard for the needs of pedestrians and bus and Green Line passengers. Stops were often resited away from the traffic objectives that they purported to serve, often on the wrong side of multi-lane traffic systems. Dedicated bus lanes were unheard of. The Hammersmith one-way system had been introduced as early as 13th June 1958 with the first phase at Bricklayers Arms following just over a year later. In the 1960s the following schemes had a significant effect on London's traffic flows – Hyde Park Corner, Marble Arch, Baker Street/Gloucester Place, the dualling of Marylebone Road and the associated Edgware Road Flyover and Euston Underpass, Elephant & Castle, Blackwall Tunnel north entrance and Victoria. In addition it became fashionable for suburban towns to introduce one-way systems during the 1960s.

The increasing traffic congestion had an adverse effect on Green Line timekeeping and reliability and late running spare coaches had to be provided at certain garages for use when the service was badly disrupted. In many cases Green Line crews were unable to complete their scheduled mileage and would have to be relieved by a crew on overtime short of their destination in order that they would be reasonably to time for their return working. In addition crews late for meal relief or finishing their duties would also be entitled to overtime payments. Measures to mitigate the effects of traffic congestion were decidedly costly!

Top Windsor was a popular destination and a considerable number of relief journeys were run between the town and Victoria on route 704. RT 603 pulls away from Eccleston Bridge working on a duplicate to Windsor. All of the roof box bodied RTs were withdrawn from the Country area in 1963. *Vectis Transport Publications*

Above After the completion of the Park Lane and Marble Arch road works Windsor's RF 65 negotiates the somewhat larger Marble Arch traffic island in order to gain Oxford Street from Park Lane. *G.A. Rixon*

RF 25 stands at St Marys Square terminus in Hitchin prior to departing for Chertsey some 65 miles away. The coach is fitted with the revised route boards with yellow lettering on a black background which were introduced in 1960. Note the concertina style blinds fitted to the glass roof panels.
Alan B. Cross

Major road improvement schemes in central London were implemented in the early 1960s often causing considerable disruption to traffic flow during the period of construction. This publicity item of November 1961 shows the location of the temporary coach stops in South Carriage Road at Hyde Park Corner during the construction of the underpass.

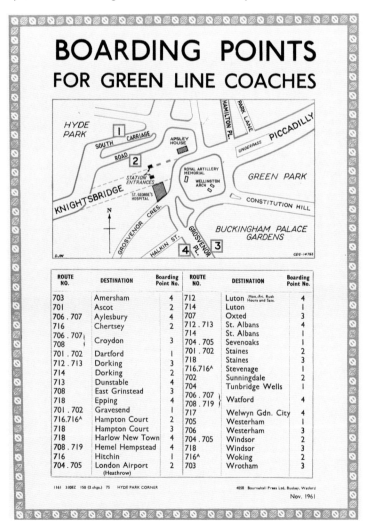

Difficulties in time keeping made the prospect of travelling less desirable and during the following decade passenger usage was to drop considerably but most of the system was to remain intact. The loss of passengers was compounded by the modernisation of the London suburban railway network starting in the late 1950s with the gradual elimination of steam working in favour of electric and diesel trains. On many lines the service outside the Monday to Friday peak periods was traditionally infrequent and irregular but with the introduction of modern trains regular interval services offering reduced journey times at greatly improved frequencies attracted passengers away from Green Line.

With all these factors applying and the ever increasing costs of operating the network it was hardly surprising that a general increase in fares took place on 15th January 1961 with the London minimum increasing to 1/6 and the Country minimum to 1/-. In order to comply with stage carriage licensing requirements at least one fare of 11d or less had to be retained. This revision increased fares progressively by amounts of between 1d and 1/6d which meant that for the first time some of the through fares for the longest journeys were now in excess of 10/- with the most expensive booking from Aylesbury to Westerham on route 706 becoming 10/11d. It must be emphasised, however, that very few passengers undertook such journeys. Less than seven months later, on 30th July, yet another fares revision put a further 1d on all fares of 8d and above except those 11d fares to satisfy licensing conditions.

The year 1961 saw little change to the system but a foretaste of things to come occurred on 25th October when the section of route 712 between St Albans and Luton was reduced to operate Monday to Friday rush hours and Saturday only.

An experiment for the summer of 1962 was the introduction of 'Ranger' tickets from 20th April until 24th September which were valid for one week and offered 25/- worth of travel for £1 on both Green Line and Country buses. Child tickets cost 10/- and offered 12/6 worth of travel. There were a few restrictions over sections where other operators' services ran in parallel. As they were not issued in subsequent years it must be assumed that the experiment was not considered a success. A further fares revision applied from 3rd June when all fares of 1/- and over were increased which brought the London minimum up to 1/8d and the country minimum generally to 1/2d.

Route 722 ran to Hornchurch Station for the last time on 3rd July 1962 and from the next day the Monday to Friday between peaks service saw a 30-minute service running to Corbets Tey. A further reduction applied from 27th October 1962 when the Saturday service frequency was reduced from 20 minutes to 30 minutes.

Above Having been closed for reconstruction on 27th September 1959 Eccleston Bridge reopened on 3rd May 1961 and was equipped with modern shelters which were fitted with tip-up seats and illuminated signage. A London Transport enquiry office was also provided (left). The shelters on the left-hand side were destined to become redundant on 26th September 1965 as a result of the Victoria one-way system. *London's Transport Museum*

Right In an age when Green Line services enjoyed stability this eight-piece enamel-iron coach directory advised intending passengers of the appropriate boarding point.
London's Transport Museum

GREEN LINE

City of Westminster
ECCLESTON BRIDGE SW
LEADING TO BELGRAVE Rᴰ

GREEN LINE

COACH DIRECTORY

	DESTINATION		DESTINATION		DESTINATION		DESTINATION		DESTINATION
2	ABBOTS LANGLEY	4	CHINGFORD	4	HARLOW NEW TOWN	6	NORTH CHEAM	3	SUNNINGDALE
4	AMERSHAM	3	CHORLEYWOOD	1	HARPENDEN	2	NORTHCHURCH	3	SUNNINGHILL
3	ASCOT	5	COLNBROOK	4	HARROW ON HILL	10	NORTHFLEET	9	SWANLEY
7	ASHFORD	10	CRAYFORD	4	HATFIELD	4	NORTHWOOD	10	SWANSCOMBE
3	ASHSTEAD	6	CROYDON		HEMEL HEMPSTEAD	8	ORPINGTON	5	TATSFIELD
4	ASTON CLINTON	10	DARTFORD			7	OXTED	9	TONBRIDGE
4	AYLESBURY	6	DORKING	4	HILDENBOROUGH	4	PINNER	3	TRING
7	BARNET	6	DUNSTABLE	3	HOUNSLOW	8	RADLETT	9	TUNBRIDGE WELLS
2	BERKHAMSTEAD	7	EAST GRINSTEAD	7	KENLEY	5	REDBOURN	3	VIRGINIA WATER
10	BEXLEYHEATH	3	EGHAM	5	KESTON	3	RICKMANSWORTH	5	WARLINGHAM
8	BIGGIN HILL	3	ENGLEFIELD GREEN	5	KINGS LANGLEY	1	ST. ALBANS	4	WATFORD
7	BOREHAMWOOD	4	EPPING	3	KINGSTON THAMES	5	SANDERSTEAD	10	WELLING
6	BOX HILL	6	EPSOM	3	LANGLEY	5	SEVENOAKS	4	WELWYN
9	BRANDS HATCH	6	ETON	7	LEATHERHEAD	8	SHENLEY	5	WESTERHAM
8	BRASTED	6	EWELL	7	LINGFIELD	10	SIDCUP		
9	BROMLEY	9	FARNBOROUGH	3	LONDON AIRPORT	5	SLOUGH	9	WEST KINGSDOWN
4	BUCKHURST HILL	9	FARNINGHAM	1	LONDON COLNEY	8	SOUTHBOROUGH	3	WINDSOR
3	BUSHEY	7	GODSTONE	4	LOUGHTON	3	STAINES		
5	CATERHAM	10	GRAVESEND	5	LUTON	5	SUNBURY	4	WOODFORD
7	CHELSHAM	3	HAMPTON COURT	5	MARKYATE	8	SUNDRIDGE	9	WROTHAM

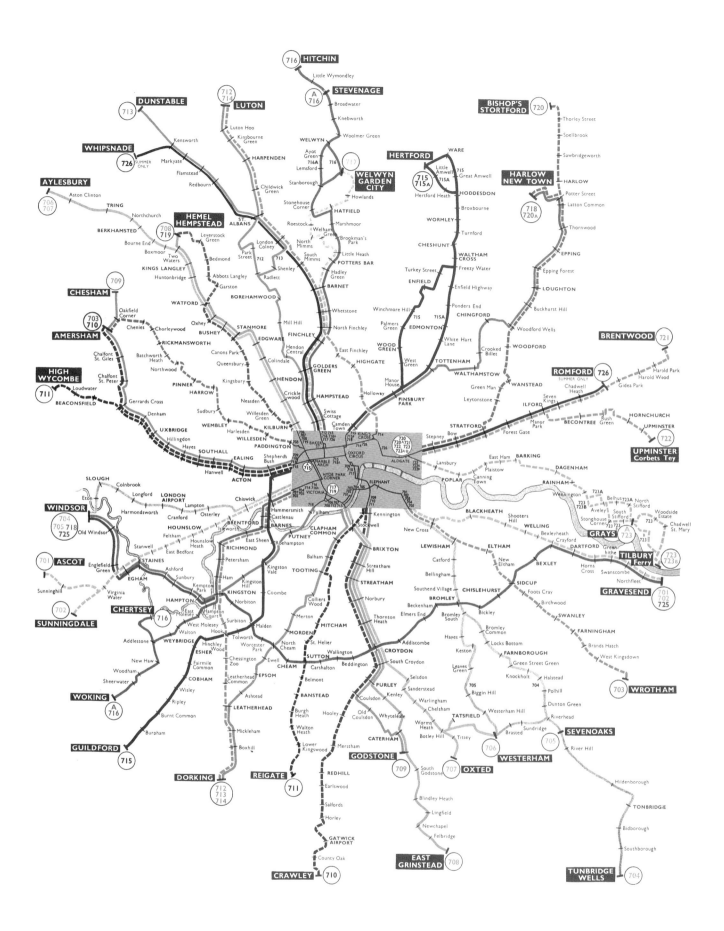

Of the four Routemaster prototypes CRL 4, which had entered service in June 1957, was the only one still in passenger service by this time. It had been extensively tested on routes 721, 711, 704 and 715 before having an extended spell on 718 and was now working on routes 716/A. It had proved to be a popular vehicle with the public, many of whom preferred the increased sightseeing opportunities afforded by the upper deck. The use of such vehicles on busier routes would offer operating economies with some 18 additional seats compared with the RF which would enable reductions in both headways and duplication to be achieved. Accordingly an order was placed for a production batch of 68 vehicles designated RMC (Routemaster Coach). They were numbered in the RM series being allocated the numbers RMC 1453 to 1520 and the first examples were placed in service on 29th August 1962 on routes 715 and 715A. They were fitted with jack-knife platform doors, deeper and more widely spaced seats than the bus version, luggage racks and fluorescent lighting. Externally they were finished in the standard Green Line livery and in keeping with tradition carried no advertisements to mar their graceful appearance.

The sting in the tail was soon apparent as route 715 was the busiest and most frequent cross-London route running every 20 minutes. The new RMC service, introduced with much publicity, saw a 30-minute frequency which did not prove popular with the Green Line travelling public. London Transport argued that the new service still offered 114 seats per hour compared with 117 offered by the RFs but the loss of one journey per hour was not appreciated by the passengers many of whom no doubt considered the 20-minute service to be so comparatively frequent that they did not need to consult a timetable. Vehicle savings amounted to six service coaches plus one duplicate at both Hertford and Guildford garages but Monday to Friday duplication was high and four extra vehicles from Hertford and two from Guildford were still needed.

In a memorandum from the London Transport Executive to the British Transport Commission it was stated that the purpose of using higher capacity vehicles was to effect cost savings by reducing headways on some routes and reducing the number of duplicate vehicles required. It was apparent that inadequacies occurred after the conversion particularly on the northern section of the route but the Executive claimed that after the adjustment of duplication timings "virtually no passengers are now being left behind at any point". Nevertheless receipts for routes 715 and 715A had dropped by 12.5 percent compared with immediately before the conversion but the seven vehicles and 20 crews saved represented a significant reduction in working expenses.

Far left This attractive map was designed by B. G. Lewis and depicts the system as it was in 1962.
London's Transport Museum

Left CRL 4 was transferred to Windsor garage for route 718 in July 1959 and in August 1960 it was painted in the light green livery used by the RFs on route 711. In August 1961 it was reclassified RMC 4 and in April 1962 the experimental bucket type seats were removed in favour of conventional bench seating over the rear wheel arches which increased the number of seats by two to 57. In November 1962 it was restored to Lincoln green as shown below. *Alan B. Cross, G.C.C Burgess*

Bottom RMC 1468 when new in service on the 715. In the original condition the RMCs carried the between decks metal Green Line bullseye, the traditional underlined fleet name, the word 'ROUTEMASTER' above the fleet number and an offside route number indicator blind. *J. Tilley*

Having converted routes 715 and 715A the future conversions concentrated on the routes serving the new towns. On 24th October 1962 route 718 received RMCs at the same frequency but the conversion of routes 720 and 720A saw the former reduced from 30 minutes to 60 minutes. Electrification of the railway service to Bishop's Stortford meant that the coach route had incurred a loss of passengers and the opportunity to gain a further economy was taken. The remaining conversions saw no further reductions in service and involved route 719 on 21st November and routes 716 and 716A on 2nd January 1963. The introduction of the RMC vehicles permitted reductions in the number of duplicate coaches operated. Duplication

Above Epping's RMC 1496 is seen in Aldgate High Street heading for Harlow. The provision of RMCs on routes 715 and 720 enabled operating economies through headway reductions. *Alan B. Cross*

Below Route 712A running from Dorking to Whipsnade Zoo was introduced on 25th May 1963 in consequence of reductions on route 726. RF 70 is seen at St Albans garage. The destination blind features the use of lower case print for the intermediate points – a practice first introduced on Central area buses in November 1961. *Photofives*

was expensive to operate as it usually involved either crews working spreadover duties of up to 12 hours in length or necessitated overtime working which attracted an enhanced rate of pay. The reduction in duplication proved to be a double-edged sword as the duplicate offered a prompt departure from central London in the evening peak. Officially duplicates were allowed to run two minutes ahead of the service coach timing, but in the event the service coach on a through journey may have been late arriving in central London.

The arrival of the RMCs allowed a number of RF coaches to be released from Green Line work. The former private hire coaches, RF 16 to RF 25, were withdrawn from service and sold and the former buses, RF 289 to RF 313, were eventually downgraded to Country area buses.

The government of the day had decided to abolish the British Transport Commission which resulted in London Transport becoming a board reporting to the Minister of Transport from 1st January 1963. Mr A. B. B. Valentine who had been Chairman since 1959 continued in the post until 1965. As previously required the Transport Act 1962 charged the new Board to provide an 'adequate' service and to pay its way – factors in the light of constantly declining bus travel which often seemed to be directly opposing each other. The financial situation was to become worse when in 1965 a succeeding government postponed fares increases.

On 22nd May 1963 a new garage at Harlow opened replacing Epping garage which was then only some 28 years old. Green Line routes 718, 720 and 720A were allocated to the new garage and much unproductive mileage was avoided without the garage journeys to and from Epping. Reductions on routes 723, 723A and 723B applied from 22nd May and meant that during Monday to Friday off peak times, Saturday and Sunday morning alternate journeys were curtailed short of Aldgate at East Ham. The result was that at certain times there was no through service between Tilbury and Aldgate. On the same day route 712 was re-routed at Park Street to run to Chiswell Green via Park Street Lane and Tippendell Lane to North Orbital Road which now meant that the low railway bridge at Park Street station was avoided and double deck duplicates could be operated. On 25th May new route 712A was introduced for the summer running from Dorking via route 712 to St Albans Garage and then running non-stop to Whipsnade Zoo. The new route consisted of two journeys each way on Saturday and four on Sunday and on the former day resulted in a two hour gap in the service between St Albans and Luton at the times when the journeys were run as 712A. Route 726 commenced on 26th May for summer Sundays and on 3rd July for Monday to Friday but no longer ran on Saturday.

The opportunity was taken to speed up the service on 28th August 1963 when route 705 was revised to run express between Victoria and Windsor observing only 12 intermediate stops and using Chiswick Flyover and Colnbrook By-Pass. On the express section of route blinds showing the route number in white on black and the destination in white on blue were employed. The coaches also carried front and side slip boards advising passengers of the limited stop nature of the service. RF 229 is seen leaving Butterwick at Hammersmith. *Alan B. Cross*

The construction of the new ticket hall at Oxford Circus Underground station which was part of the Victoria Line project meant that traffic flows across Oxford Circus became one-way from 2nd June. Northbound coaches on routes 709, 710 and 711 were obliged to run via Hanover Square, Cavendish Square and Chandos Street between Regent Street and Portland Place. Northbound coaches on routes 715 and 715A were diverted away from Oxford Circus via Old Cavendish Street, Cavendish Square and Chandos Street. Over the August Bank Holiday weekend (3rd to 5th August) a steel umbrella to facilitate the construction was installed.

Yet another fares revision applied from 23rd June with the London minimum increasing from 1/8d to 2/- and the Country minimum from 1/2d to 1/3d. The 2/- London minimum fare would remain for the rest of the period covered by this book.

Two interesting developments to the system took place during 1963. The first was on 28th August when route 705 was run express over the section from Victoria to Windsor. The coaches proceeded from Hammersmith via Great West Road and Chiswick Flyover and also ran via Colnbrook By-Pass instead of Colnbrook. Only 12 intermediate stops were served between Victoria and Windsor and the running time over this section was reduced by 19 minutes to exactly one hour. The coaches displayed limited stop slip boards and special blue and white blinds over the express section which were changed at Victoria to show the standard black and amber blinds on the London to Sevenoaks section of route. On 18th November the Dartford–Purfleet Tunnel opened and, in

addition to a bus service from Grays to Dartford, Green Line route 722 was extended from Corbets Tey via Ockendon, Belhus and Aveley through the tunnel to terminate at Dartford Garage. A 30-minute service was provided daily but on Sunday only alternate coaches ran beyond Corbets Tey to Dartford. There was no late evening service over this section and additional journeys were run on Monday to Friday peak hours between Corbets Tey or Romford and Aldgate. In addition to the fare a toll surcharge of 6d (3d child) was payable.

What was then referred to as the Dartford–Purfleet Tunnel opened on 18th November 1963 and route 722 was extended from Corbets Tey through the tunnel to Dartford. In practice very few passengers wished to use the facility and the route ran to Dartford for the last time on 3rd November 1964. RT 3251 does no business in Westgate Road, Dartford. In September 1963 the Country Buses and Coaches operating department reduced the use of garage code stencils by painted the garage code onto the vehicles. *Alan B. Cross*

In November 1963 the practice of displaying the route number on the offside of double deck Central area buses and Green Line coaches was discontinued. RMC 1503 stands outside the attractive frontage of Windsor garage having had the offside route number indicator painted over. When the RMCs were subsequently overhauled the aperture was panelled over. *Barry LeJeune*

On the non-express section of route 705 between Victoria and Sevenoaks the conventional amber and black blinds were displayed. RF 133 shares Sevenoaks bus station with RT 3652 and Maidstone & District AEC Reliance S328. A blue limited stop slip board is displayed on the RF. *Barry LeJeune*

When the Sunday service on route 726 resumed on 10th May 1964 the coaches were re-routed between Temple Fortune and Friars Wash away from Barnet and St Albans to run via Great North Way, Mill Hill, Watford By-Pass to Berrygrove and then the M1 motorway. When the Monday to Friday service was introduced on 1st July an additional stop at Mill Hill Dawes Lane was provided.

Constantly rising costs of operation, principally staff wages (the crews had received eight wage awards since the 1958 strike) and fuel, and progressively declining passenger usage led to fares revisions becoming an annual event. From 19th July a further increase applied which increased the Country minimum fare to 1/4d with certain exceptions. In 1960 some 36.0 million passenger journeys were made on Green Line but by 1964 this figure had fallen by 23.6 per cent to 27.5 million while car miles run had only fallen by 1.9 per cent from 25.1 million to 23.2 million. The five fares revisions between 1960 and 1964 meant that traffic receipts of £3.2 million in 1960 were virtually the same in 1964 and clearly drastic action was needed in an attempt to check the disparity between the falling passenger figures and the minimal reduction in car mileage.

Apart from the Chislehurst Arch (demolished in May 1963) low railway bridges at Shortlands and Worcester Park prohibited the use of double-deck vehicles on route 725. The rebuilding of the bridge and the lowering of the road surface at Worcester Park in late 1962 meant that double-deck buses could operate reliefs between Windsor and West Croydon. RT 4654 lays over at West Croydon bus station on one such working. *Alan B. Cross - W.R. Legg collection*

By the summer of 1964 the old order was set to change and the days of route 703 were numbered. Amersham's RF 57 is captured at Eccleston Bridge heading for Wrotham. It was common practice for some Green Line vehicles to spend the night away from their home garage at the other end of the route and on the following day they would be allocated a duty to return them home – hence the SJ stencil. *G. Mead*

CHANGE
1964–1968

The winter programme of 1964 which applied from 4th November set about addressing the problems facing Green Line and saw significant changes to the system. Route 703 was withdrawn completely with the northern section from Victoria and Amersham via Rickmansworth disappearing from the Green Line map. It will be recalled that London Transport did not originally wish to re-introduce this section in 1946 and the electrification of the Metropolitan Line to Amersham in 1961 had resulted in a decline in patronage. The southern section from Victoria to Wrotham was covered by an extension of route 717 which ran hourly from Welwyn Garden City to Victoria via South Hatfield and Brookmans Park. At the same time the route was converted from RF operation to RMC with Hatfield and Swanley garages using the vehicles released from routes 720 and 720A which after just two years reverted to RF operation. The electric train service from Bishop's Stortford to London had abstracted further passengers. London Transport maintained that the RFs on the routes could accommodate all passengers but in practice inadequacies in the service were shown up at busy times. Following the success of express operation to Windsor route 709 was revised to run express from Oxford Circus to Amersham with only 17 intermediate stops by being diverted at Shepherds Bush to run via Wood Lane and Western Avenue to Hillingdon Circus thence Hercies Road to Uxbridge. In the event it proved a very difficult manoeuvre

RMC 1469 was given a new look in July 1964 in order to assess the appearance planned for the forthcoming RCL class. There were no brake cooling grills at the front end and the air intake grill under the destination box was reduced in size to allow the cant rail to be carried across the front of the vehicle. The metal between decks bullseyes were replaced with transfers placed further forward and the fleet name was revised. The green relief colour became lighter – so called 'porcelain' green and the plastic roundel over the radiator grill was replaced by a triangle. The coach is seen at Chiswick Works fitted with experimental blind displays in the via boxes – these designs were not perpetuated. *Colin Curtis*

Following the successful express operation on the 705, route 709 was revised on 4th November 1964 to run express between Oxford Circus and Amersham by running to Uxbridge via Western Avenue instead of the traditional route via Uxbridge Road. RF 57 is seen on Western Avenue at Northolt en route to Caterham. The destination blinds displayed on the express section of the route were produced in black and yellow rather than the blue and white used on route 705. *David Bosher*

Right When it entered service the front intermediate points blind box on RMC 1469 had been extended in width to be the same size as the destination box. It was then allocated to Hertford garage for use on routes 715 and 715A and is seen at Oxford Circus en route to Hertford on route 715. *Laurie Akehurst collection*

to get from Hercies Road onto Western Avenue thus southbound coaches ran from Uxbridge to Western Avenue via Park Road. The Sunday service on 709 ran from Godstone to Baker Street Station only so on that day route 710 was extended from Amersham to Chesham to cover the loss of 709.

Routes 712 and 713 were reduced to a basic 60-minute service from Dorking to Dunstable on Monday to Friday with a 30-minute service between St Albans and Dorking at peak periods when alternate journeys terminated in London. Luton was only served during Monday to Friday peak periods and Saturday morning and early afternoon. On Saturday a 30-minute service was run between Dorking and St Albans except early am and evenings when the interval was 60 minutes. Sunday saw a basic 60-minute service from Dorking to Dunstable with additional afternoon and evening journeys between St Albans and Victoria. Generally alternate coaches ran via Park Street and Shenley which led to a somewhat passenger-unfriendly route numbering scheme. The numbers 712 and 713 remained unchanged (Dorking – Park Street – Luton and Dorking – Shenley – Dunstable respectively) with a new 712B becoming Dorking – Park Street – Dunstable and 713A Victoria – Shenley – Luton. At the time of the changes route 712A was suspended for the winter. This pattern of service which was progressively introduced onto some other routes no doubt lost a great deal of public goodwill.

A new route, 727, between Tring and Victoria was introduced on 4th November 1964. The route made use of the M1 motorway between Hemel Hempstead and Berrygrove, its then southern extremity, and continued via Watford By-Pass and Golders Green. RF 70 is seen at Oxford Circus with black and yellow destination blinds and boards. Fortunately the tiny lower case lettering on the side-board was not perpetuated.
London's Transport Museum

Below left A new Green Line guide was issued in summer 1963 using a larger format and 24-hour clock notation. The printing plates were utilised for a new style of timetable leaflet issued from October 1963.

Below right The express operation on the northern section of route 709 was not a success and on 31st October 1965 the route was revised to run between Godstone and Baker Street daily. RF 177, heading for Baker Street, is seen on Victoria Embankment having been diverted away from Whitehall on Remembrance Sunday 1965. The RF carries the new style of yellow and black destination blind which first appeared on the 709 and 720 at this time and quickly spread across the system replacing the amber style blinds. *Alan B. Cross*

GREEN LINE

COACH ROUTE

727

TIMETABLE AND FARES

(From 4 November 1964)

LONDON TRANSPORT, 55 BROADWAY, S.W.I.
Tel. ABBEY 1234

No vehicles were saved and while six fewer late turn duties were required on Monday to Friday these were off-set by the additional cost of 'spread-over' duties which involved staff working in both peak periods. On Saturday when there was probably a demand for a 30-minute service throughout the day there were now insufficient crews to provide it.

Changes took place on all of the east London routes with 721 being reduced from every 10 minutes to every 12 minutes on Saturday evenings. It had been a difficult task for the planners to accurately predict the demand for travel through the Dartford – Purfleet Tunnel and in the event the people of Essex obviously had little affinity with Kent and vice versa thus the provision of both a bus and a Green Line coach through the tunnel had proved somewhat excessive. Accordingly route 722 was withdrawn from Dartford to run from Aldgate to Corbets Tey on a 30-minute daily headway with some additional journeys at Monday to Friday peak periods. Further changes in south Essex involved the routes to Tilbury and Grays. Route 723, Tilbury – Chadwell St Mary – Grays – Aldgate was re-routed away from Purfleet to serve the estate at Belhus. Route 723A, Grays – Belhus – Aldgate was extended to Tilbury via Dock Road and route 723B Tilbury – Dock Road – Grays – Purfleet – Aldgate was curtailed at Grays. This facilitated a reduction of one journey per hour between Grays and East Ham during Monday to Friday off peak periods and Sunday with very few journeys on route 723B running further west than East Ham. On Saturday more journeys were curtailed at East Ham with only a 30-minute service being run through to Aldgate.

Ashford Town Centre saw Green Line for the first time since 1942 when route 725 was diverted away from the main road. By far the most innovative development was the provision of an express route from Tring to Victoria via Hemel Hempstead, the M1 motorway to its then southern extremity at Berrygrove, Watford By-Pass and Golders Green. Route 727 was worked by Tring Garage using RFs for the 1 hour and 31 minutes journey with only 19 stops with the route running on Monday to Saturday only providing a basically hourly service with two 90-minute gaps. The new 727 made great inroads to the Amulree rules as the route followed from Baker Street was via Marylebone Road, Portland Place, Oxford Circus, Piccadilly Circus, Trafalgar Square, Whitehall and Victoria Street to Victoria. Another nonsense was also abolished when the 1946 boarding restrictions at the Piccadilly Circus stop were removed. Similar restrictions at the Selfridge's stop were removed on 8th February 1965.

An adjustment to route 709 was made from 2nd December between Hillingdon Circus and Uxbridge when the coaches

were diverted via Long Lane and Uxbridge Road in both directions. Three additional stops were provided on the route on 24th March 1965. From 27th January route 727 was allowed six minutes extra running time and the two 90-minute gaps were closed on Monday to Friday. From 14th April all suffix letters on routes 712 and 713 were withdrawn and irrespective of northern destination, including Whipsnade Zoo, all journeys via Park Street ran as 712 and via Shenley as 713. Further motorway running was authorised from 16th April when certain duplicates on route 704 could be instructed to run between Hammersmith and Langley via Great West Road, Chiswick Flyover and the M4 motorway. The express nature of route 727 suffered a set-back during May with the sudden closure of the M1 motorway due to the road surface breaking up. The coaches were diverted at Maylands Avenue roundabout to run via Leverstock Green then route 719 to North Watford, The Dome and Watford By-Pass to line of route at Berrygrove. The situation was ratified from 30th June when stops on the diversion were provided at Garston and North Watford, together with one at Boxmoor, and when the M1 reopened the route was via the motorway from Hemel Hempstead to Bricket Wood and then running via Garston to Berrygrove.

From 26th April 1965 cheap off-peak day returns became available on Monday to Friday on the northern sections of routes 709, 710, 711, 712, 713, 714, 715 and 715A to central London. Issued after 0930 hours they were available in both directions but could not be used to return from central London between 1630 and 1830 hours. The return fare from Hertford to London was 7/6d which gave a saving of 3/- on twice the single fare. Yet another fares revision was proposed to be implemented in June but the Wilson Government was trying to overcome inflation by restricting wage awards and restraining prices. The Government stepped in and, in an unprecedented action, halted the fares increase and gave London Transport a subsidy of £3.8 million instead.

London Transport decided to replace the Green Line liveried RTs working on the east London routes and ordered a batch of 43 RCL coaches which were a 30-foot version of the RMC seating 65 passengers instead of 57. Allocated fleet numbers RCL 2218 to 2260 they entered service on route 721 on 2nd June 1965, 722 two weeks later and on routes 723 and 723A on 1st July. It had been proposed to use them on route 723B but problems with limited clearance at a railway bridge in South Stifford meant that RMCs had to be used with the balance of RCLs going to route 715A in exchange for its RMCs. Route 726 resumed for the season on 6th June and was RCL worked.

This panel bill was produced to advise passengers of the arrival of the RCL coaches and to highlight the new standards of comfort compared with the RTs that they replaced. In practice clearance difficulties with a railway bridge at South Stifford meant that route 723B had to be operated with the shorter RMCs.

Above The RCLs – the finest of the Routemaster sub-classes – finally brought a touch of luxury to east London Green Line passengers who were used to some years of RT travel. The fleet name was further modified from the arrangement applied to RMC 1469. The destination blinds were produced in yellow instead of amber and the ultimate destination display was reversed to appear on a black background. This change in style was introduced on the RMCs earlier in 1965. *Brian Speller*

Right The RCLs intended for route 723B were sent to Hertford garage in exchange for the RMCs from route 715A. RCL 2249 is seen on 14th July 1965 on route 715A – the wide via blind box has been masked at the edges to accommodate the narrower RMC blind. After a time wide blinds were produced for the front boxes. *Alan B. Cross*

Despite the arrival of new vehicles London Transport was so concerned about the spiral of declining traffic that during 1965 a confidential report was produced about the hypothetical withdrawal of Green Line services. The report found that, if the withdrawal was considered in isolation, after taking operating costs, passenger receipts, depreciation and interest charges into account the Board would be some £421,000 per annum worse off. It was accepted in the report that this action was not a realistic option as some additional 55 Central buses and 89 Country buses would be required to handle the traffic caused by the loss of Green Line. A second option of the retention of only the most profitable routes such as 704, 715, 716 and 725 was suggested but without giving financial details. It was estimated at the time that the cost of operating Green Line services which required some 328 coaches, including spares, was just in excess of £3 million per annum.

The winter programme of 1965 brought further significant changes to the Green Line system. From 3rd October certain Sunday journeys on route 707 were extended every two or three hours from Oxted to Holland to cover the loss of local bus 464 on that day. Due to changes in the crews' pay week new timetables were now introduced on Sundays and 31st October saw the route 709 running from Baker Street to Godstone daily. The express running north of London had failed to attract sufficient passengers. In compensation route 710 was extended from Amersham to Chesham daily and two additional Monday to Friday peak hour coaches were run between Amersham and Lambeth North. Route 720A from Harlow Bus Station to Aldgate was withdrawn to be covered by a diversion of route 720 between Potter Street and Old Harlow to serve Harlow town centre. The effect of this was to reduce the overall service to Aldgate to 60 minutes during Monday to Friday off peak periods, Saturday early am and evenings and Sunday mornings. Companion route 718 was also reduced to a 60-minute service outside Monday to Friday peak periods, and Saturday early am and evenings. Alternate journeys during Monday to Friday peak periods were split in London running from Windsor to Victoria and Harlow to Oxford Circus. The 30-minute service was maintained on Sunday but an irregular service was provided on Sunday evenings. The reductions on 718 were a winter measure with the through 30-minute service being restored from 15th May 1966 until 1st October 1966 inclusive. Route 719 was reduced to every 60 minutes during Monday to Friday off peak periods. Route 722 suffered an even more severe fate when it was reduced to run during Monday to Friday peak periods only. Some coaches were stabled in Bow garage between the peaks in order to save the cost of returning to Romford with few or no passengers. A new five-day weekly ticket was introduced issued to and from the route's freehold section left without a Saturday service. Route 727 had failed to attract custom and was withdrawn, running for the last time on 30th October.

In an attempt to overcome the ever-increasing problems of traffic congestion routes 701 and 702 were split into two sections on Monday to Friday. Route 701 ran every 30 minutes from Gravesend to Hammersmith and every 60 minutes from Victoria to Ascot and route 702 ran every 60 minutes from Victoria to Sunningdale. The normal through service continued to run on Saturday and Sunday. Initially passengers could not book through on Monday to Friday but from 22nd November passengers were allowed to transfer at Victoria or Hammersmith to any coach to travel within the availability of their ticket. Route 714 was split into two non-overlapping sections at Baker Street on Monday to Friday with

Route 720A from Aldgate to Harlow Bus Station was withdrawn from 31st October 1965 and route 720 was diverted between Potter Street and Old Harlow to run via Harlow Bus Station on its way to Bishop's Stortford. RF 112 fitted with a new route board which includes Harlow Bus Stn as an intermediate point passes RT 2427, awaiting a new crew, outside Loughton garage.
Vectis Transport Publications

the through service between Dorking and Luton running on Saturday and Sunday. Through bookings were permitted and passengers could complete certain journeys on routes 716 and 716A.

The Green Line image on route 705 changed when 14 new AEC Reliance 49-seat single-deck coaches, designated RC class, with Willowbrook bodies replaced the RFs on 28th November 1965. The new coaches, 36 feet long and 8ft 2½in wide, were in a striking silver and grey livery with a broad green waist-band and offered passengers panoramic windows, high-backed seats, foot rests and forced-air ventilation. Despite a big publicity launch the RCs proved to be mechanically unsatisfactory and were in trouble from day one. They were simply not up to the arduous requirements of Green Line work that the fourteen year old RFs performed effortlessly under any conditions.

A fares revision took place on 16th January 1966 which brought the Country minimum to 1/6d, but by this time over a number of sections cheaper fares were

On 28th November 1965 a striking new look came to Green Line with the arrival of fourteen AEC Reliance coaches. The attractive appearance and improved passenger standards were not supported by their mechanical performance and they were dogged by problems from the very start. RC 8 takes on passengers at Eccleston Bridge at the start of the express run to Windsor.
Essex Transport Group

offered in country districts, some only Saturday and Sunday where parallel bus services had been increasingly reduced or withdrawn. From 6th June the experimental Monday to Friday cheap day off peak return fares, introduced the previous year, now marketed as 'Greenliners' were introduced on all routes except 722, 725 and 726. Unlike the experimental facilities they were issued only on journeys towards London. From 19th September they were revised in some cases to allow passengers to overlap the central London fare stage in order to reach such points as High Street Kensington and Baker Street.

The new RCL coaches were somewhat wasted on route 715A and the peak hour only 722 so from 12th June 1966 they were transferred to Windsor and Tunbridge Wells garages for the busy route 704. RFs were provided for route 715A and the 722 reverted to RT operation after just one year.

In the mid-1960s the future of the single-deck fleet was under review as the RFs had been given a book life of 14 years at the time of their introduction. It was decided to improve radically both the external and internal appearance of the RFs and to this end RF 136 was selected as a prototype vehicle and entered the works in July 1965 to emerge in March 1966 as a remarkably transformed vehicle. Its appearance was striking, retaining the basic Lincoln green paint work but with a broad light green waist-band with the fleetname in the style of the RC coaches. Detail differences included twin-headlamps, repositioned trafficators, the removal of the bullseye radiator flap, and curved mudguards. The side route-boards colours were reversed with black letters appearing on a yellow background. The interior was fitted with fluorescent lighting and the seat moquette

Top In 1965 London Transport gave some thought to the future of the single-deck coach fleet. Rather than obtain new vehicles a decision was taken to completely refurbish the RFs, both externally and internally, and RF 136 was selected as a prototype vehicle to receive a new look. London Transport used the services of the design consultant Misha Black and after eight months in the works RF 136 emerged in its new form in March 1966. The effect was striking with the coach appearing in two-tone green with a broad waist-band, and having twin headlamps, repositioned trafficators and a number of other detail differences. The side route boards were changed to black lettering on a yellow background which complemented the black and yellow destination blinds. After spending just five days on route 705, on 21st March the coach was transferred to Tunbridge Wells garage for use on route 704 and is seen here passing through Grosvenor Gardens, Victoria. *Bruce Jenkins*

Right In an attempt to boost off-peak travel, cheap day returns were offered on most routes for journeys to London from 6th June 1966.

and panelling was finished very much the same as on the RMC and RCL vehicles. It entered service at Dunton Green garage on 16th March on route 705 alongside the RCs but just five days later moved to Tunbridge Wells for route 704. It proved to be a success and the Board decided to refurbish a further 174 members of the class in order to meet the requirements of the single-deck coach fleet. The refurbished coaches entered service on a progressive basis between August 1966 and July 1967 and differed from the prototype vehicle by retaining square mudguards. One coach driver remarked that to drive one was akin to driving a new vehicle and many passengers thought that they were just that!

An innovation for Green Line was the introduction on 10th July of a cross-country express one-man operated route from Romford to High Wycombe using RFs. Numbered 724 the hourly route was worked by Romford and High Wycombe garages and linked the two towns in three hours running via Harlow, St Albans, Watford and Amersham with only 25 stops. The longer boarding times required by one-man operation were under-estimated and from 7th August an additional 15 minutes running time was allowed. The senior drivers who volunteered to work Green Line's first one-man operated route were very enthusiastic and friendly to their passengers and the route quickly became a success. Weekly tickets were available from garages and enquiry offices and could be obtained from drivers by prior arrangement. A further change took place on 10th July when route 706 gained a Saturday and Sunday summer extension from Westerham to Chartwell, the home of the late Sir Winston Churchill, which had recently opened to the public. In the following summer seasons the route also ran to Chartwell on Wednesdays and Thursdays.

The new requirement was 248 coaches on Monday to Friday, 238 on Saturday and 224 on Sunday. In addition to these figures so called late running spare coaches were held in reserve on certain routes to cover contingencies. The need for duplication had fallen considerably by this time with 13 vehicles being required on Monday to Friday, eight on Saturday. Sunday was still a popular day for Green Line travel when some 38 additional vehicles were needed.

What was now becoming an annual programme of severe cuts to the system applied from the last day of 1966. Further changes in the pay week consequential to crews now working five days a week meant that service changes now took place on Saturdays. Route 709 was reduced to just two Monday to Friday peak hour journeys in the direction of the peak plus two on Sunday for visitors to Caterham Hospital using RCL coaches. Officially the coaches ran dead against the peak but at least one

The northern area cross-country route 724 was introduced on 10th July 1966 and was Green Line's first one-man operated route, with the drivers using the standard Setright Speed ticket machines. The coaches were fitted with the standard orange perspex 'Pay as you enter' slip boards which were used on Country buses at the time. RF 204 stands on High Wycombe garage forecourt. *Ken Glazier*

crew always ran in service albeit unofficially; a position that London Transport ratified from 27th February 1967. Special five-day weekly tickets were available on the route's freehold section but 'Greenliners' were no longer issued. Route 710 lost its Monday to Friday two additional peak hour coaches from Amersham to London and was withdrawn on Monday to Friday between Amersham and Chesham. Route 711 was diverted to serve Banstead Village. The through service was reinstated on route 714 on Monday to Friday but the Sunday service was reduced to operate every 60 minutes. The split service had required two additional coaches and additional crew duties and it was highly improbable that the additional costs were offset by any significant increase in traffic receipts. Another 1946 proposal was finally realised when routes 714 and 718 were diverted between Marble Arch and Great

Portland Street station away from Baker Street to run via Oxford Circus. Route 718 also suffered a reduction to an hourly service on Sunday. Route 715A was reduced to run only during Monday to Friday peak hours and Saturday morning and afternoon. Turning to south Essex, route 721 was reduced from four to three journeys per hour on Sunday late mornings and early afternoons and route 722 was further reduced. Route 723A running from Tilbury to Aldgate via Dock Road and Belhus was withdrawn. Companion route 723B was revised to run from Grays to East Ham via Purfleet during Monday to Friday peak periods and on Saturday morning and afternoon, losing the section on to Aldgate. This left 723 to provide a 60-minute service from Tilbury, 30 minutes from Grays to Aldgate via Belhus with an additional hourly journey from Grays to East Ham at busy times on Monday to Saturday.

On 10th July 1966 route 706 gained a summer extension to Chartwell, the home of the late Sir Winston Churchill, which was open to the public. RF 235, seen at Chartwell, was one of 174 RF coaches refurbished in the style of RF 136. During 1962 the side boards for routes 701/2, 706/7, 712/3 and 720/A were modified to incorporate both destinations at the expense of not showing the route number for when coaches interworked. *Essex Transport Group*

An innovative fare experiment took place on route 724 from 24th March 1967 when after 0930 hours on Monday to Friday and all day Saturday and Sunday the maximum single fare was reduced to 10/- and a cheap day return fare of 15/- without any return restriction was introduced. This gave a considerable saving on longer journeys as the through single fare from Romford to High Wycombe had previously been 15/-. The 724 had revolutionised cross-country travel as the quicker journey times made longer-distance trips viable whereas prior to the route's introduction existing Country bus facilities, involving changes and prolonged running times, made such journeys somewhat tedious. Harlow to Amersham could be covered in two hours on the coach whereas before such a journey would require three or four different buses and after allowing for waiting would take something in the region of double that time.

Based on the success of route 724 another cross-country route appeared from 13th May when the 727 was introduced from Crawley to Luton Station via Gatwick Airport, Kingston, Heathrow Airport, Watford Junction and St Albans. The one-man operated route ran every 60 minutes with Reigate and St Albans each supplying four RFs which were specially modified by having luggage accommodation installed at the rear at the cost of four seats. The route was operated on an express basis with only 25 stops. New Almex ticket machines were used for the first time on Green Line. An extensive range of tickets from British Rail stations via Luton and Watford Junction to Heathrow were accepted on the coaches. The provision of luggage facilities at the rear of the coaches was not an ideal arrangement but some of the more enthusiastic drivers, keen that the new venture should be a success, would load and unload luggage through the rear emergency exit at stopping places such as Watford Junction, Heathrow and Gatwick.

From 2nd July until 24th September inclusive cheap day returns were available on Sunday on routes 712, 713 and 714 from London and intermediate points to Dorking. Staff shortage at Dorking garage meant that from 22nd July the through Saturday service on route 714 was reduced to 60 minutes with two coaches per hour being provided between Luton and Oxford Circus. So-called duty schedule efficiency resulted in a poor, passenger unfriendly timetable which resulted in an uneven service interval over the northern section at worst giving 15 and 45 minute gaps; hardly a measure designed to attract custom. Severe staff shortage at Staines garage caused route 702 to be withdrawn between Sunningdale and Victoria on Saturday. The staff shortage was caused by enhancements to the annual leave entitlement for crews which put particular pressure on summer Saturdays. With the resumption of the Monday to Friday service on route 726 on 24th July the route was diverted to join the M1 at the recently opened Brockley Hill junction instead of Berrygrove.

The introduction of winter schedules from 7th October 1967 saw the full Saturday service restored to routes 714 and 702 but the peak hour route 722 lost some further journeys. With the introduction of the summer service on 13th May route 718 had not received the full summer service on Monday to Friday – the half hourly service was only reinstated between Windsor and Victoria leaving two coaches per hour between Oxford Circus and Harlow during the peak hours only. Hardly surprisingly the route was now reduced to a 60-minute service daily with no future summer enhancements. This action meant that some of the best-patronised Monday to Friday peak hour journeys disappeared without replacement. The Windsor to Staines section suffered further reduction at the same time when on Sunday morn-

ings route 725 was run in two sections, Gravesend to Staines and Dartford to Windsor. This proved to be a winter measure and the full Sunday service was restored from 19th May the following year. Route 721 was increased by one coach per hour from Romford to Brentwood Post Office on Monday to Friday during the between peaks period.

The problems of ever increasing traffic congestion and timekeeping were closely monitored by London Transport and some timekeeping tests made at Victoria southbound showed that 80 per cent of coaches were within 10 minutes of right time, but a London traffic census revealed that now 2¼ times the number of private cars were licensed in London compared with 10 years ago.

London Transport were seeking further economies and looked at the possibility of garage closures but the only feasible option was Tunbridge Wells which operated route 704 alone. Accordingly from 2nd December 1967 the garage closed and route 704 was reallocated to Dunton Green garage. The

On 2nd December 1967 route 723 lost its RCLs to route 705 and gained RMCs. RMC 1476 pulls away from the stop at Aldgate while working to Tilbury Ferry. The RMCs were overhauled between May 1967 and January 1968 and appeared with transfers and fleet name similar to that used on the RCL class. They lost the pale green window relief which resulted in a duller appearance.
John Herting

route was revised together with route 705 which lost its express section and was converted to RCL operation with the RCs going into store. Apart from an additional coach during Monday to Friday peak hours over the southern section route 705 was reduced to 60 minutes. Route 704 ran on a 20/40-minute headway to provide a combined 20-minute frequency from Windsor to Bromley with route 705. Alternate coaches terminated at Sevenoaks except during Monday to Friday peak hours and Saturday afternoons. The original proposal had been to run 705 express between Victoria and Windsor but running via Heathrow Airport Central. In the event this did not happen but both routes were diverted westbound, away from the Bath Road to stop on the East Ramp at Heathrow North. The RCLs for the 705 came from Grays which received RMCs for route 723 and it was proposed to replace the offside longitudinal seats in the lower saloon with luggage racking. It seems that at least one coach was actually converted but the seats were soon restored.

The northern section of route 717 was withdrawn and the route ran from Wrotham to Baker Street Station in its revised form worked by Swanley which continued to use RMCs until 30th December when RFs took over. To cover the northern section route 716A was diverted to serve Welham Green and South Hatfield. There was no service provided between Welwyn Garden City and Stevenage daily during afternoons and late evenings except Saturday solely due to the allocation being changed from Stevenage to Hatfield.

Further changes took place on 30th December 1967 went route 701 was extended at Ascot from Horse and Groom to Heatherwood Hospital. Route 708 was reduced from 30 to 60 minutes and converted from RF to RMC in order to avoid the need for duplication but as with 718 some of the best-patronised peak journeys were withdrawn. The RMCs came from route 719 which reverted to RF operation. At the same time an application for a joint service with Eastern National from Victoria to Stansted Airport to be numbered 728 was refused by the traffic commissioners.

Route 717 was curtailed to operate from Wrotham to Baker Street on 2nd December 1967 with the northern section to Welwyn Garden City being covered by a diversion of route 716A. Prior to the change RMC 1469, fresh from overhaul, pulls away from the northbound coach stop in Golders Green station forecourt. From December 1963 a long tradition of Green Line vehicles not carrying advertisements was broken when RTs and RMCs were fitted with them on the rear lower panels.
Essex Transport Group

For what was destined to be its last season, when 726 reappeared on Easter Monday, 15th April 1968, it was re-routed away from Kings Cross to run via Oxford Circus where a stop was permitted. In the event major diversions were taking place at Oxford Circus during the Easter weekend in connection with the removal of the Victoria Line umbrella. Route 726 ran for the last time on 6th September and did not reappear the following year. The Monday to Friday sectionalised service on routes 701 and 702 was abandoned from 18th May principally due to Staines garage being some 20 conductors short of requirements. A through service was run every 60 minutes on route 701 with some Gravesend to Hammersmith peak hour strengthening. Route 702 ran from Sunningdale to Victoria during Monday to Friday peak periods and through to Gravesend on Saturday and Sunday but with no early or late service. On the same day staff shortage at Dorking saw the Saturday service on route 714 reduced as in the previous year.

The continuing need for further economies hit Green Line hard during 1968 when on 15th June route 715A lost its Saturday service being reduced to just two Monday to Friday peak hour journeys. Five-day weekly tickets were introduced for journeys to and from the freehold sections of the route. Route 707 was withdrawn on Sunday from 16th June with the 30-minute interval being maintained between Aylesbury and Chesham on that day running as 706 but there was no provision southwards to Oxted and Holland. The death of route 722 had been a long, drawn

Top With the progressive decline in Green Line passengers the Monday to Friday peak hour RT relief workings were gradually phased out. The last example on route 701 from Northfleet garage was withdrawn, as far as can be established, after 2nd February 1968. In this view taken a few years earlier RT 620 from Northfleet, RT 3624 from Dunton Green and RT 3612 from Northfleet lay over between the peaks at New Cross garage. The Dunton Green bus is displaying an 'Extra' slipboard. *M.G. Webber*

Centre RCL 2258 was transferred from Hertford to Tunbridge Wells garage for route 704 on 12th June 1966. It is seen at the Buckingham Palace Road stops which replaced the southbound stops at Eccleston Bridge on 26th September 1965 in consequence of the introduction of the Victoria one-way system. *Capital Transport*

Left Route 726 ran for the last time on 6th September 1968 and was not introduced for the following season with the Whipsnade service being provided by routes 712 and 713. RCL 2228 heading for Whipsnade turns from Marylebone Road into Baker Street to reach Gloucester Place via York Street. When the RCLs were repainted in 1968 they lost the pale green window relief in keeping with the RMCs. *John Herting*

From 18th May 1968 route 702 was reduced to operate during Monday to Friday peak hours and on Saturday and Sunday. In this view the rear of refurbished RF 201 is shown at Butterwick, Hammersmith. The standard of vehicle turn-out on Green Line was usually very high; the failure to fit correct route boards was an exception. *Essex Transport Group*

Route 722 suffered a long lingering death being reduced to run during Monday to Friday peak hours, losing its RCLs for RTs and having the number of journeys progressively reduced. It was withdrawn completely after 2nd August 1968 but not before an immaculate RT 3438 was photographed at Aldgate. *John Herting*

out process, but it was finally put out of its misery running for the last time on 2nd August. Severe staff shortage at Guildford garage saw the busy route 715 reduced from 24th August when on Monday to Friday alternate coaches from Hertford ran only as far as Oxford Circus. Some additional peak hour coaches between Guildford and Oxford Circus supplemented the basic 60-minute service over that section. The 30-minute service was maintained on Saturday and Sunday but with three gaps of one hour. It would seem that increases in wages and holiday allowances had done very little to attract staff as it was reported in September that the Country Buses and Coaches operating department was short of some 312 drivers and 273 conductors which represented 11.1 per cent of an establishment figure of 5,284. The 715 reverted to its normal timetable from 5th October when the summer annual leave period was over.

From 29th June 1968 the availability of 'Weekender' tickets which gave unlimited travel for any consecutive Saturday and Sunday on the Underground, Central buses and Country buses was extended to include all Green Line coach routes. The tickets cost 25/- adult and 12/6d child and were also available for travel on a Sunday and consecutive bank holiday Monday. On the following day the special cheap day return tickets from London to Dorking were re-introduced for the summer season. The first Green Line fares revision since January 1966 applied from 7th September when fares of 2/11d and above involving travel of 11 miles or more were increased. Some 4d and 8d local fares which had not been increased by 1d on 4th August were increased in this revision. In line with practice on route 724 a maximum single fare of 10/- now applied across the network. This meant a considerable reduction for certain journeys, for example the through fare on route 727 from Luton to Crawley was previously 15/- while the most expensive through fare on a cross London route from Aylesbury to Chartwell on route 706 had been 14/-. It must be remembered that only comparatively few passengers ever under-

took such lengthy journeys. With certain exceptions child rate half fares which previously counted fractions of 1d as 1d now calculated fractions of 3d as 3d. The long-standing monthly return booking on route 721 from Brentwood to Romford was withdrawn at this time.

A general reduction of frequency was implemented on route 721 from 5th October 1968; principally, one fewer coach per hour was provided on Saturday and Sunday but more journeys were projected in Brentwood to London Hospital Annex. Route 723B from Grays to East Ham following the traditional route via Purfleet ran for the last time on 4th October. This left 723 to provide generally two coaches per hour from Grays to Aldgate (one per hour from Tilbury) which was supplemented during Monday to Friday peak times and Saturday mornings and afternoons by an additional hourly journey between Grays and East Ham. The service on Monday to Friday evenings was cut to hourly.

Special blinds were produced for RTs covering RMC duties as depicted by Addlestone's RT 3605 in Green Line livery on route 716A. During the latter half of 1967, when the RMC overhaul programme was in full swing, it was quite common to see RT substitutions. *Essex Transport Group*

Former Green Line RF 96 has been downgraded to Country bus status but was captured at Butterwick whilst covering for an RMC on route 715. Note that the Green Line E plates are displayed in triplicate both over and inside the passenger shelter. *Essex Transport Group*

DECLINE
1968–1969

The question of London bus crews' rates of pay continued to be a contentious issue. The Wilson government (1964–1970) attempted to pursue a policy of both price constraint and wage restraint and referred matters to the Prices and Incomes Board which concluded that increased pay was warranted in exchange for increased productivity through one-man operation. In 1966 London Transport published a plan for reshaping London's bus services but only scant reference was made to Green Line other than to state that it was envisaged that the system would be converted to full one-man operation. As might be imagined the negotiations between the Transport and General Workers' Union and the Board were very protracted and proposals to convert routes 701, 702, 714 and 720 to one-man operation in October 1967 had to be deferred. One-man operation of services necessitated the allowance of additional running time to reflect the extra time needed by the driver to collect the fares and issue tickets. This meant that the driver could not always complete the same mileage in a duty that was achievable with crew operation. Various proposals were considered including the retention of the existing running times for one-man operated routes on Saturday and Sunday but in practice this option was considered impracticable. Eventually a scheme was imposed on Green Line in two stages during the winter of 1968/9 which resulted in all single-deck routes being worked with one-man operation.

Above The major casualty of the Green Line one-man operation conversions was the London to Crawley section of route 710. Amersham's RF 106 stands at Crawley Bus Station prior to working to Chesham, some 67 miles away. *Essex Transport Group*

Below The decline in Green Line services was such that from March 1968 twenty-four of the refurbished RF coaches were converted into Country buses. Most were reduced to 37-seaters by the removal of the front near-side seat in favour of a luggage pen, had the brackets for the side boards removed and were finished with a broad yellow band carrying the London Transport fleet name. This livery had been adopted for the generation of rear-engine single-deck buses then being introduced. They still tended to turn up on Green Line duties as circumstances required. RF 83 stands at Dartford garage between journeys on route 725. As virtually all Country area single deck operation was one-man operated the pay as you enter slip boards were replaced by transfers on the vehicle but route 725 was still crew operated when this photograph was taken. *John Herting*

Route 717 ran for the last time on 22nd November 1968 to be replaced by an extension of route 719 from Victoria to Wrotham. RF 218 stands in Allsop Place at Baker Street station. *Essex Transport Group*

The first phase applied from 23rd November 1968 and reintroduced variable running times, according to time of day and day of the week, which had not been used since 1942. Routes 701, 702 and 720 were converted on existing frequencies. Route 710 (Crawley to Amersham) could not be converted as it stood as the additional running time involved would have made the driver's duty length excessive. The route was revised to run from Amersham garage to Baker Street Station being diverted at Lancaster Gate to run via Marble Arch and Portman Square. The sections from Chesham to Amersham and London to Crawley were abandoned. In part compensation an additional journey was provided in each peak period on route 709 with Godstone receiving an additional RCL. Route 711 was reduced from 30 minutes to 60 minutes during Monday to Friday off-peak times (with alternate peak journeys split at Baker Street), Saturday early am and evenings and Sunday while route 714 was reduced to every 60-minutes at all times. Route 717 from Wrotham to Baker Street was withdrawn in favour of an extension of route 719 from Victoria to Wrotham with Garston and Swanley garages supplying the coaches. Additional coaches were provided during Mon–Fri peak periods and Saturdays except evenings to give two journeys per hour between Garston and Victoria. Some augmentation to the service for hospital requirements was provided on Sunday afternoons which resulted in a Leavesden Hospital becoming a new destination for Green Line.

Before the conversion of route 719 to one-man operation and extension to Wrotham, RF 80 stands at Hemel Hempstead Bus Station. *Essex Transport Group*

Above Another casualty of the one-man operation conversions was route 707 which ran for the last time on 14th February 1969. RF 65 is seen in Sparrows Herne, Bushey heading for Oxted. *John Herting*

Right After just over a year of RMC operation route 708 was converted to RF one-man operation on 15th February 1969. RMC 1505 is seen at Colindale. *J.G.S. Smith*

Below right Route 713 was converted to one-man operation on 15th February 1969. After the conversion RF 43 is seen opposite St Albans garage bound for Dorking with the drivers exchanging a few words while changing over. *Barry LeJeune*

The second phase which involved routes 706, 708, 712, 713 and 725 was introduced from 15th February 1969. Route 707 was withdrawn with route 706 providing a daily 30-minute service from Aylesbury to Chelsham. The route was projected to Westerham during Monday to Friday peak periods and coaches only double ran to Tatsfield in the direction of the peak flow. Coaches continued to run to Chartwell on Wednesday, Thursday, Saturday and Sunday during the summer season. In order that running times would be equated over the common section with route 706 between South Croydon and Two Waters route 708 was converted from RMC operation to RF omo. Routes 712 and 713 were converted without change of service pattern except that Luton was served by one coach only in each peak period and lost its Saturday service. Route 725 was converted without major change except that the Monday to Friday duplicates over the Dartford to Croydon section were now shown in the timetable and part of the Staines allocation was transferred to Windsor.

RMC worked route 715 was revised at the same date to run every 30 minutes from Hertford to Oxford Circus with alternate coaches continuing to Guildford on Monday to Friday with some peak hour journeys supplementing the southern section. The Saturday service was every 30 minutes throughout but the Sunday service was reduced to 60 minutes. As with the one-man services variable running time was introduced to the route. Companion peak hour only route 715A was withdrawn at the same time.

Under agreements with the trade union there was no compulsory redundancy of conductors due to one-man conversions and many coach conductors were redeployed as Country bus conductors, offered driver training, found alternative employment within London Transport or opted for voluntary redundancy. The run-down of Green Line services enabled some RMCs to be used as Country buses from 15th February 1969 when some were allocated to Hatfield garage for routes 303 and 303A (New Barnet – Hitchin) and to Addlestone garage for route 461A (Botleys Park – Walton). The vehicles concerned retained their Green Line livery and were interchangeable with those operated by the garages concerned on Green Line work.

One-man operation proved not to be the panacea for all ills that the Wilson government's advisers would have had everyone believe. In theory the cost of employing conductors was saved and everything just carried on as before. In practice the situation was rather different. There were delays caused by drivers having to consult the complex fare charts. On some routes lengthy country sections offered cheaper fares on Saturday and Sunday to supplement withdrawn or reduced bus services.

The Green Line travelling public expected to be advised if it was cheaper to take a return on Monday to Friday and often requested travel information concerning onward connections or the times of return coaches – all information which the conductor could readily assist with but not the driver while the coach was still standing at the stop! Some of the more enthusiastic conductors would assist passengers with luggage and even the odd tip from a grateful passenger was not unknown.

Numerous public complaints about the protracted boarding times and running times associated with omo were received and passenger usage dropped. Figures for week ended 30th March 1969 compared with 1968 showed receipts on omo routes to be 16 per cent down overall with the following routes coming out worst – 710 down 60 per cent, 711 down 25 per cent, 714 down 28 per cent and 719 down 25 per cent. By July it was reported that passenger journeys in the 15 to 20 mile range had fallen considerably on Green Line which was attributed to one-man operation and service reductions. Passenger usage for the four weeks ended 13th July 1969 was down by 18 per cent compared with the previous year. Weekly tickets could not be issued by the driver on the one-man coaches but could be obtained at garages and enquiry offices or on a specific coach by prior arrangement. It was hardly surprising that weekly ticket issue had dropped from 2,346 for a test week in March 1962 to just 468 for a week in July. The timetables for the omo routes were determined by duty schedule requirements rather than the need to provide a robust service. At certain times when two coaches per hour were provided especially during the Monday to Friday periods against the peak flow, the courtesy

of providing an even interval service was forgotten. The worst example was on route 701 where during Monday to Friday afternoons the timetable provided for two coaches per hour from Gravesend arranged on a 3/57-minute headway!

The opportunity seems to have been lost with the introduction of one-man operation to adjust the cross-London linkings as clearly by this time a system planned in 1946 was not necessarily suited to the additional running times required by one-man operation. This course of action may have meant that the Crawley to London section of the 710 could have been saved. The savage reductions in frequencies and reversions from double-deck to single-deck operation that took place over the previous five-year period undoubtedly caused inadequacies with intending passengers left behind. It is not pleasant to be so treated, most people will not be caught out twice and no doubt many turned to other forms of transport, especially the private car. The introduction of local fares where Country bus services had been reduced also caused problems as in some instances coaches left terminals full with many short-distance riders which meant that genuine coach passengers further along the route could not be certain of boarding. On those sections where the coaches were performing bus work, delays were often caused as far more calls at request stops for the need of local riders were required. The nature of Green Line had changed and average length of passenger journeys made had gradually fallen over the years.

Severe crew shortage at Windsor garage was a continuing problem with records showing that the garage was some 38 bus and coach drivers short of requirements in March. It was somewhat unfortunate that

During 1969 the RCs appeared in conventional livery, were equipped for one-man operation and fitted with additional luggage accommodation for use on route 727. They were drafted onto the route in May but were again dogged by mechanical problems. RC 2 is seen in Reigate. *Barry LeJeune*

RFs frequently substituted for RCs on route 727 and during the autumn of 1969 they were officially back on the route. In contrast to the RCs the 17 year-old RFs had no problems in performing the arduous duties. RF 79 is seen at Heathrow Airport. *John Herting*

the most profitable Green Line route 704 was to suffer a service reduction because of this problem. From 19th April the Windsor to Sevenoaks journeys (extended to Tunbridge Wells during peak periods and Saturday afternoon) were withdrawn when scheduled to be worked by Windsor crews. This meant an awkward 20/40-minute interval with route 705 and the evening peak coach from Victoria to Sevenoaks on route 705 was switched to the 704.

Since their withdrawal at the end of 1967 the RC class had been in store but during 1968 three were painted in conventional Green Line livery and were used at Dartford garage for relief duties on route 725 until the route was converted to omo in February 1969. The class was then fitted with additional luggage accommodation, converted for one-man operation, and all now appeared in conventional livery and replaced RFs on route 727 during May. Mechanical problems had plagued the class on the arduous route 705 and they proved

little better on the 727 being withdrawn during the autumn with the reliable RFs taking up the duties once again.

A revision of fares took place on 7th September 1969 which, in line with other London Transport road and rail services introduced standard and inner zones. The latter was the area approximately within the Circle Line which attracted a higher level of fares. The London minimum remained at 2/- but for journeys to or from the inner zone allowed six miles of travel instead of the standard seven. The Country minimum remained at 1/6d but the 11d fares which had been retained to fulfil stage carriage licensing requirements were withdrawn in favour of 9d fares which were inserted in country districts. Route 716 lost its long standing special return fares to be replaced by the standard off-peak cheap day returns. The weekly ticket minimum rate was now 27/- for journeys where the normal single fare was 3/-. As a prelude to decimalisation of the coinage some 9d and 1/3d fares were increased by 3d in two phases on 30th November and 28th December.

The last timetable revision to Green Line under London Transport applied from 4th October 1969 when route 704 was reduced to a 60-minute service following the emergency staff-shortage timetable introduced on 19th April. One peculiarity of the new timetable was that a late Sunday evening journey from Tunbridge Wells ran to Westerham. The surplus RCLs from route 704 were transferred to Grays for route 723 which now ran with a mix of RCL and RMC coaches. Variable running times now applied to all routes with the exception of 724 and 727 from this date. The route allocation and vehicle requirements as at 4th October are shown on page 144.

Dating from pre-war days it was the practice to use Green Line coaches on Country bus working as permitted by the scheduling requirements. Such journeys were usually performed during the morning peak period. RF 172 sits on Amersham garage forecourt prior to working a schools journey on route 332. After the short trip on route 332 the coach will return to Amersham garage in order to run to Baker Street on truncated one-man operated route 710. One of the new generation of double deck buses, XF 7, can be seen in the background on a temporary visit to Amersham. *John Herting*

The requirement was now for 204 service coaches on Monday to Friday, 207 on Saturday and 178 on Sunday with the figures for duplicate coaches being just one, two and five respectively.

A fundamental change to the method of financing London Transport was to be implemented under the terms of the Transport (London) Act, 1969 which, from 1st January 1970, was to transfer control and financing away from central government to the Greater London Council. Country Bus and Green Line operations extended far beyond the area covered by the GLC and it was obviously inappropriate that they should continue to form part of the London Transport empire. Accordingly from that date the Country Buses and Coaches operating department was passed to a new company called London Country Bus Services Limited, one of 54 subsidiary companies of the National Bus Company which had been established under separate legislation on 1st January 1969. Thus London Transport's 36 year span of operating Green Line Coaches regrettably came to an end.

At the close of 1969 217 coaches, including traffic spares, were still required on Monday to Friday compared with 316 some 10 years earlier and the number of passenger journeys at 20.5 million represented a fall of 43 per cent over the same period. Mileage operated in 1969 was 16.4 million, which had fallen by 35 per cent in 10 years, and traffic receipts were £2.6 million compared with £3.1 million in 1959 but operating costs had risen considerably over the period. The system had been in a state of progressive decline over the last five years but much of the 1946 map was still recognisable, albeit with reduced levels of service over most sections of route. Under the new company, London Country Bus Services, the rate of decline would be destined to increase considerably.

GREEN LINE COACH
704·705

WINDSOR AND TUNBRIDGE WELLS
WINDSOR AND SEVENOAKS
via
Heathrow Airport   Slough
LONDON Victoria
and Bromley

TIMETABLE AND FARES

DECEMBER 1969

LONDON TRANSPORT   55 Broadway SW1
Telephone 01-222 1234

Starting 1 January 1970, Green Line Coaches will
be taken over by a new company:-
LONDON COUNTRY BUS SERVICES LTD.
with head office at Bell Street, Reigate, Surrey.

1269/4228C/7M

The last timetable leaflets to be issued under London Transport auspices in December 1969 set out the new ownership arrangements which would apply from 1st January 1970 thus bringing 36 years of London Transport's responsibility for Green Line services to an end.

No.	Route	Type	Garage	No. of coaches MF	Sat	Sun
701	Gravesend – Victoria – Ascot	RF	Northfleet	6	7	7
702	Gravesend – Victoria – Sunningdale	RF	Staines	6	7	7
704	Tunbridge Wells – Victoria – Windsor	RCL	Dunton Green	4	3	3
			Windsor	4	4	4
705	Sevenoaks – Westerham – Victoria – Windsor	RCL	Dunton Green	5	4	4
			Windsor	3	3	3
706	Westerham or Chartwell – Victoria – Aylesbury	RF	Chelsham	9	9	8
			Tring	7	8	7
708	East Grinstead – Victoria – Hemel Hempstead	RF	East Grinstead	4	4	4
			Hemel Hempstead	4	5	4
709	Godstone – Oxford Circus – Chesham	RCL	Godstone	3	–	1
710	Amersham – Baker Street	RF	Amersham	4	4	4
711	Reigate – Oxford Circus – High Wycombe	RF	Reigate	7	7	6
			High Wycombe	7	7	6
712	Dorking – Victoria – Dunstable/Whipsnade/Luton	RF	Dorking	5	6	3
713	Dorking – Victoria – Dunstable/Whipsnade/Luton	RF	St Albans	8	9	6
714	Dorking – Oxford Circus – Luton	RF	Dorking	4	4	4
			Luton	4	4	4
715	Guildford – Oxford Circus – Hertford	RMC	Guildford	7	6	4
			Hertford	8	8	4
716	Chertsey – Marble Arch – Hitchin	RMC	Addlestone	4	4	4
			Stevenage	4	4	4
716A	Woking – Marble Arch – Stevenage	RMC	Addlestone	3	3	3
			Hatfield	5	5	5
718	Windsor – Victoria – Harlow	RMC	Windsor	4	4	4
			Harlow	4	4	4
719	Wrotham – Victoria – Hemel Hempstead	RF	Swanley	3	3	4
			Garston	6	7	5
720	Bishop's Stortford – Aldgate	RF	Harlow	7	8	7
721	Brentwood – Aldgate	RCL	Romford	13	13	7
723	Tilbury Ferry – Grays – Aldgate	RCL/RMC	Grays	9	9	7
724	Romford – St Albans – High Wycombe	RF	Romford	5	5	5
			High Wycombe	3	3	3
725	Gravesend – Croydon – Kingston – Windsor	RF	Northfleet	4	4	4
			Dartford	6	4	4
			Staines	4	4	3
			Windsor	3	3	4
727	Crawley – Heathrow Airport – Luton Station	RF	Reigate	4	4	4
			St Albans	4	4	4

Although a spare RF was kept at both Riverside and Victoria garages they were sometimes not available and it was not unknown for Central area buses to be pressed into service. A breakdown or minor traffic accident has caused an RMC on route 718 to be replaced with RM 1220 from Putney Central area garage. The destination blinds have been hastily amended in chalk. In 1968 and 1969 an RMC was allocated as spare coach to Riverside garage instead of the RF. *Colin Routh*